LONDON TROLL
MEMORIES

Julian Bowden

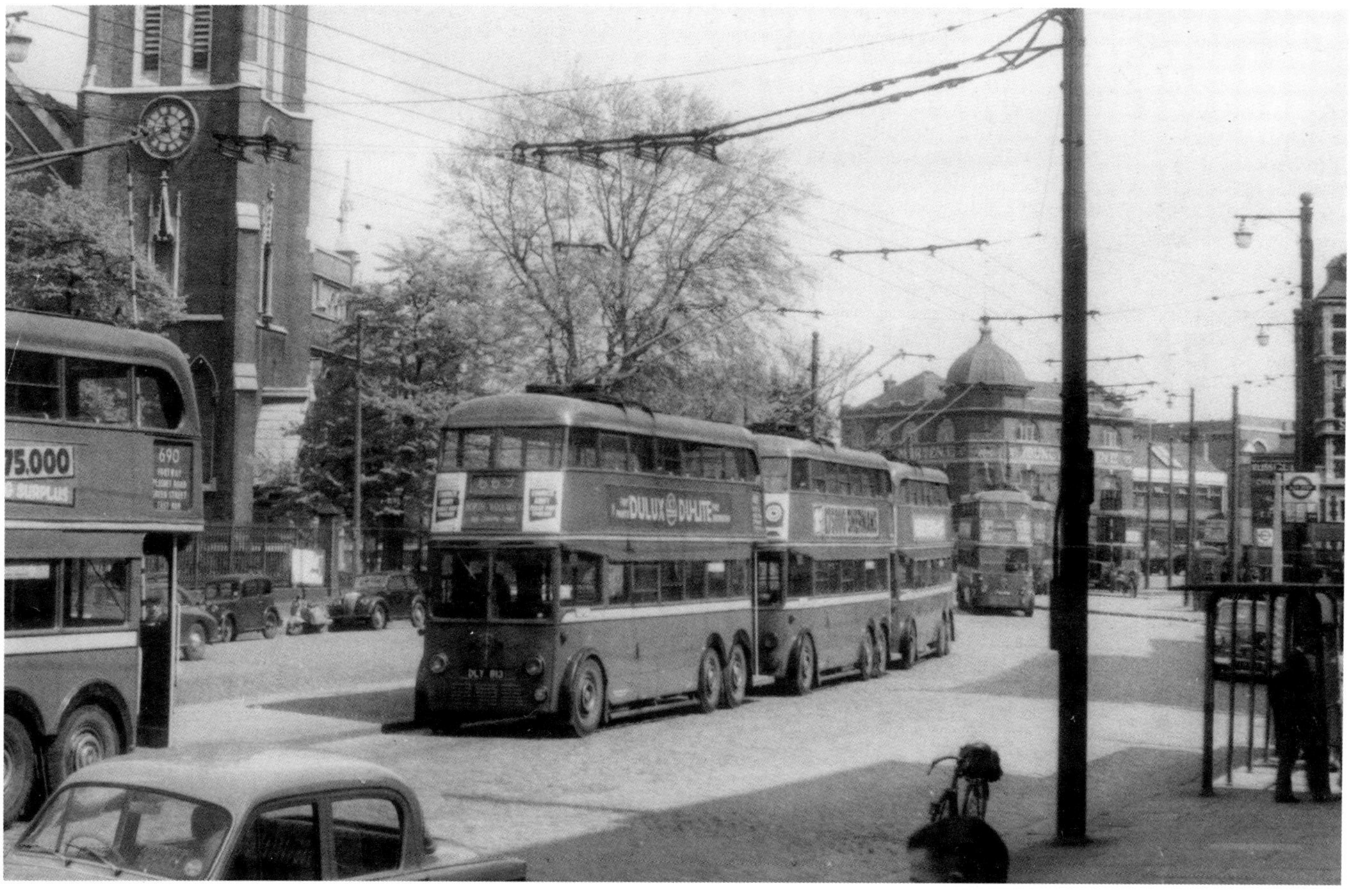

Stratford Broadway was a major hub of trolleybus operation in east London with both through and terminating routes. Although this 'trolleybus scape', viewed on 2 May 1959, was taken after the trolleybus to bus conversion scheme had begun, Stratford at that time had not lost any of its trolleybus routes, the only decline in local trolleybus workings being the reduction in overall service levels which affected all of London. Thus the scene here remains trolleybus dominated. E2 class trolleybus 613 on route 669 takes centre stage.
Fred York

Bowden Publishing

LONDON TROLLEYBUS
MEMORIES

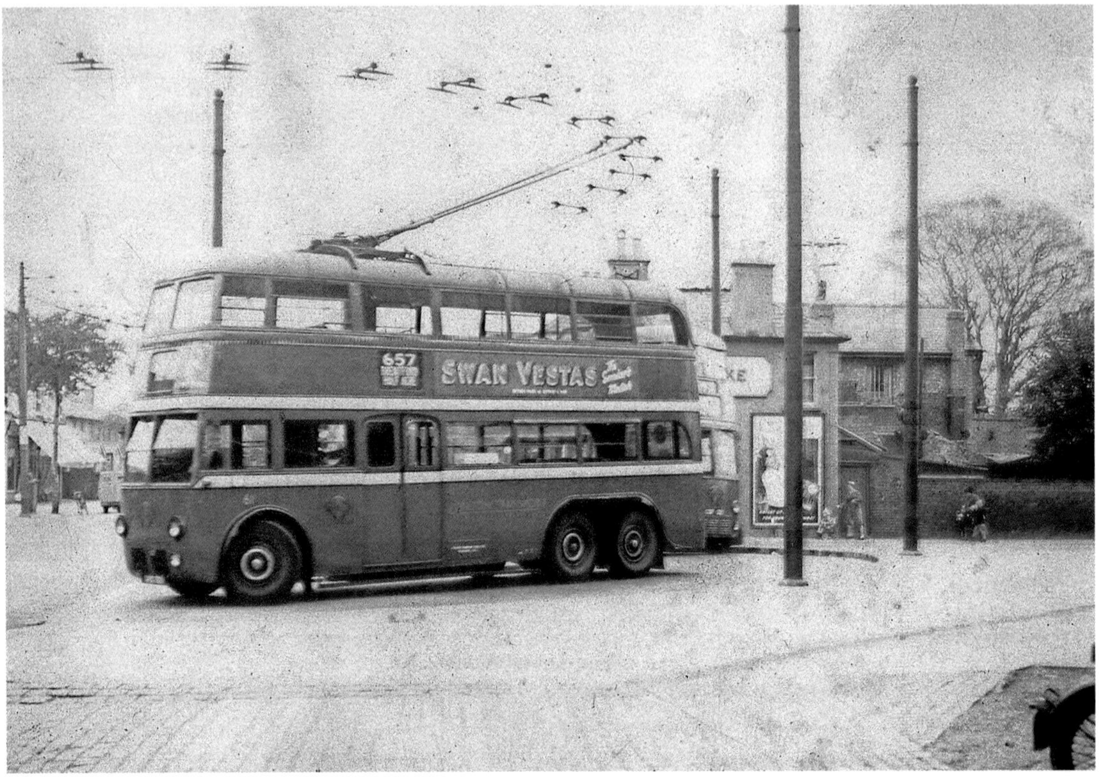

61 (AHX 601) is seen in it's last few years of service on route 657 whilst allocated to Isleworth Depot. The western terminus of the 657 was Hounslow where this photograph was taken. 61 was the first experimental trolleybus (class X1) originally delivered new to London United Tramways in March 1933.
John Aldridge collection

Front Cover: It is Easter Monday 23 April 1962, a warm and sunny day, and L3 class 1483 is about to leave on a short working to Malden on route 604. In a little over two weeks, the trolleybuses will be but a memory. RF 108 passes by on the 718 on its way to Windsor, completing the busy scene at Hampton Court.
Mick Webber

Rear Cover: It is Stanley Road, by the rear entrance to Fulwell Depot. It must be the most quiet part of 8 May 1962, for there appears to be no enthusiasts milling around as L3 class 1479 waits to leave for Twickenham, although the blind still shows Tolworth.
Peter Horner

Published by Bowden Publishing, 21 Forde Avenue, Bromley, BR1 3EU

Designed by Ramport Design, Bromley.
Printed by Ian Allan Printing Ltd, Hersham, KT12 4RG

LONDON TROLLEYBUS *MEMORIES*

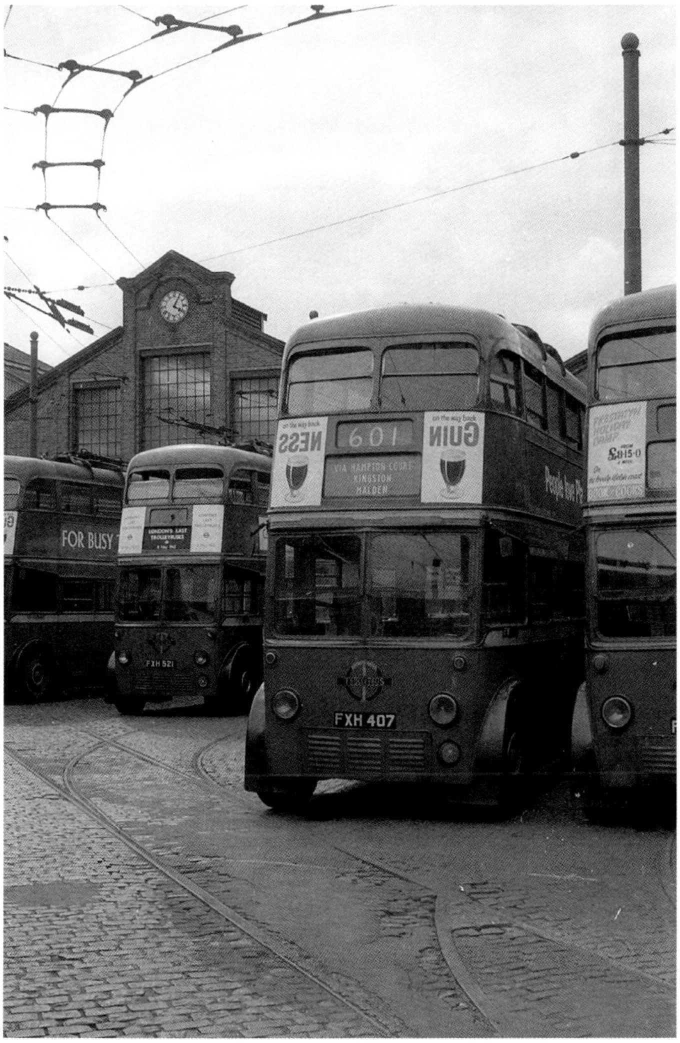

Taken on 18 May 1962 ten days after trolleybus operation came to an end, L3 1407 stands at the rear of Fulwell Depot. The very last trolleybus 1521 is parked to the left and will be spared from the scrap yard.
Brian Speller

INTRODUCTION

It is now over fifty years since the last trolleybus ran in service, yet even today there is a remarkable level of interest in this form of public transport. This is reflected in the number of younger and not so young enthusiasts maintaining the trolleybuses at the main museums where they can still be seen running in service, carrying realistic loads, usually crowds of passengers at special events. As well as these trolleybuses, there are others equally worthy of mention on static display in various museums across the country.

This book has arisen because of this interest and an awareness by myself that there are some fantastic photographic collections of all forms of public transport that very rarely see the light of day. This manifests itself in the large number of collectors and enthusiasts who willingly pore over hundreds, if not thousands of photographs at transport rallies and other similar events often buying copies to expand their collections or as a happy memory of something that they recollect from the past.

So, this book is a collection of photographs, hopefully many previously unpublished, that commemorate an era that lasted nearly 31 years through the middle of the 20th century. The first London trolleybus started public service on 16 May 1931 on a network of routes based at the Fulwell Depot of London United. Ironically the last London trolleybus ran officially on 8 May 1962 but finally entered Fulwell Depot in the early hours of Wednesday 9 May. In between these dates London Transport built up the largest fleet of trolleybuses in the world, having purchased or acquired 1891 trolleybuses between 1931 (under London United auspices) and 1952 when the last Q1 trolleybus was delivered. The London Transport network, at its maximum, covered 255 route miles.

The photographs used in this book are from a number of sources, some of which are well known, others may be not. I am most grateful to all of them and their families for their help and cooperation in this project. I hope you the reader enjoy the selection provided.

ACKNOWLEDGEMENTS

Thanks are due to all the people who have given me encouragement and provided assistance, whether it is in the form of photographs or factual information. These include John Aldridge, Brian Botley, Alan Cross, Michael Dryhurst, Jim Hawkins, Dave Jones (LCCTT), Geoff Lumb, Vic Nutton, John Shearman, Lesley and Michael Speller, Mick Webber, Tony Wilson (Travel Lens Photographic), Fred York and last but not least my immediate Bowden family. I have attempted to identify and credit accurately all photographic sources. Should any error or omission have occurred, then this is entirely unintentional.

Julian Bowden

April 2012

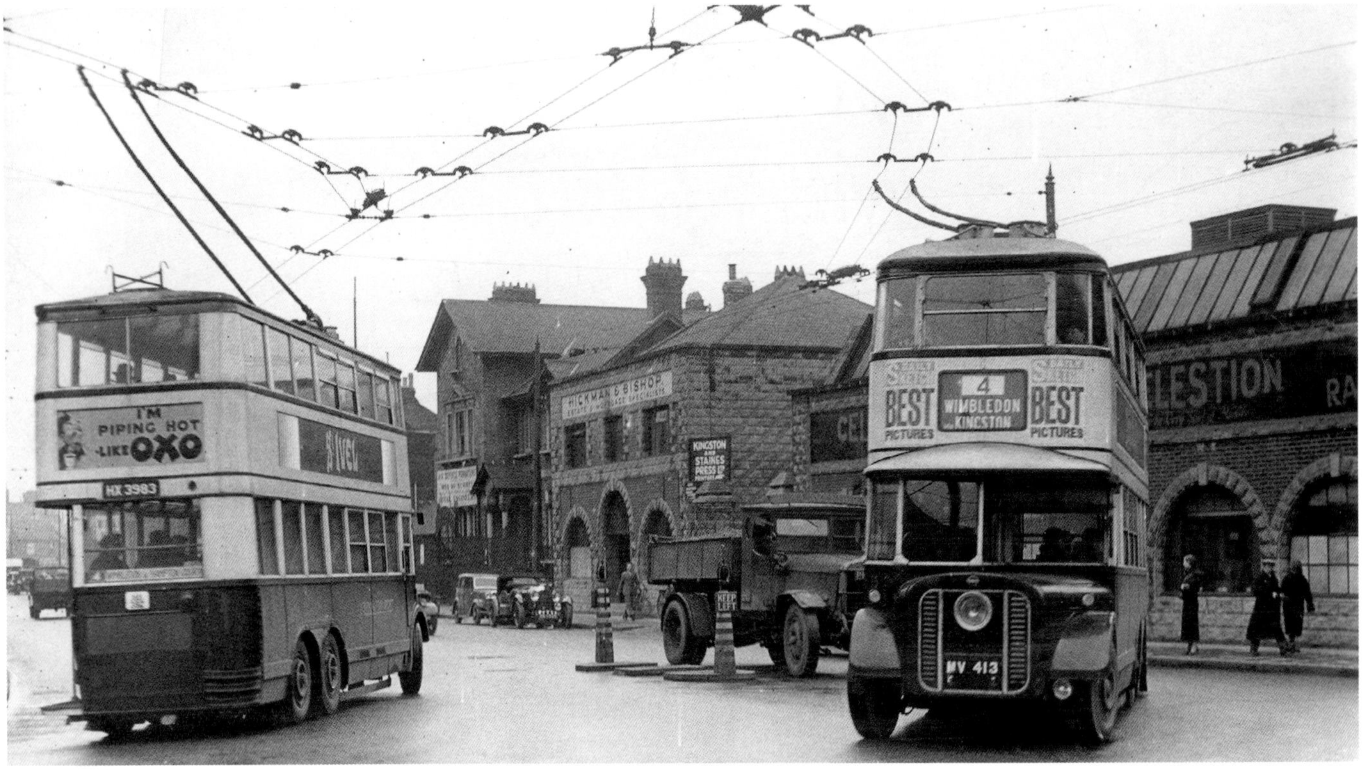

Diddler 55(MV 413) is turning in Kingston to head towards Wimbledon. In the opposite direction 4(HX 3983) is heading towards Hampton Court.
John Aldridge collection

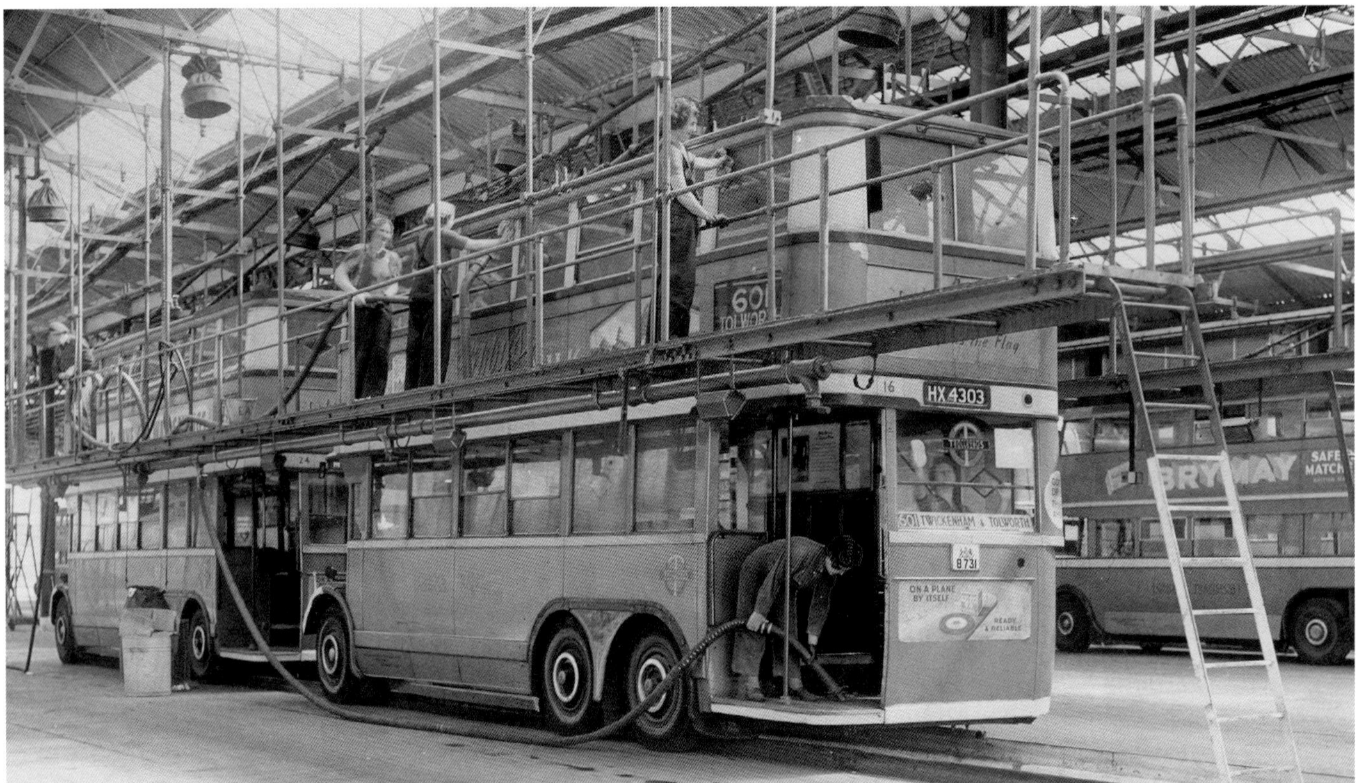

Diddler 16 (HX 4303) with 24 (MG 102) in front being cleaned and vacuumed in Fulwell Depot. This wartime photograph from 1942 illustrates the use of female staff to help the 'war effort'.
John Aldridge collection

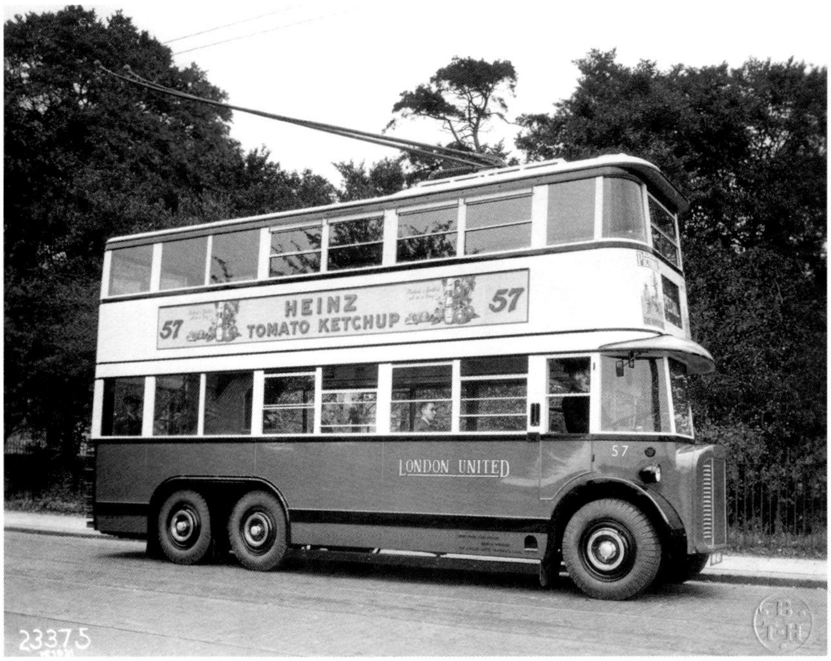

BTH supplied the electrical equipment for the Diddlers numbered 36-60, and commissioned a photographer to capture 57, posed here at Fulwell in October 1931. The curved front upper deck corner windows soon began to fail under body stress, and were later replaced with two smaller panes.
BTH/ Mick Webber Collection

The Red Lion terminus of route 603 at Tolworth is the setting here, as 29 waits for the return trip to Kingston, and a turn around the loop past Richmond Park gate. Vehicles 1 – 35 are classified A1, and the remainder of the 60 buses delivered are class A2, the first batch having English Electric equipment, the others having BTH equipment.
Mick Webber Collection

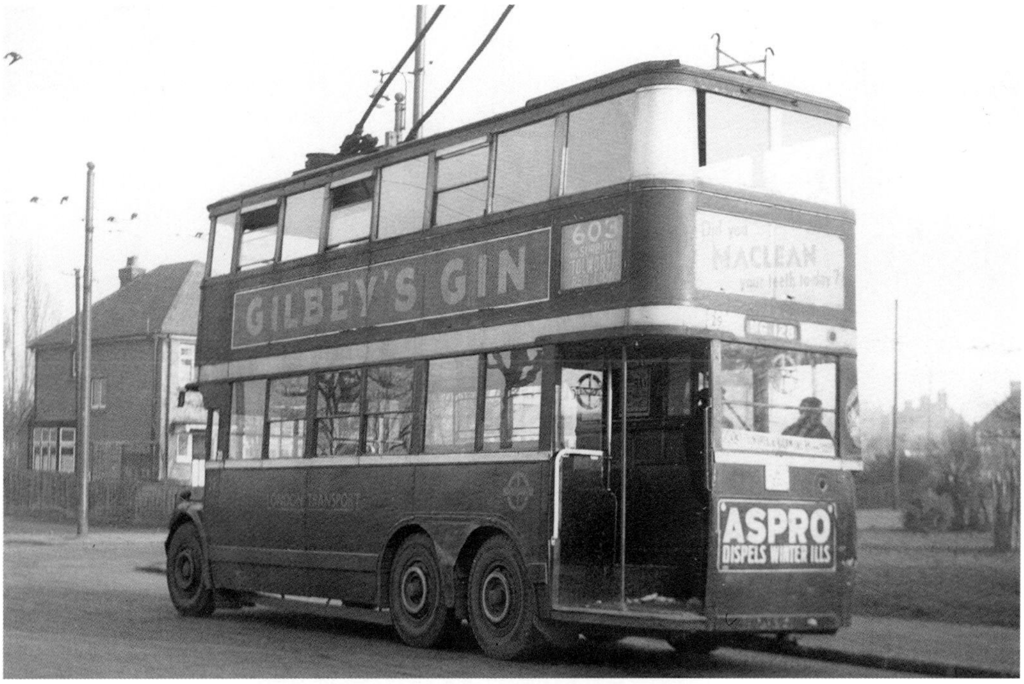

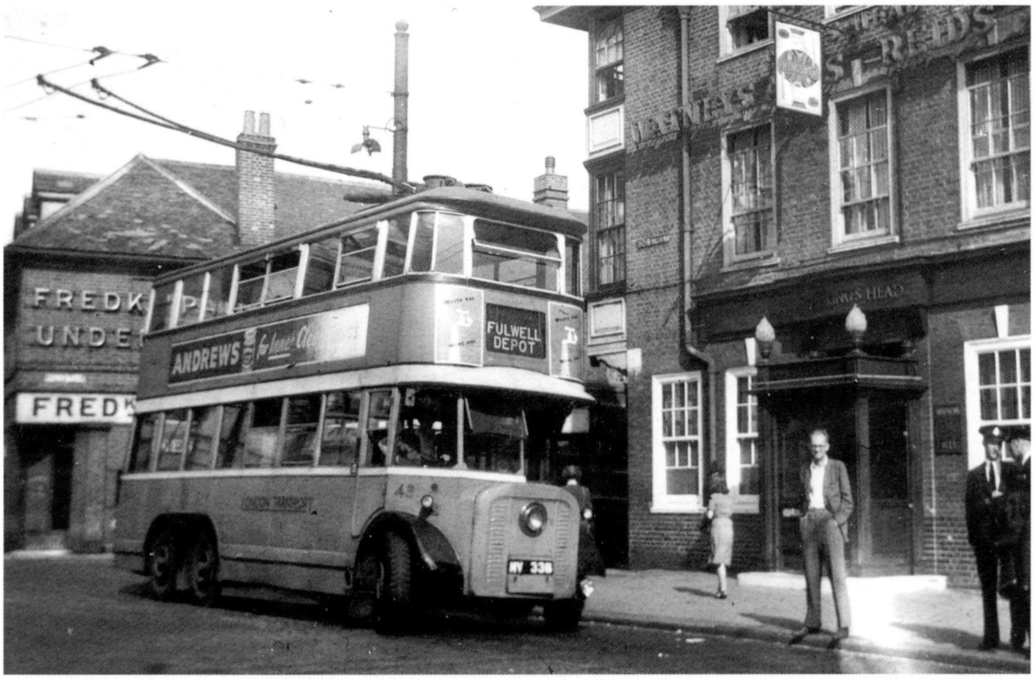

Diddler 43 is parked in King Street, Twickenham, waiting to work back to Fulwell Depot. This post war view shows the vehicle near the end of its service life, being withdrawn in 1949. The front advertisements urge the public to be mindful of its use of water, so thats nothing new now.
J.H.Price

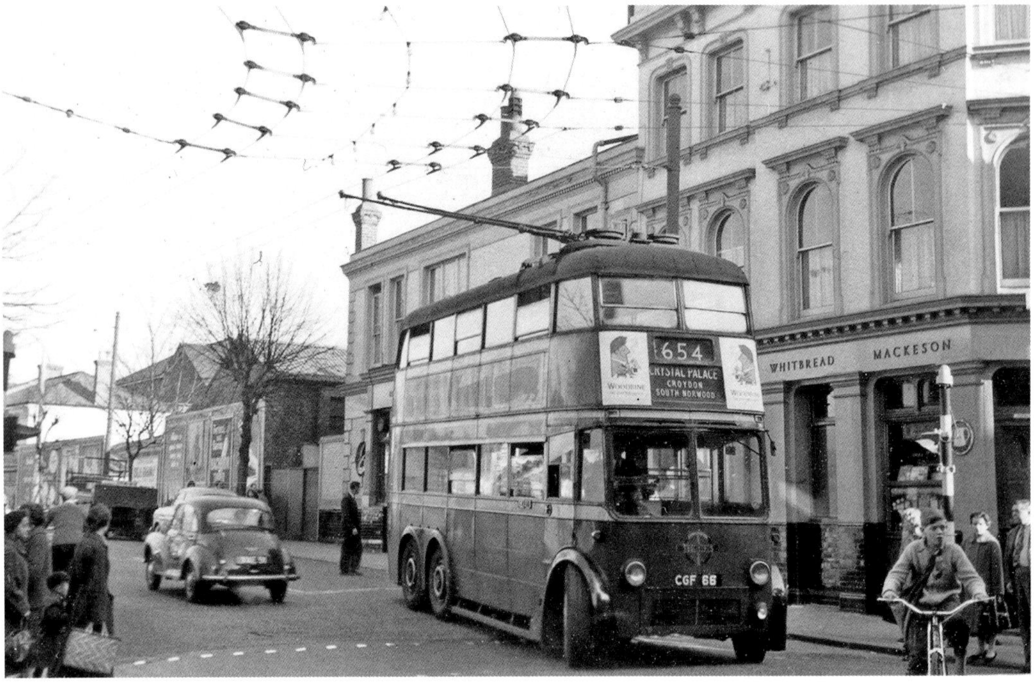

66 is one of 30 B1 class trolleybuses that spent their working lives at Sutton (later re-named Carshalton) Depot.
John Aldridge

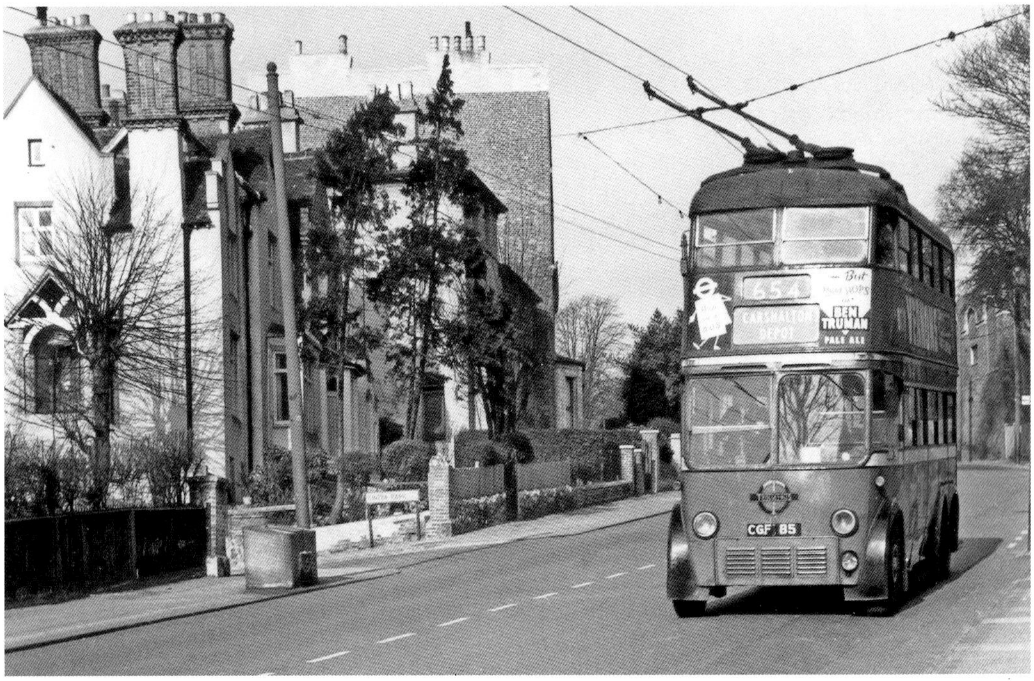

85 is seen just before its withdrawal from service in March 1959 at 'Stage 1' of the trolleybus replacement programme descending Anerley Hill. It has just started it's journey back to Carshalton Depot.
John Aldridge

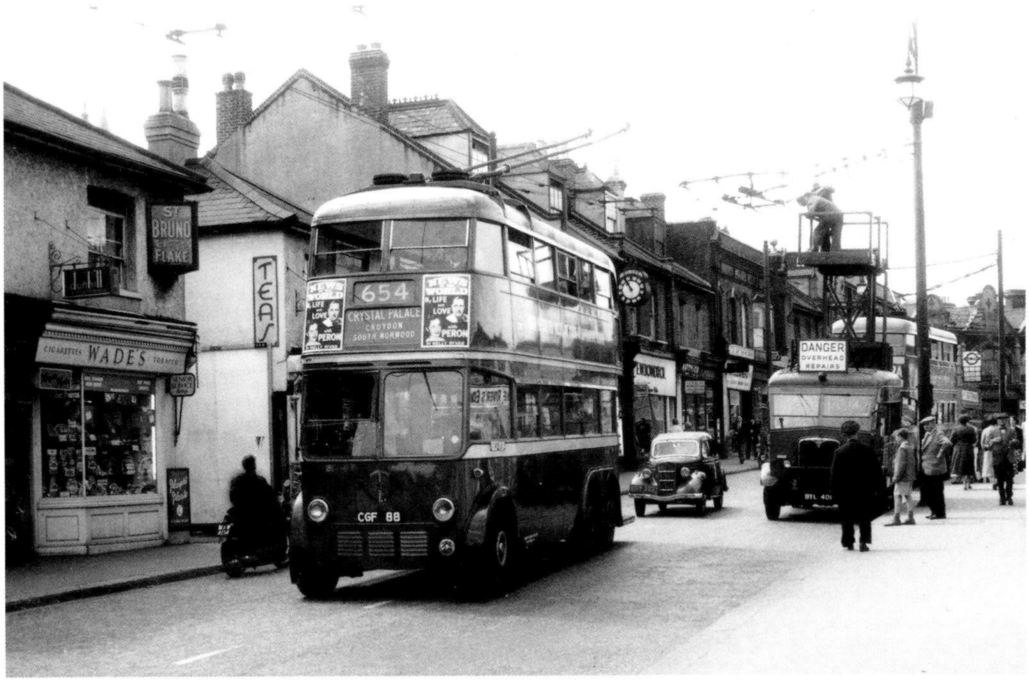

The B1 and B2 classes were short wheel base 60 seat trolleybuses. All were Leyland vehicles, and have bodywork by Birmingham Railway Carriage and Wagon Co (B1) and Brush (B2). B1 class 88 is pictured on the 654, Sutton Depot's only route and which traversed the steep Anerley Hill. Because of this, the B1s are equipped with coasting and run back brakes, to prevent runaways. AEC tower wagon 76Q, a 1935 AEC Mercury, is in the background, with a crew attending to the overhead.
Mick Webber Collection

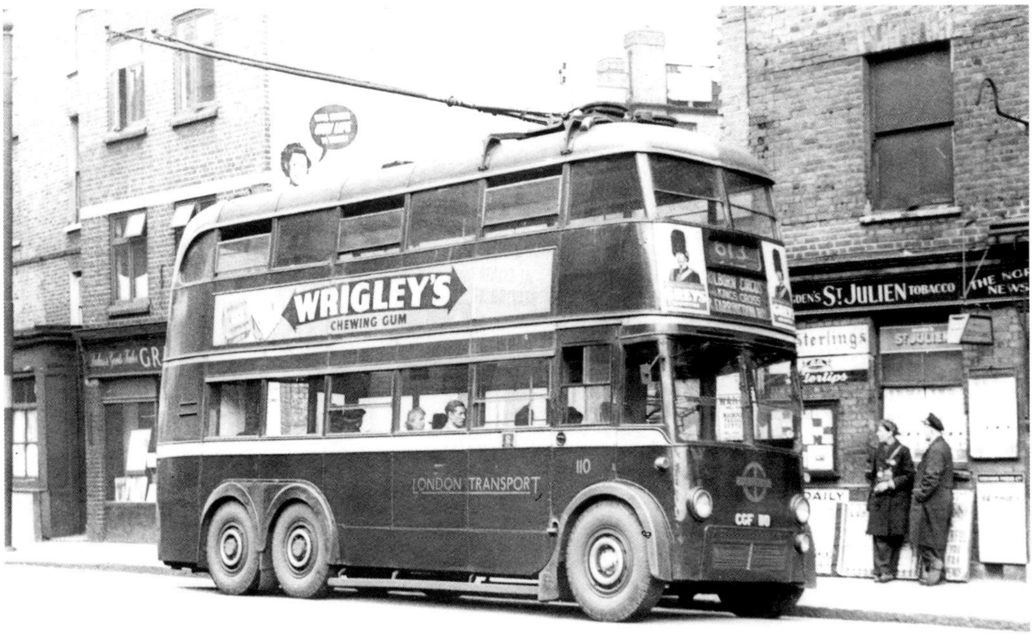

110 is a B2 class vehicle, a Leyland short wheelbase 60 seater with Brush bodywork. Holloway Depot (re-named later Highgate) operated a number of these on the Hampstead routes, and the 639 is featured here at Kentish Town.
Mick Webber Collection

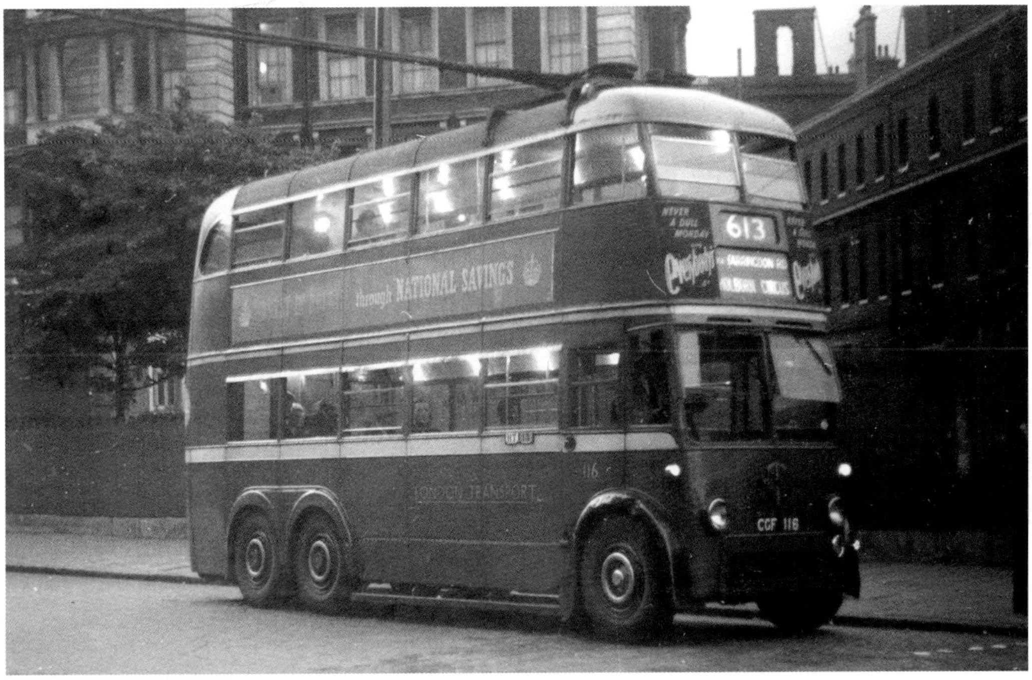

B2 class 116 is working the 613 one late afternoon in 1952, and does not seem to be attracting much custom. It was withdrawn later that year, having been in stock since November 1935.
Alan Cross

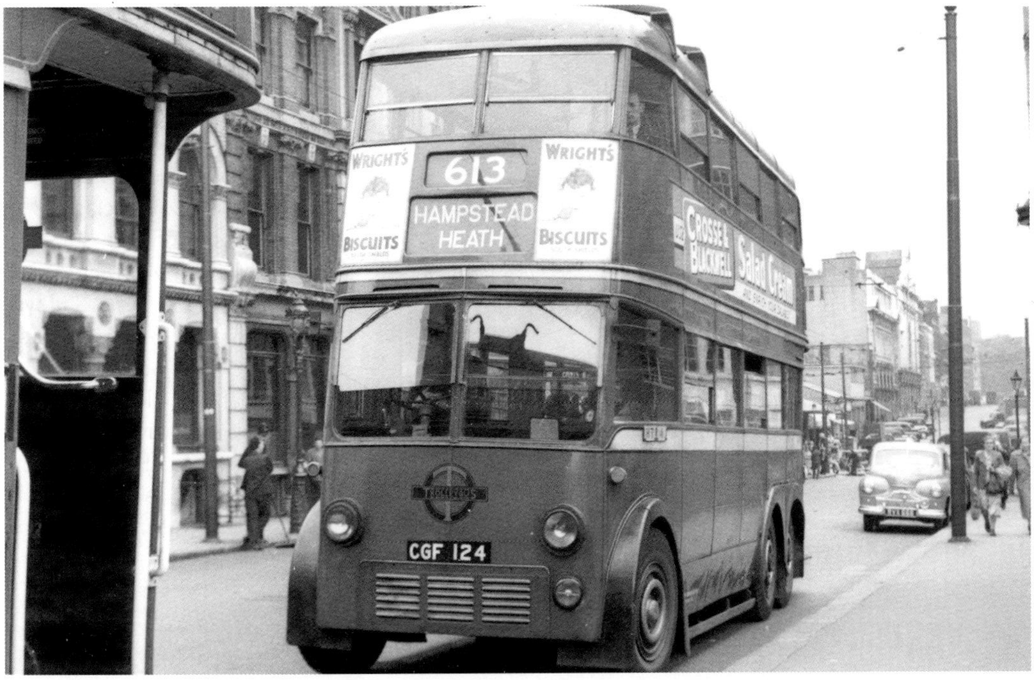

The 513 and 613 linked Hampstead with Holborn Circus, and as other routes, operated a loop via Farringdon Road and Grays Inn Road, the 500 series working in an anti clockwise direction, and the 600 series, clockwise. B2 class 124 waits here at Holborn on the 613.
F.G.Reynolds

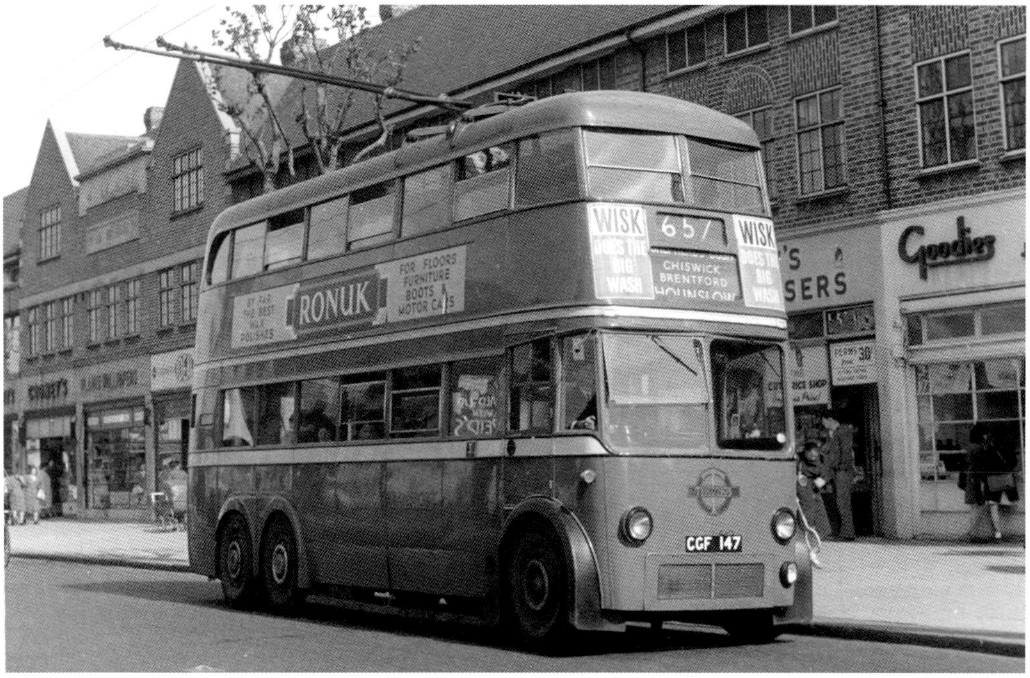

Route 657 took over from tram route 57, a former London United route, in October 1935. The trip from Shepherds Bush to a new terminus at Hounslow Heath, was scheduled to take 40 minutes, and was operated by trolleybuses from Hounslow (later Isleworth) Depot. C1 class 147 is smartly turned out here in this post war view taken before July 1950, when trolleybuses first carried depot code plates, upon the tram and trolleybus operations being merged with Central buses.

JH Aston

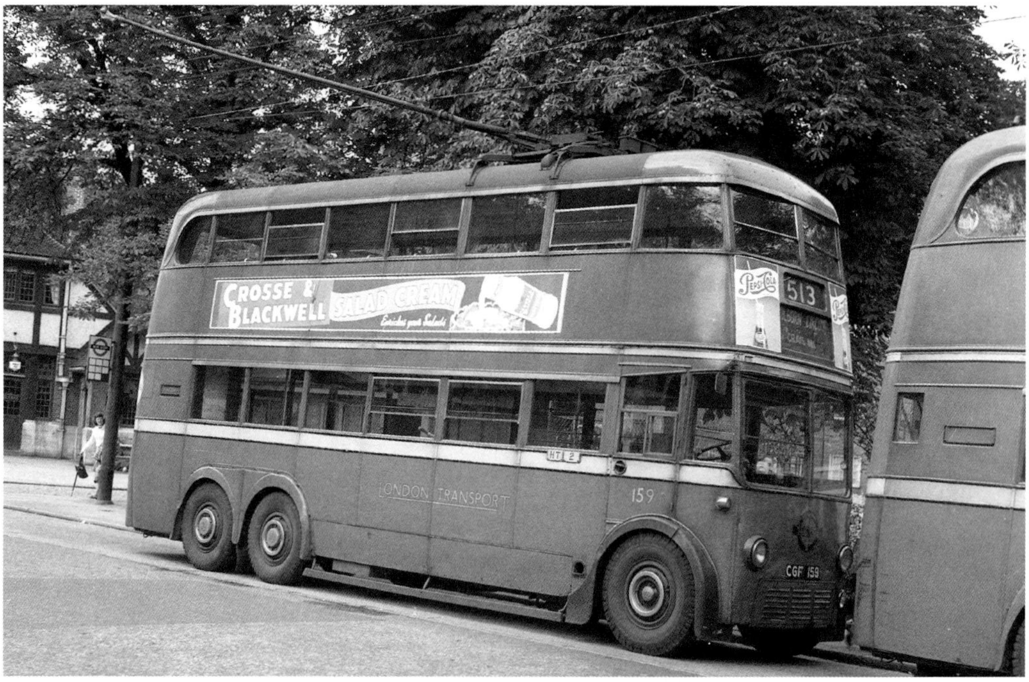

The first order placed by London Transport for AEC trolleybuses comprised the C class, the first dating from 1935. Seen at the 'Hampstead Heath' terminus is C1 class 159, bodied by Metropolitan Cammell Carriage & Wagon Co, which had not retained its offside platform signalling window, unlike the trolleybus ahead.

Michael Dryhurst

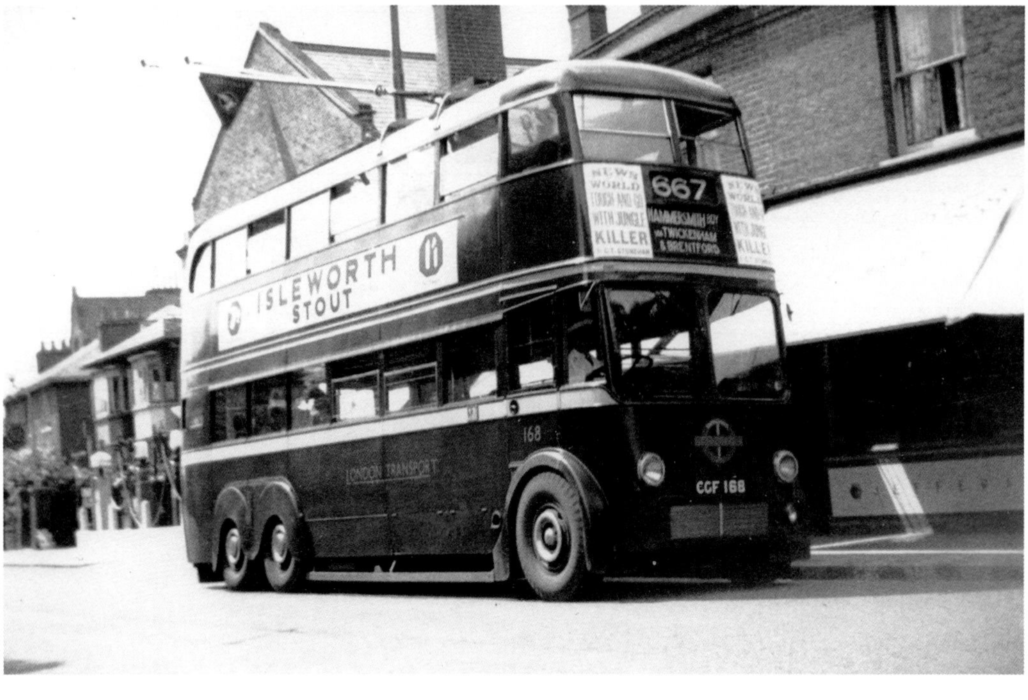

C1 class 168 proudly advertises Isleworth stout at a bargain price of 1/1d, as it sits in the sun on route 667. The driver is wearing his summer white coat in this pre war picture. This C1 was delivered in October 1935.

Mick Webber Collection

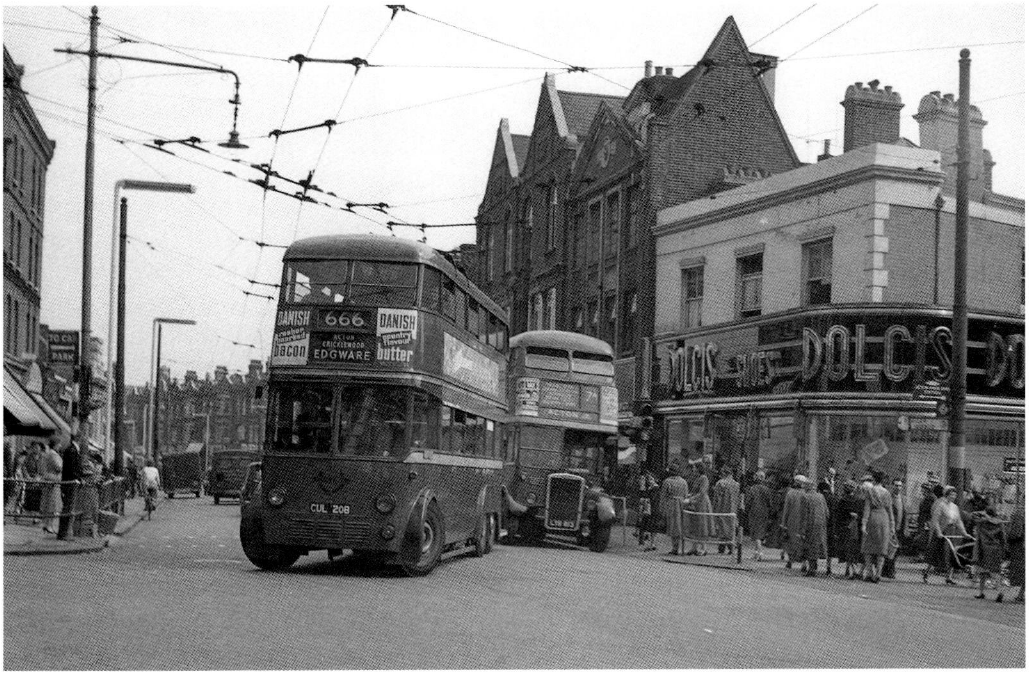

C2 class 208 turns out of Acton High Street into Horn Lane, whilst RTL1281 edges past on route 7A, which became a victim of the post-1958 strike service cuts.
Michael Dryhurst

A Thursday in March 1958 and half-day closing in Harlesden, as C2 class 187, heads to Hammersmith replete with original grille and rear-wheel 'spats'.
Michael Dryhurst

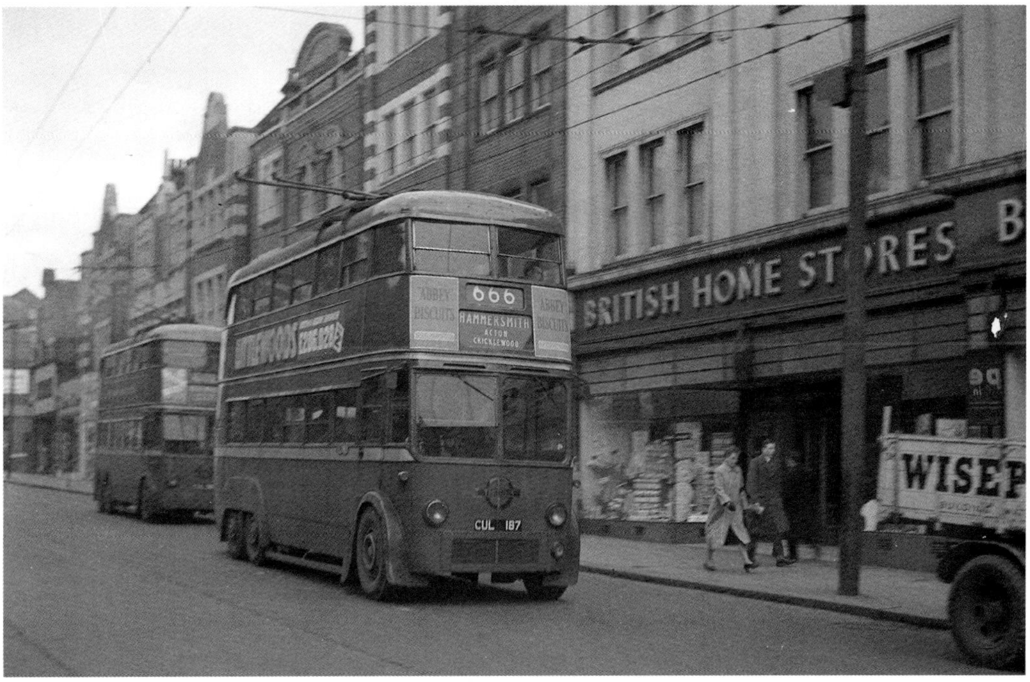

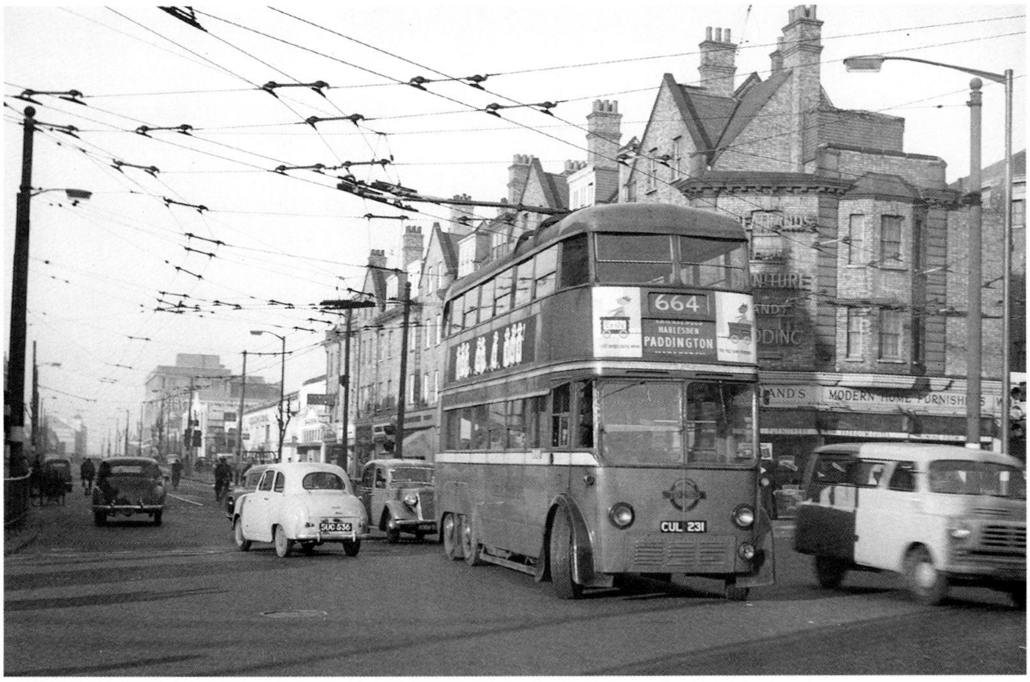

C2 class 231 is at Cricklewood Broadway on the last Saturday operation of the 664. Together with routes 683 and 695, this was a trolleybus casualty of the post-1958 strike service cuts.
Michael Dryhurst

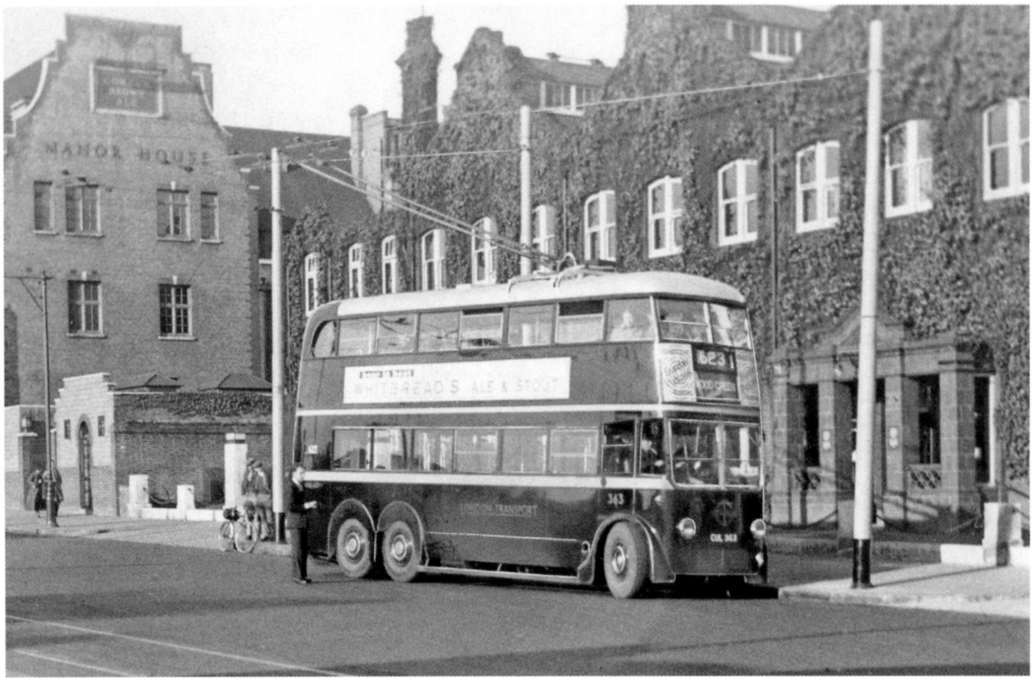

This is the first day of service (18th October 1936) of C3 class 363 on route 623, allocated to Walthamstow Depot. Manor House was the western terminus of this route that continued until 26 April 1960.

John Aldridge collection

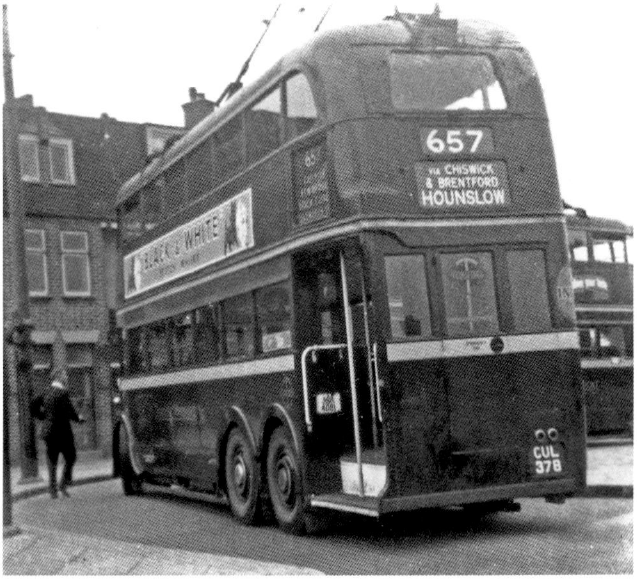

This view of 378 shows the modifications made to the platform area of this trolleybus for 'Pay As You Board' trials with a seated conductor in a cabin over the rear nearside wheel. This reduced the seating capacity from 70 to 64 seats.

BA Chaplin, courtesy of John Aldridge

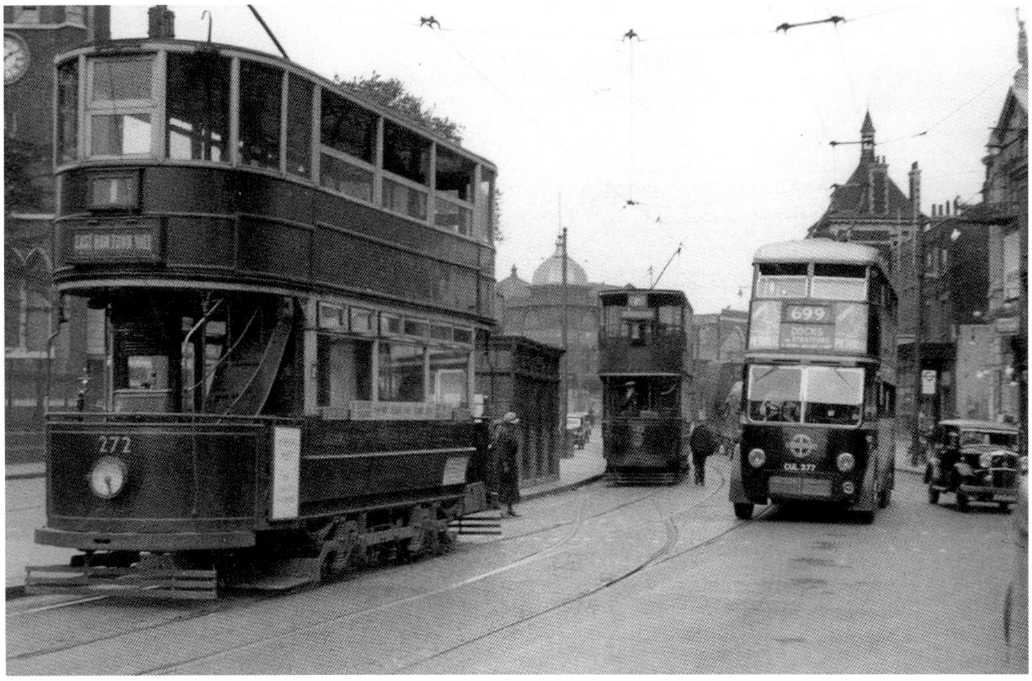

New C3 class 377 sets off for the docks on route 699. It is passing the old order in the shape of tramcar 272 which is working the soon to be replaced route 1.

DWK Jones

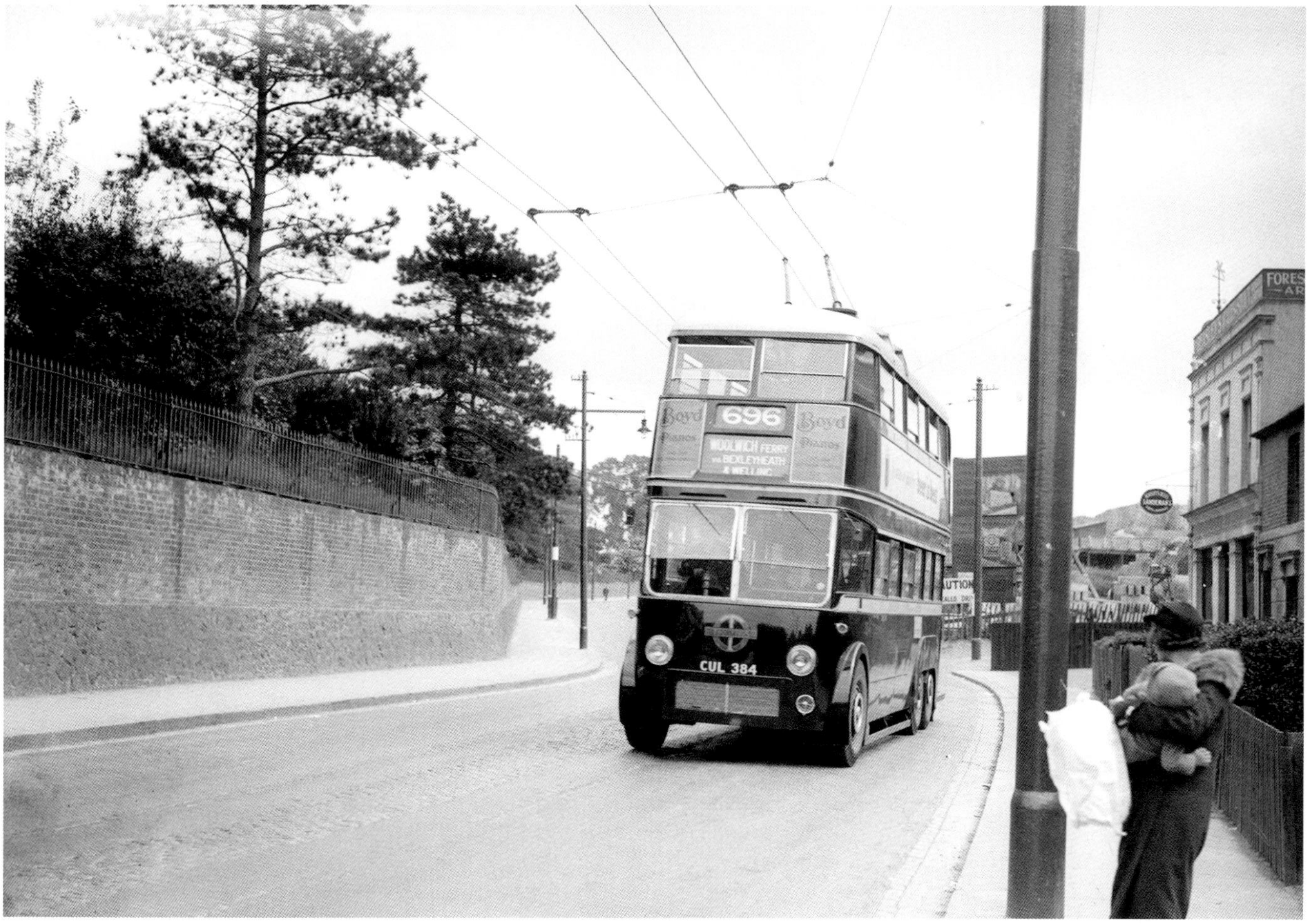

The first trolleybus to be completly built by Leyland, was D1 class 384. It was first used at Bexley, and is seen here on route 696 in Wickham Lane when new. *BCVM*

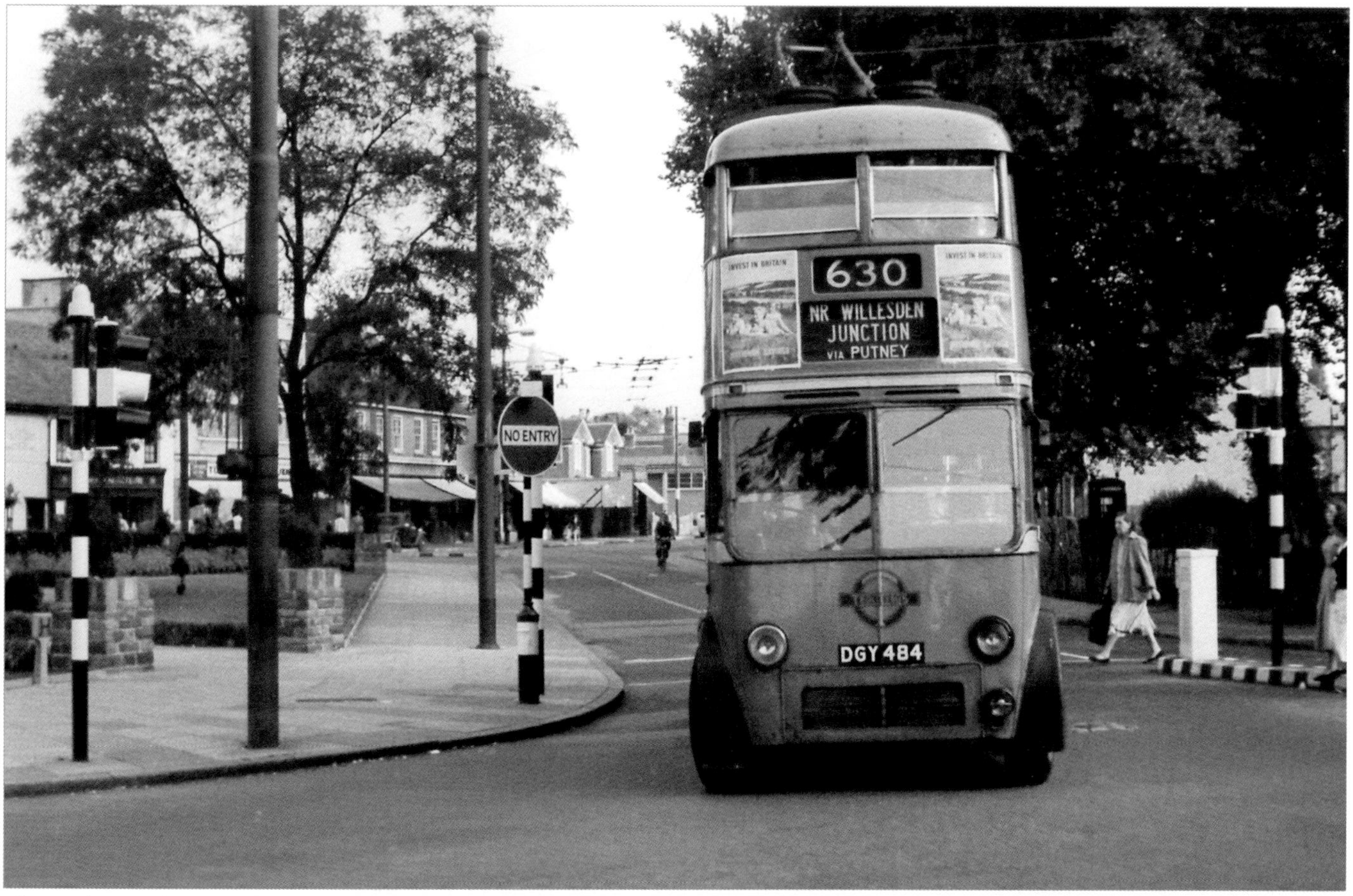

This early 1950's view of B3 class 484 was taken at Mitcham on route 630. The B3s were five short wheelbase 60 seat vehicles. *Geoff Morant*

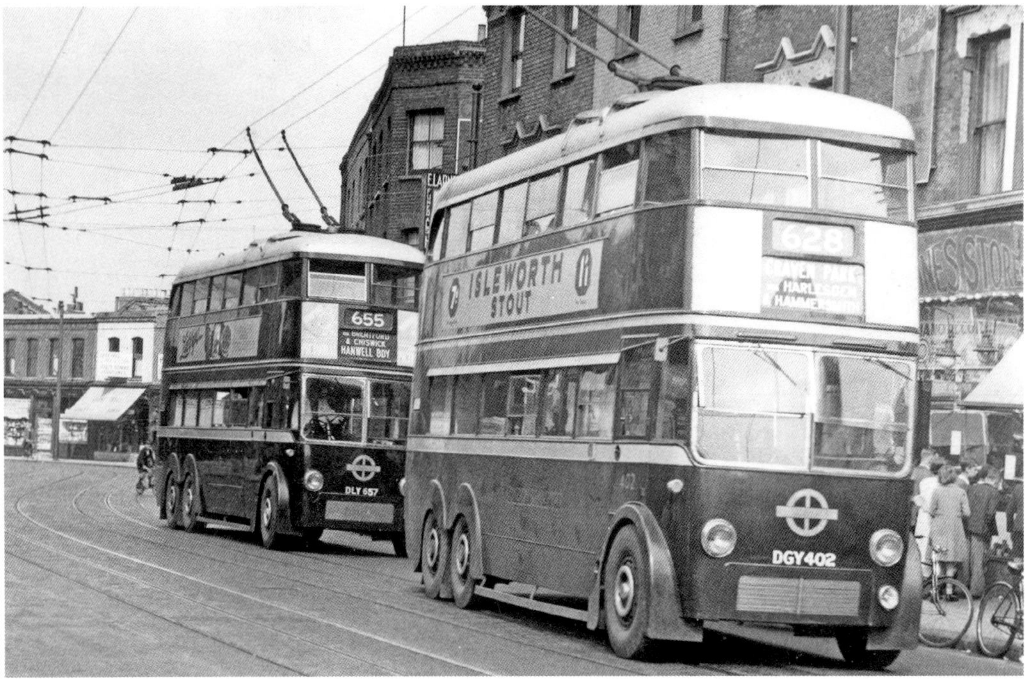

D2 class 402 was allocated to Hammersmith Depot for service on route 628 when this veiw was taken late in 1937. The body of this vehicle was destroyed by enemy action in 1944 and later rebodied by Northern Coachbuilders. F1 class 657 is at the rear.

John Aldridge collection

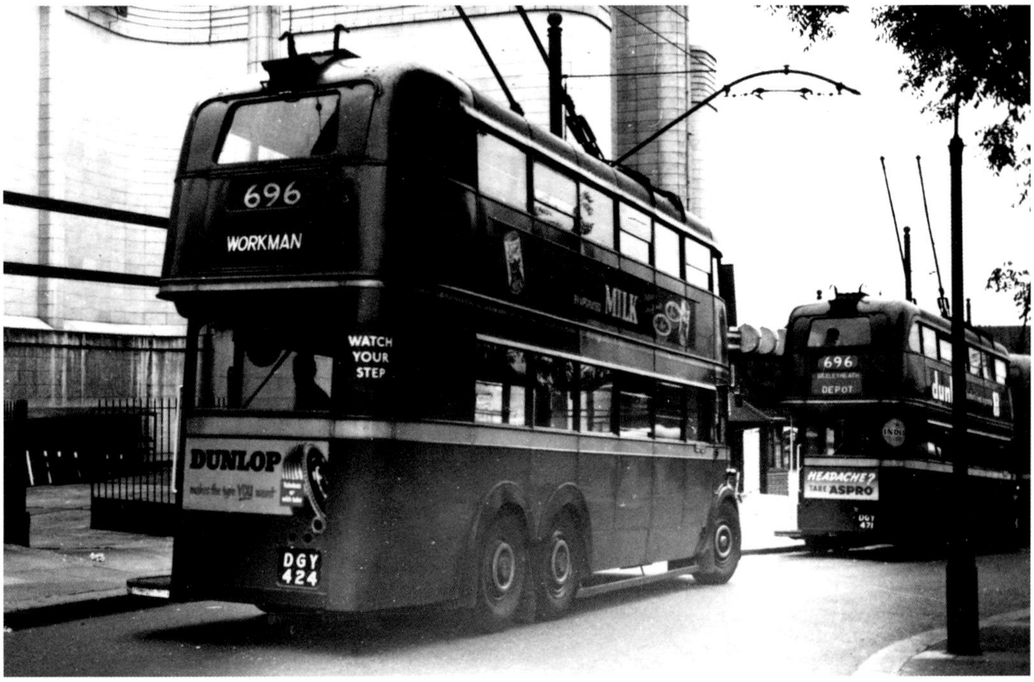

The D2 class are Metro Cammell bodied Leylands which arrived during 1936 and 1937. 424 is working the 696 from Bexleyheath Depot, and is seen on a workmans journey, waiting to depart from Parsons Hill, Woolwich. Workmen were entitled to discounted fares on these workings in the early mornings.

Mick Webber Collection

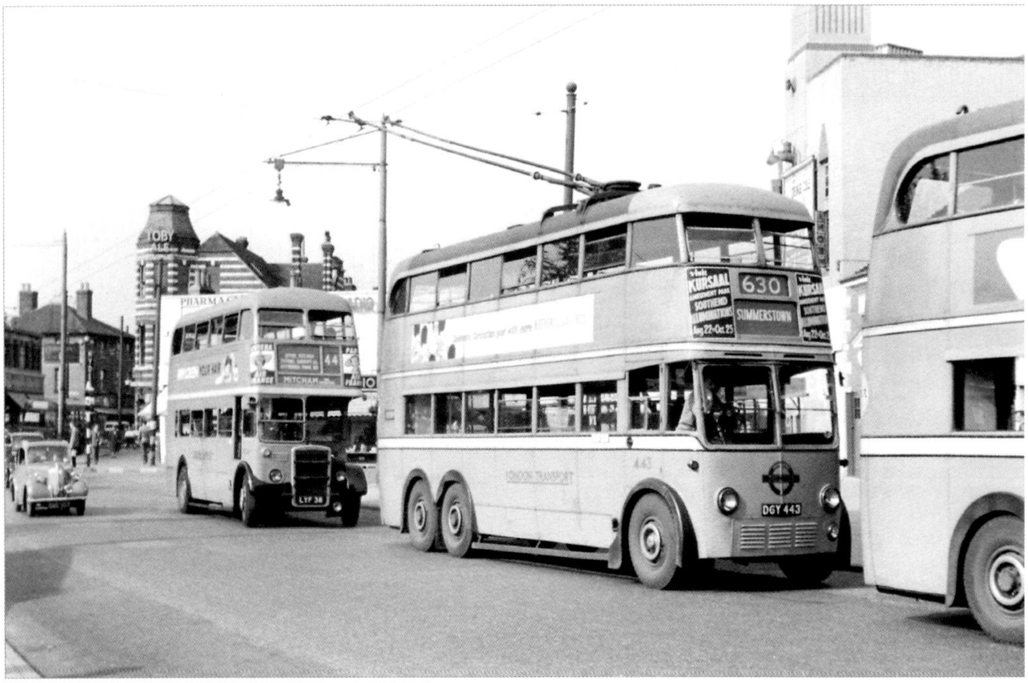

Mitcham is the scene here, as D2 Class 443 works a special to Summerstown. RTL 1114 is at the rear on route 44.

Geoff Morant

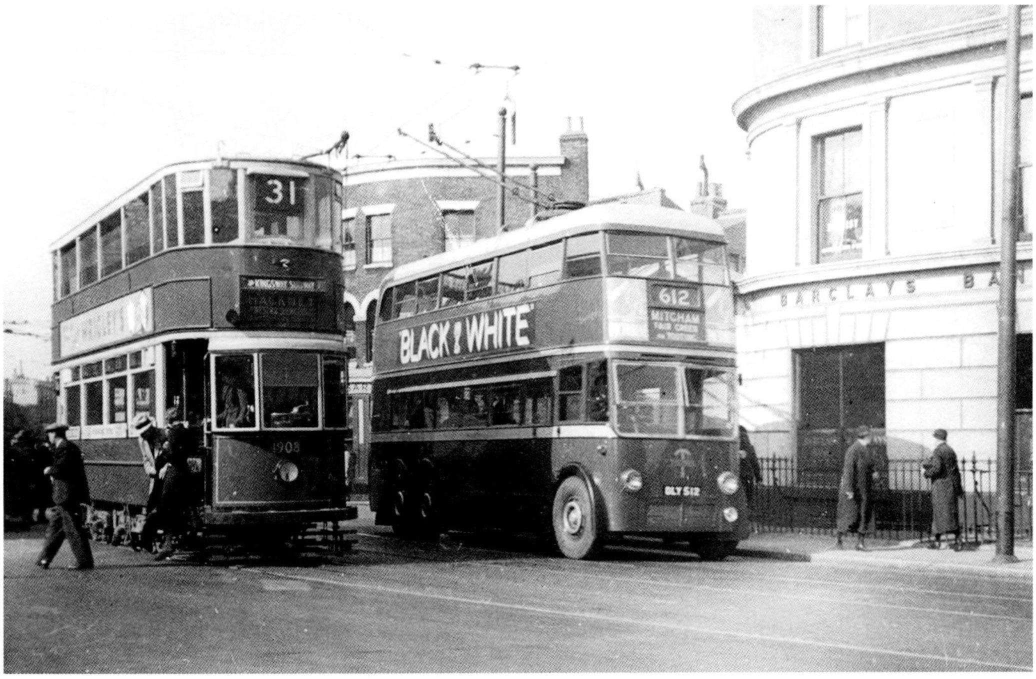

A section of tram route 12 had been replaced by new trolleybus route 612 in September 1937, and Wandsworth Depot supplied the vehicles. New D3 class 512 is seen here alongside 1908, an E3 class tram, the old with the new. The D3s are BRCW bodied Leylands.
Mick Webber Collection

The first full-length Leylands to be bodied by BRCW are those of the D3 class, as exemplified here by 511 seen passing through Hammersmith Broadway on one of the few trolleybus routes to be worked jointly by two Depots, in this instance Hammersmith and Stonebridge.
Michael Dryhurst

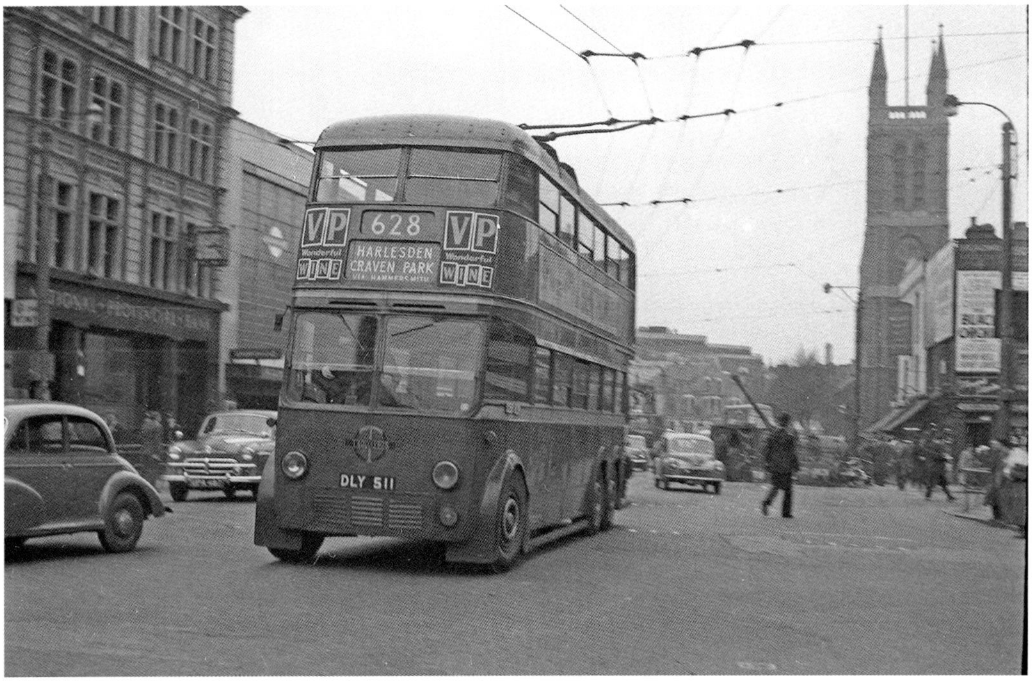

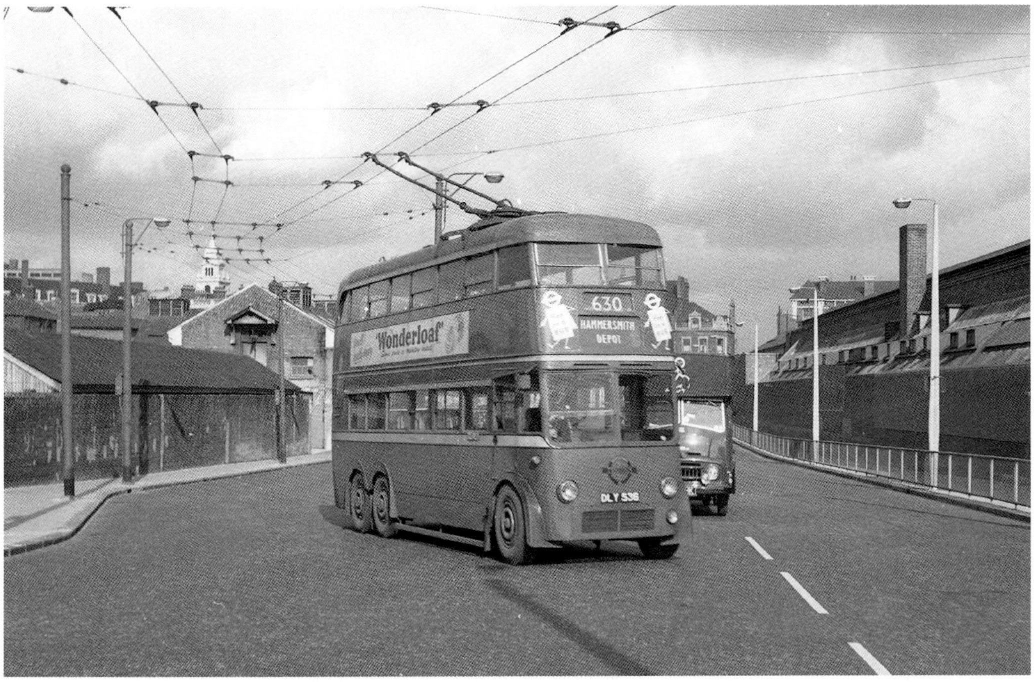

D3 class 536 makes the somewhat tortuous crossing of Butterwick from the bus station to access Hammersmith Depot.
Michael Dryhurst

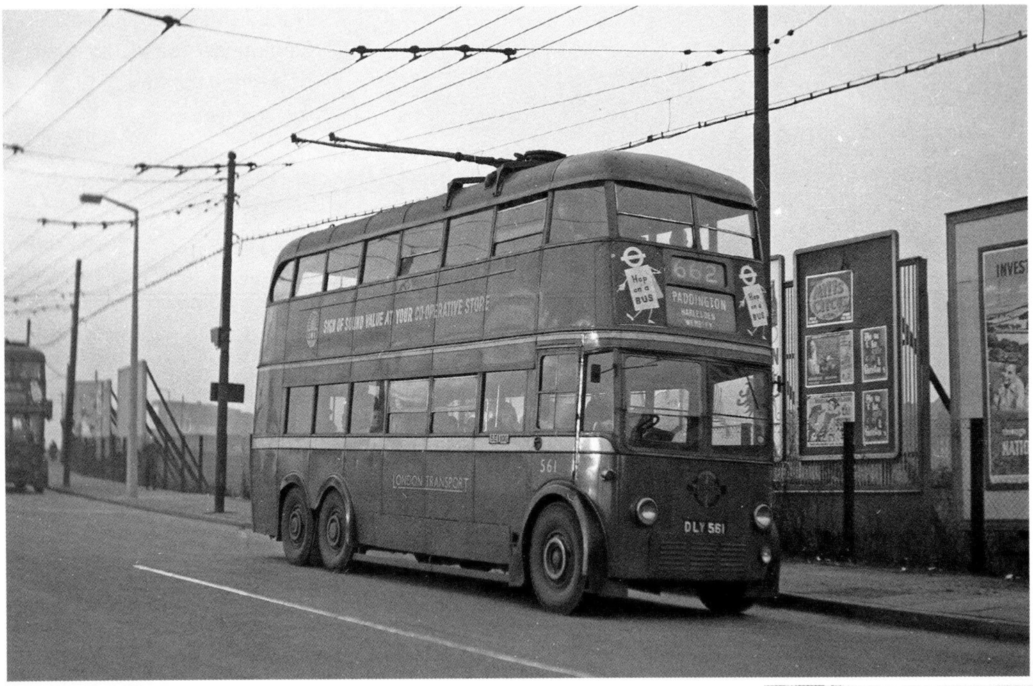

The 50 E1 class trolleybuses are AECs with Brush bodywork, distinguishable by the more deep dome. 561 passes through College Park, for many years denoted as 'Nr. Willesden Junction'.
Michael Dryhurst

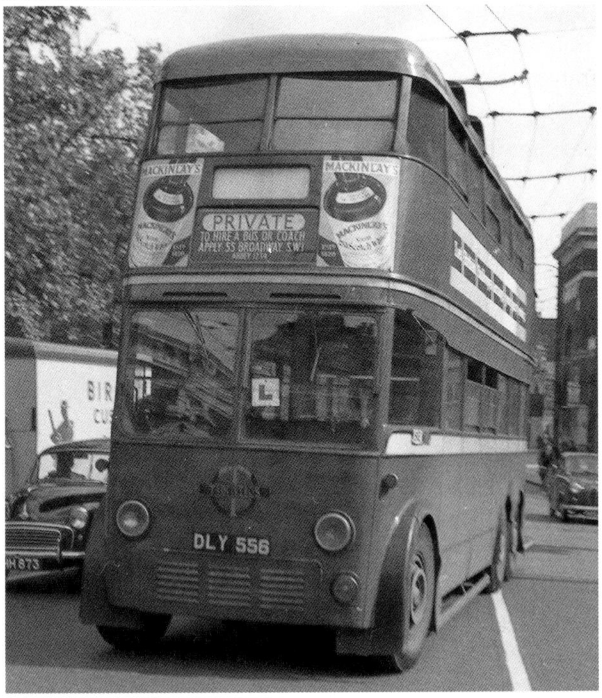

Each depot had its 'dedicated' trainer (usually two) trolleybuses, whereby the bulkhead window behind the driver could be removed. One such Stonebridge Depot vehicle E1 class 556, is seen here at Shepherds Bush Green. Trolleybus drivers were being trained until three months before the final conversion.
Michael Dryhurst

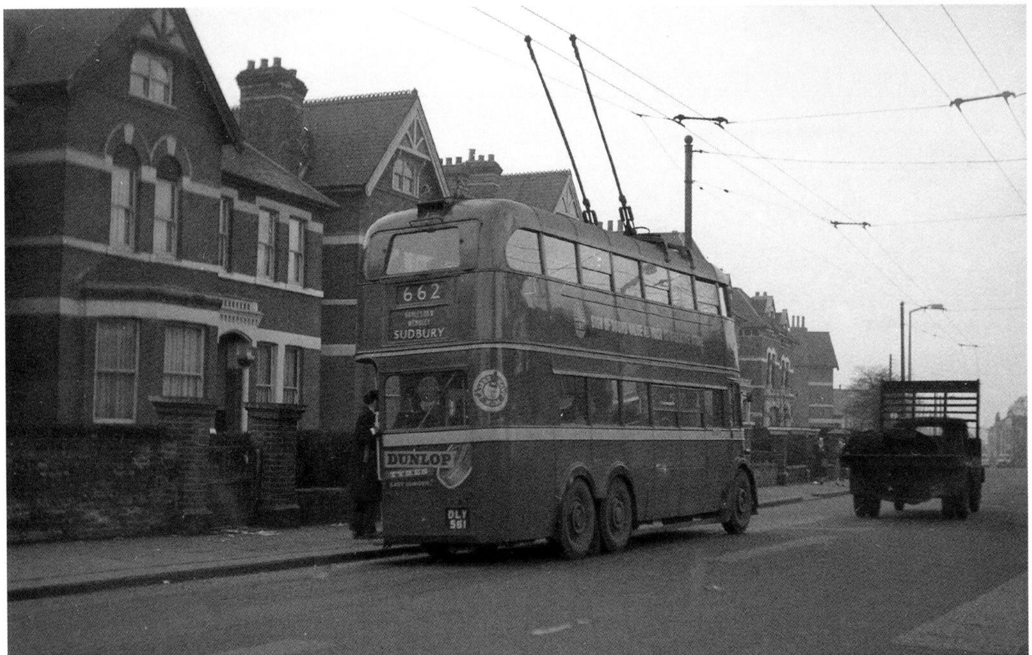

Seen leaving Craven Park for Sudbury is E1 class 561 on route 662.
Michael Dryhurst

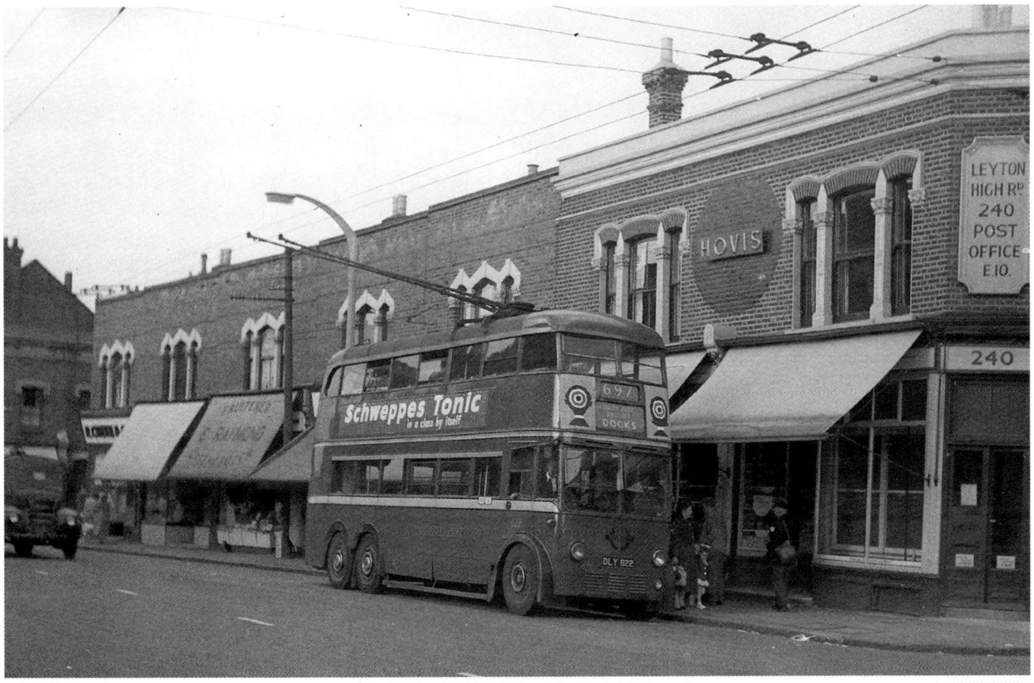

The E2 class trolleybuses were always based at West Ham depot, and 622 was made famous by the fact that it inaugurated trolleybus operation there, and in the early morning of 28 April 1960, was also the last trolleybus ever to operate into that Depot.
Michael Dryhurst

Weymann supplied very few trolleybus bodies to London Transport. However, the 25-strong E2 class was bodied at Addlestone. 619 is seen at the specially constructed 'Docks' terminus.
Michael Dryhurst

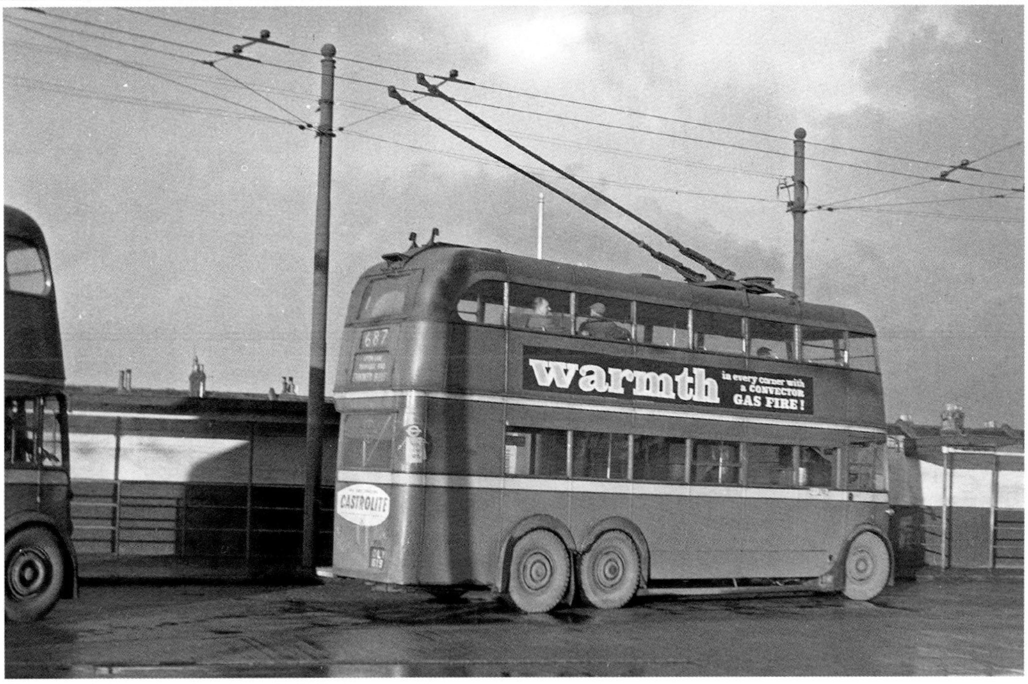

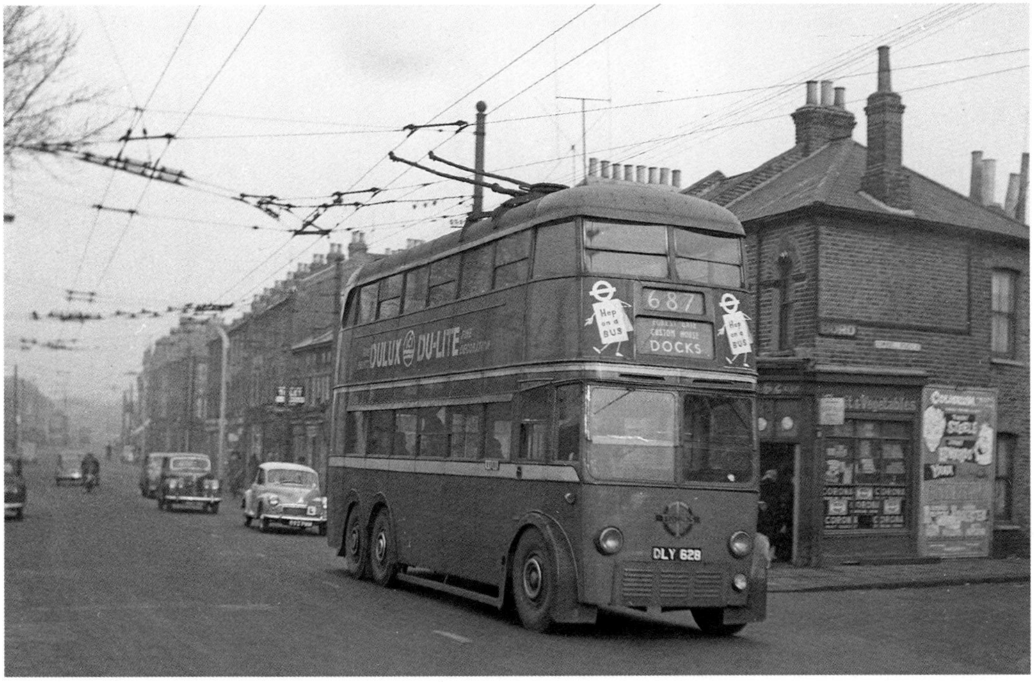

628 was not fitted with fireplaces, the chimney pots belong to the building behind. This E2 class trolleybus is seen passing the Downsell Road terminus, at Leyton.
Michael Dryhurst

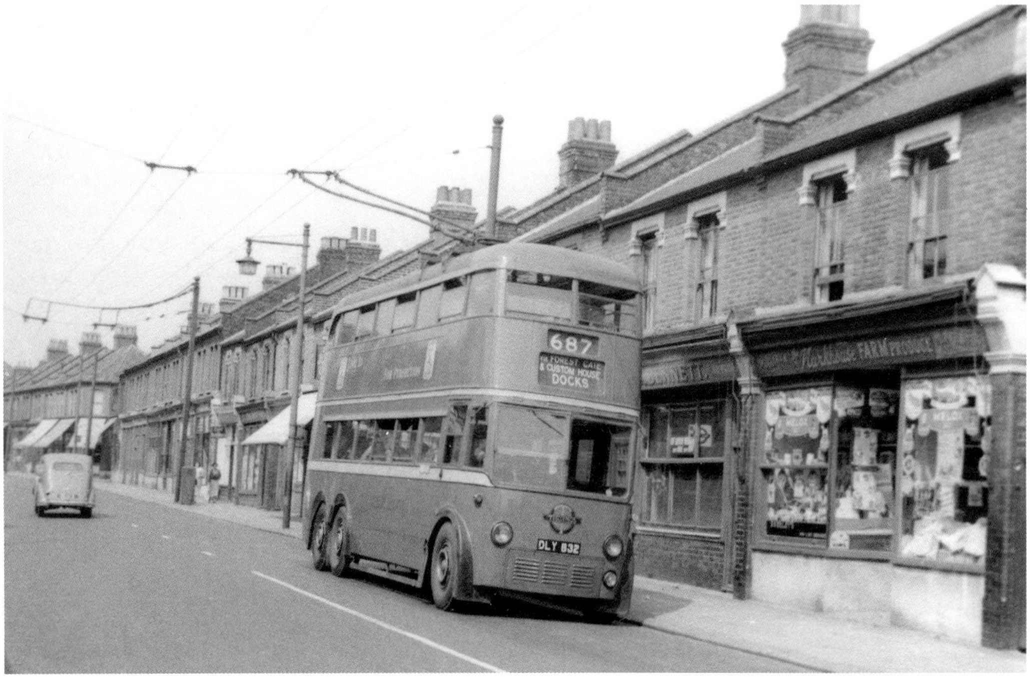

The E3 class were AECs with Park Royal bodies, which were not as robust as most other vehicles. Consequently, the whole class, apart from those rebodied after war damage, had been withdrawn by the end of 1956. 632 is shown on the Docks route 687 at Markhouse Road.
C. Carter

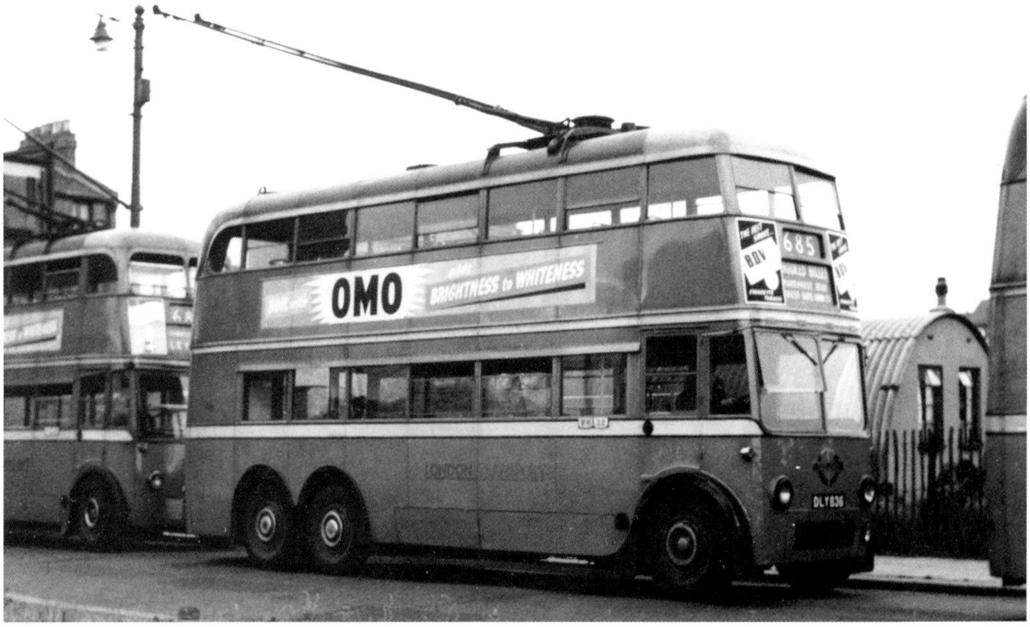

The E3s were easily distinguished by the row of four vents at the front between decks, which 636 shows here while waiting at the Canning Town stand on route 685.
Alan Cross

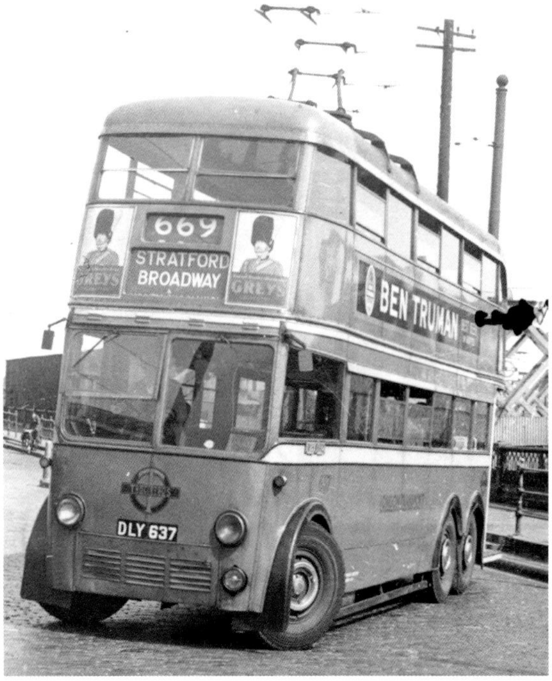

The Woolwich Free Ferry linked Bexleyheath trolleybus routes on the south side, with others at North Woolwich. Here, 637 is turning on route 669, from West Ham Depot. The E3s spent their whole operating lives at that depot.
LCC Tramway Trust

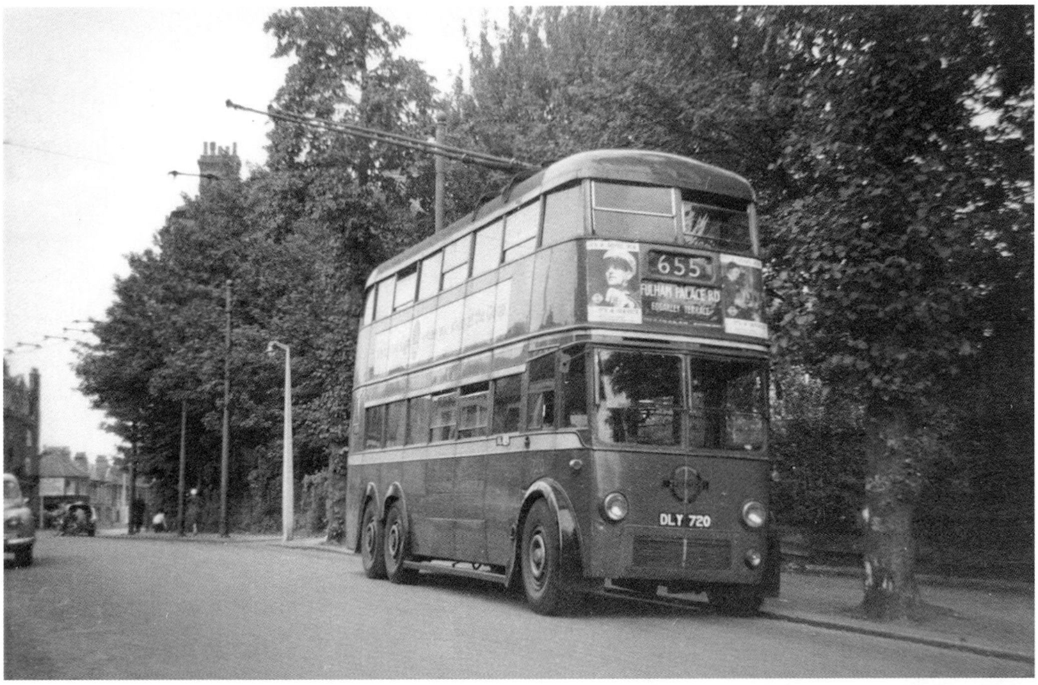

Hanwell Depot's F1 class 720 is working the 655. It has turned short at Fulham Palace Road, Edgarley Terrace, where it is standing in this 1960 view. The F1 class were delivered in 1937, and most, including this one, survived until Hanwell Depot was converted for bus operation in November 1960.
Mick Webber Collection

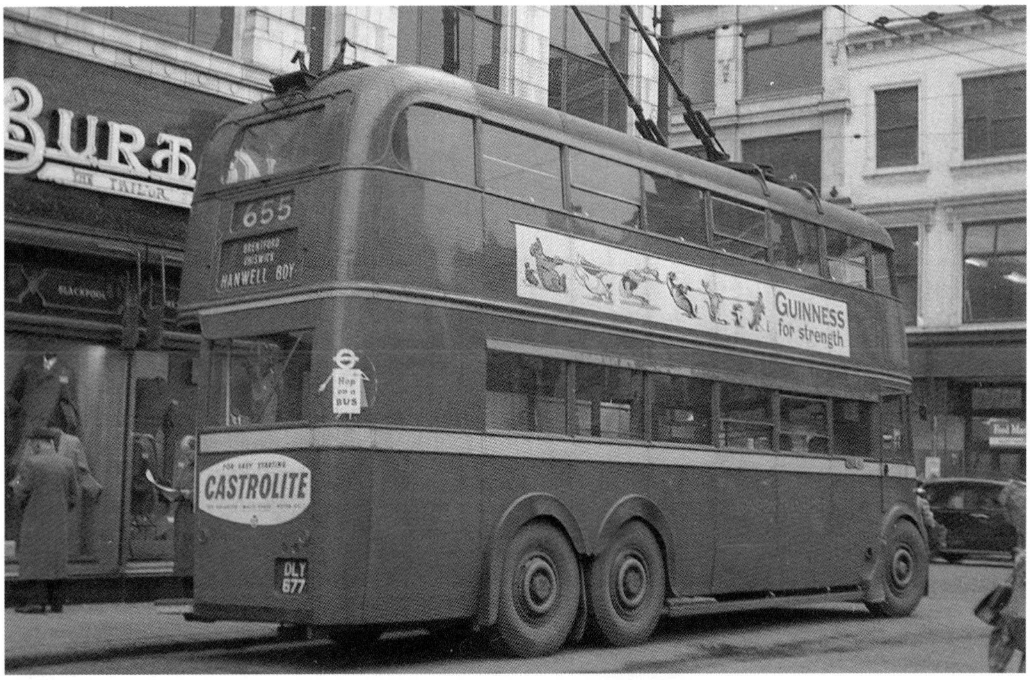

In recent years, much criticism has been levelled at the paucity of information on the destination screens of buses. But one doesn't recall trolleybuses ever having been so criticised, such are the brief details seen here on F1 class 677, an all Leyland trolleybus, which type was associated most particularly with Hanwell Depot.
Michael Dryhurst

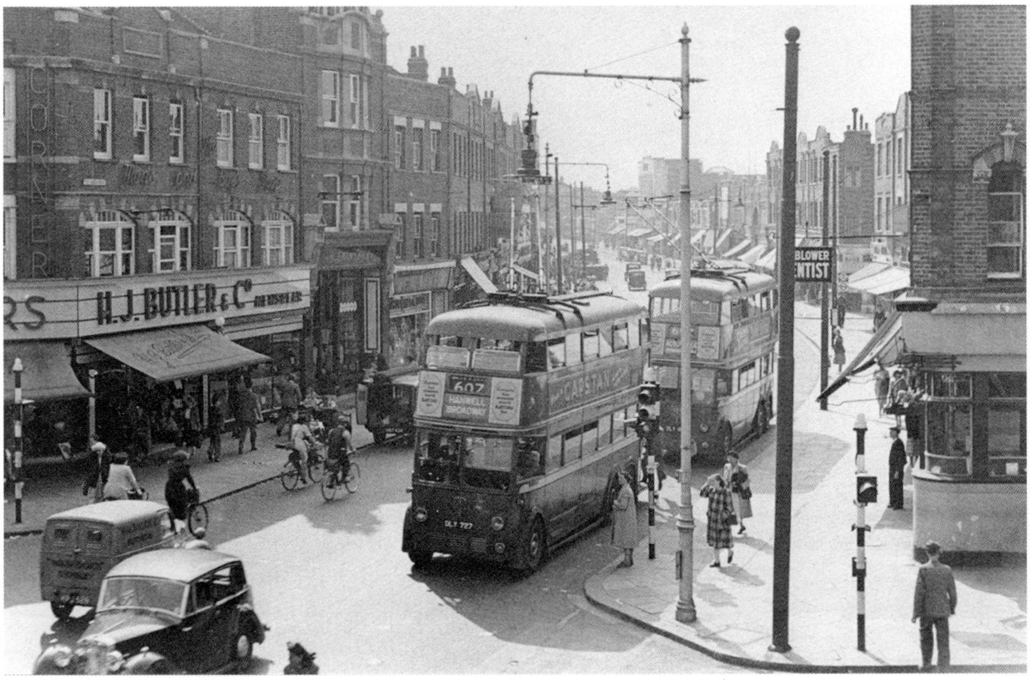

F1 class trolleybuses were the mainstay of route 607 throughout its period of operation. They were an all Leyland product, and 727 is working short to Hanwell Broadway, closely followed by another short working to Acton Vale, Bromyard Avenue. The Uxbridge to Shepherds Bush route was formally tram route 7, and after trolleybuses, became bus route 207. A later express bus route also re-used the number 607.
Mick Webber Collection

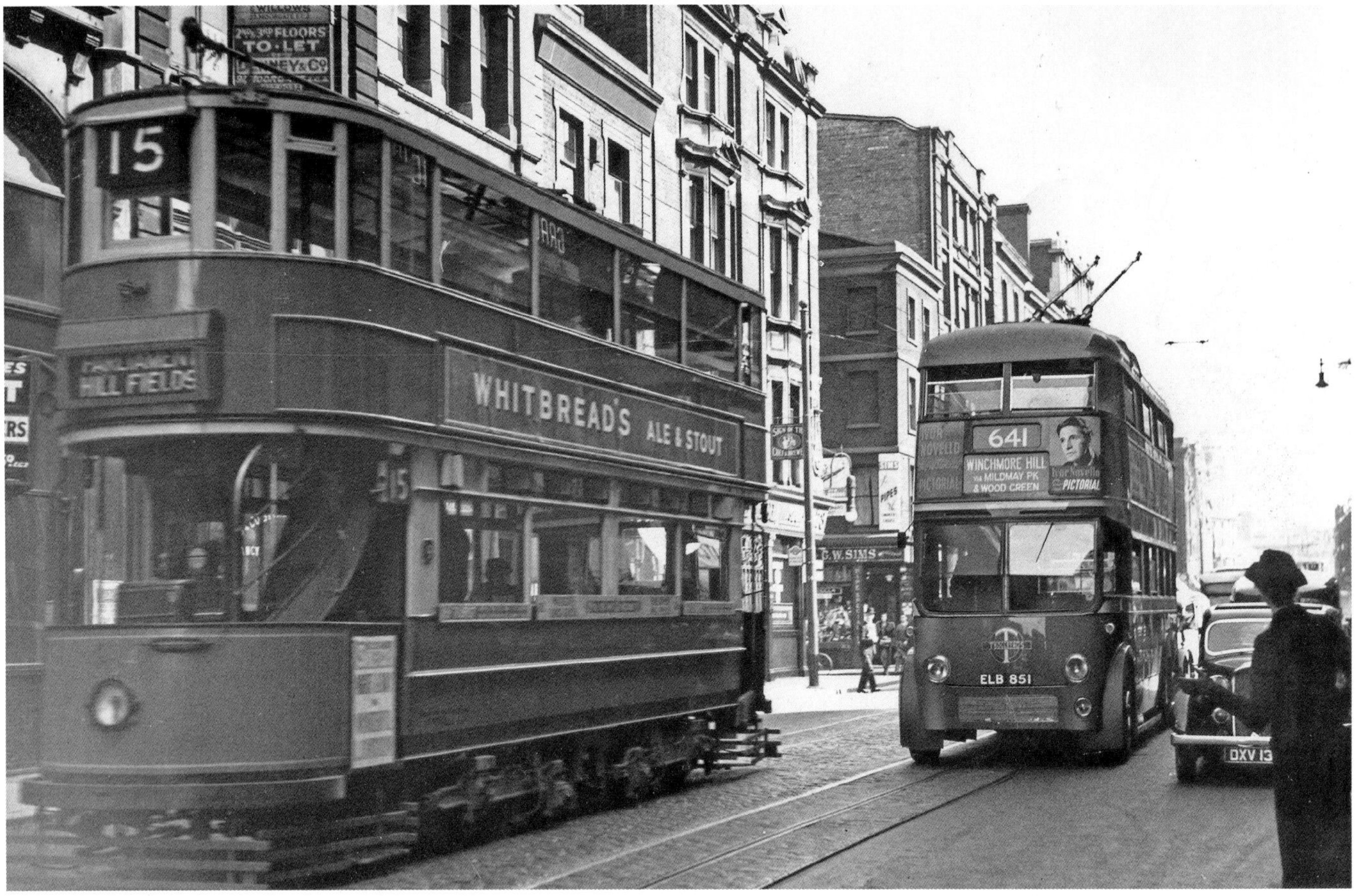

The Metro Cammell bodied Leyland H1 class of which 851 is an example, had recently begun service when this photograph was taken in June 1938 on newly introduced trolleybus route 641. This route ran daily between Winchmore Hill and Moorgate until its withdrawal in November 1961. *John Aldridge collection*

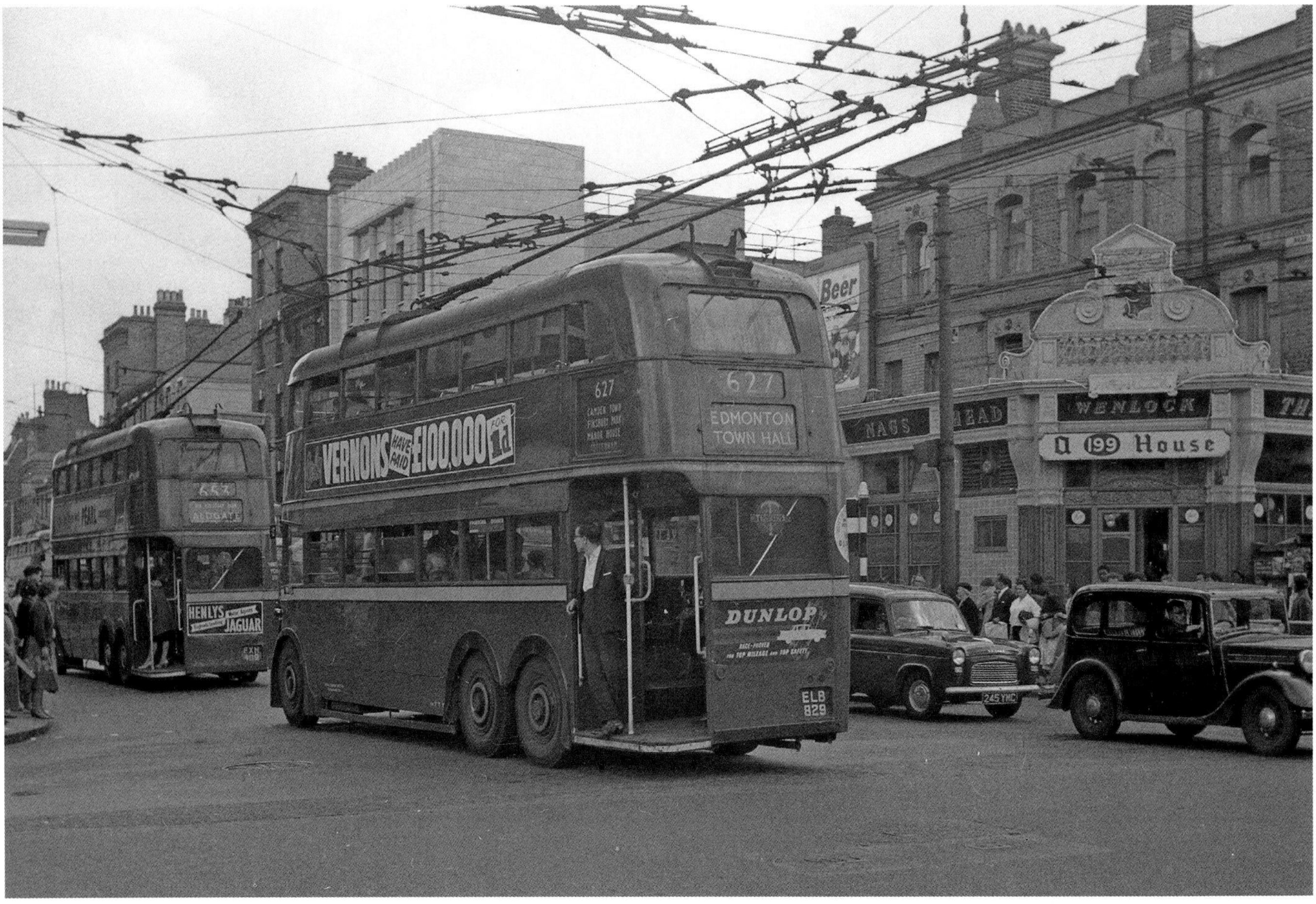

Wood Green was the Depot most readily associated with the H1 class. Although route 627 did not go anywhere near that Depot it had some peak-hour workings on that route, as seen here with 829 at The Nag's Head, Holloway. *Michael Dryhurst*

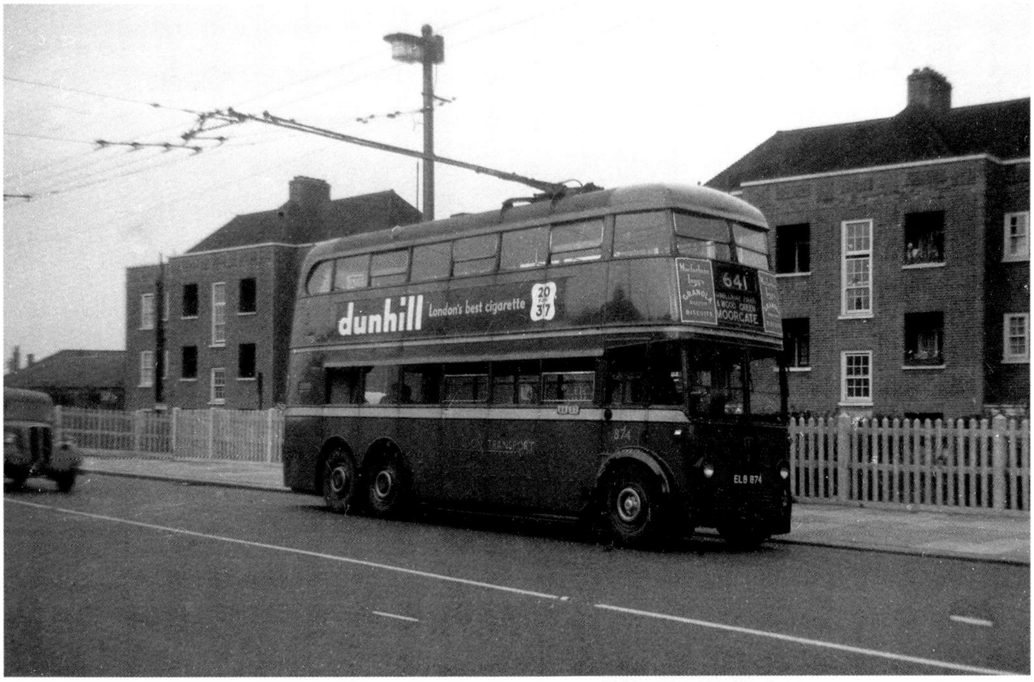

H1 class 874 is here photographed on 14 June 1955 at the Winchmore Hill terminus of route 641. Soon after the photograph was taken this trolleybus was overhauled and then reallocated from Wood Green Depot to Walthamstow Depot.
John Shearman

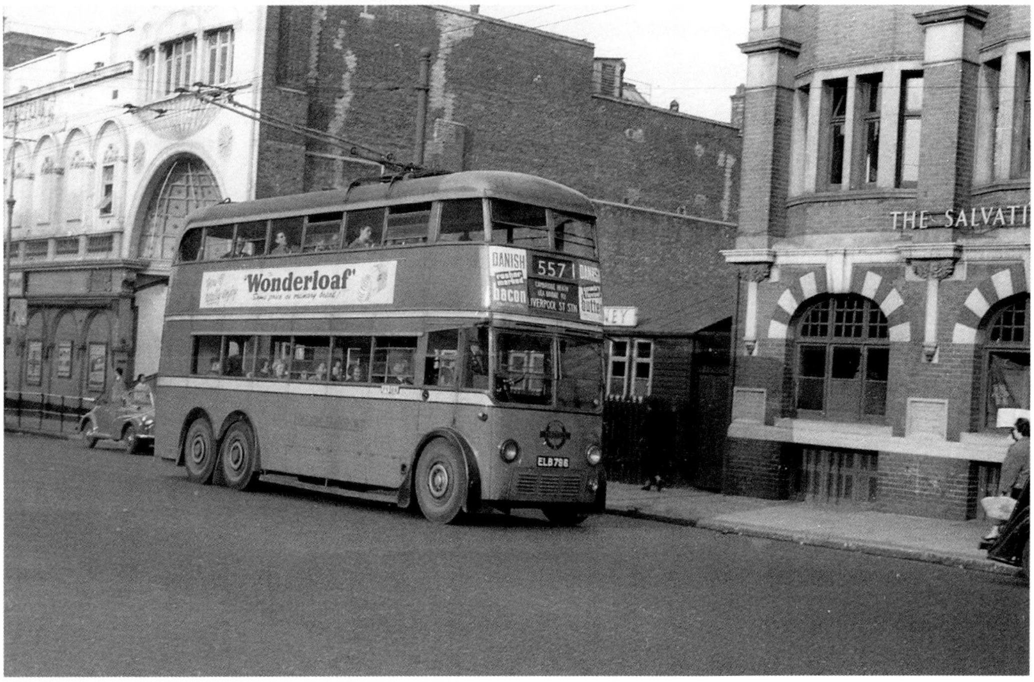

H1 class 796 is seen here in Mare Street, Hackney in March 1959 after its transfer from Bexleyheath Depot to Walthamstow Depot where it had spent almost all its working life. This trolleybus subsequently found fame when it was exported to France and was displayed at the AMTUIR Transport Museum in Paris. It was subsequently repatriated to the UK in October 2010 and has been restored for use in service at the East Anglia Transport Museum.
Brian Speller

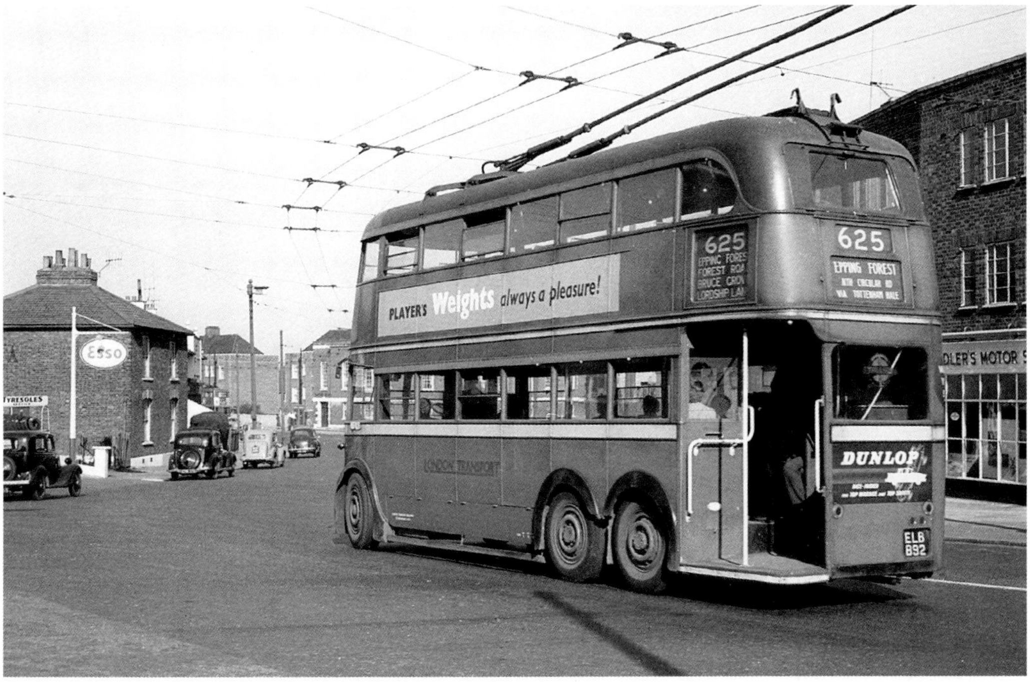

Trolleybus route 625 last ran on 26 April 1960 and H1 class 892 is seen here having left Winchmore Hill and is travelling along Green Lanes on 21 April 1960.
Brian Speller

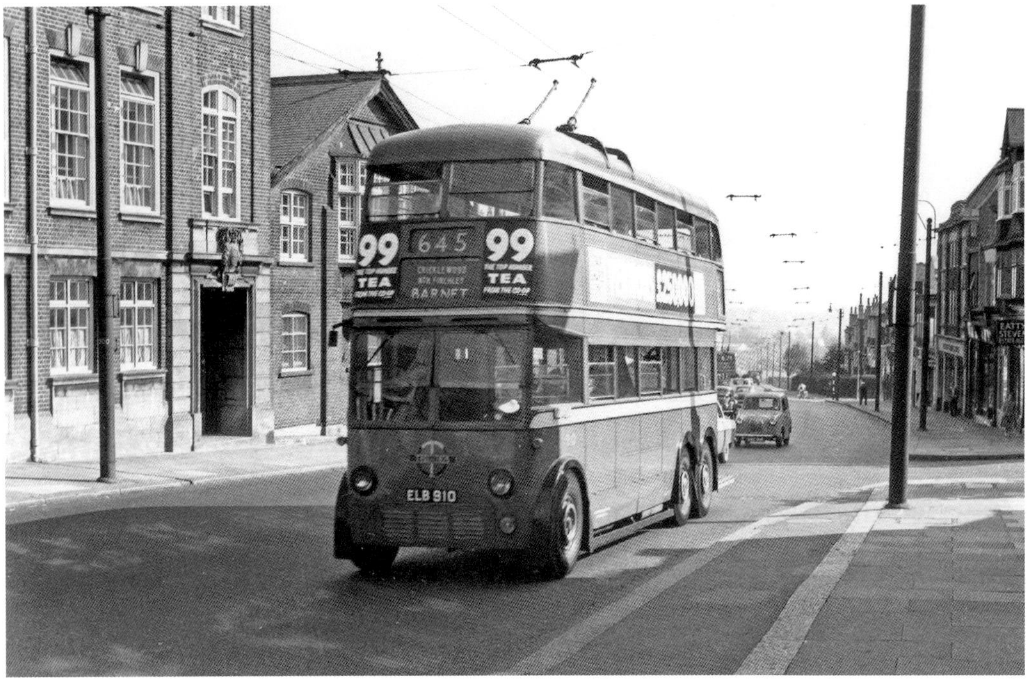

J1 class 910 was allocated to Finchley Depot and is seen heading towards Barnet on route 645.
John Aldridge

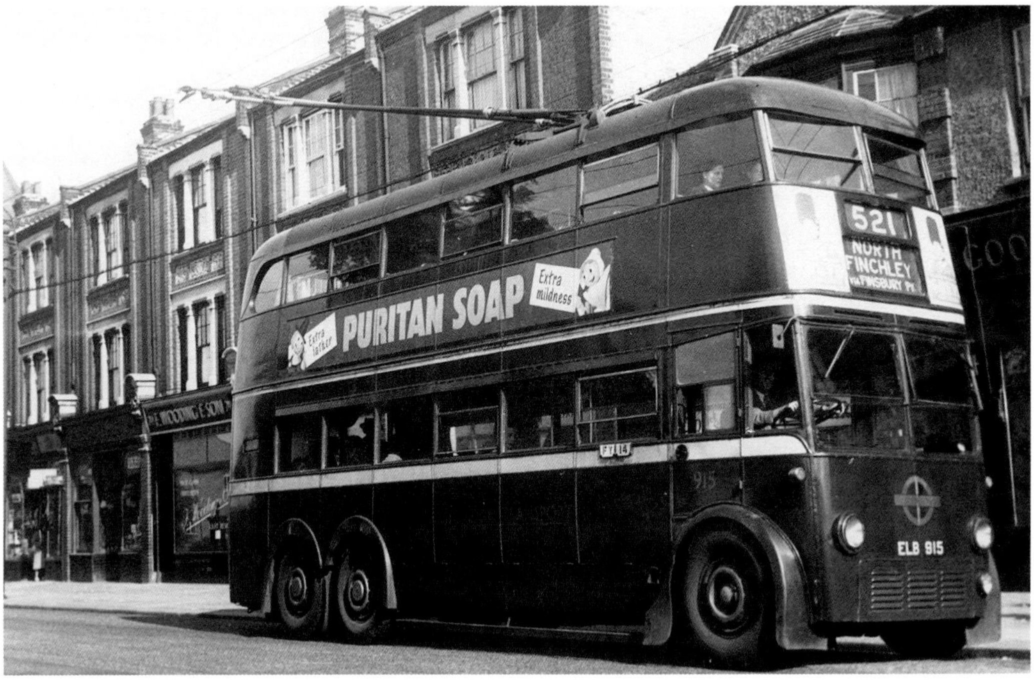

This early 1950s picture shows Finchley Depot's J1 class No 915, working route 521. All J class vehicles were taken into stock in 1938, and all have chassis built by AEC. The J1s have bodywork by Weymann.
Mick Webber Collection

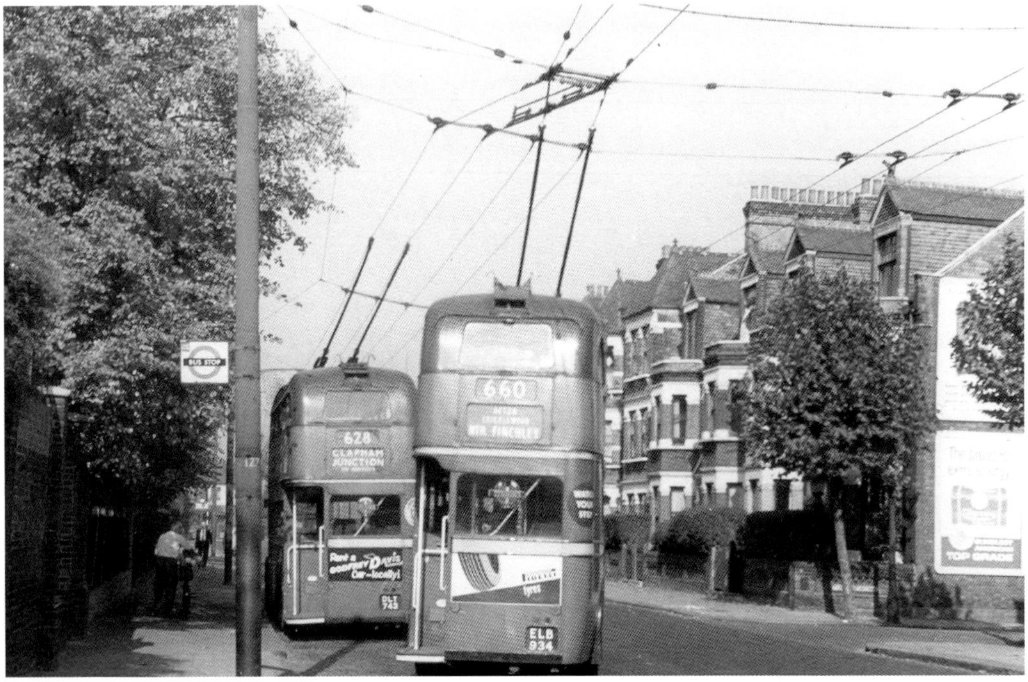

J1 class 934 is seen passing F1 class 743 in Craven Park Road, Harlesden on 4 October 1959.
John Aldridge

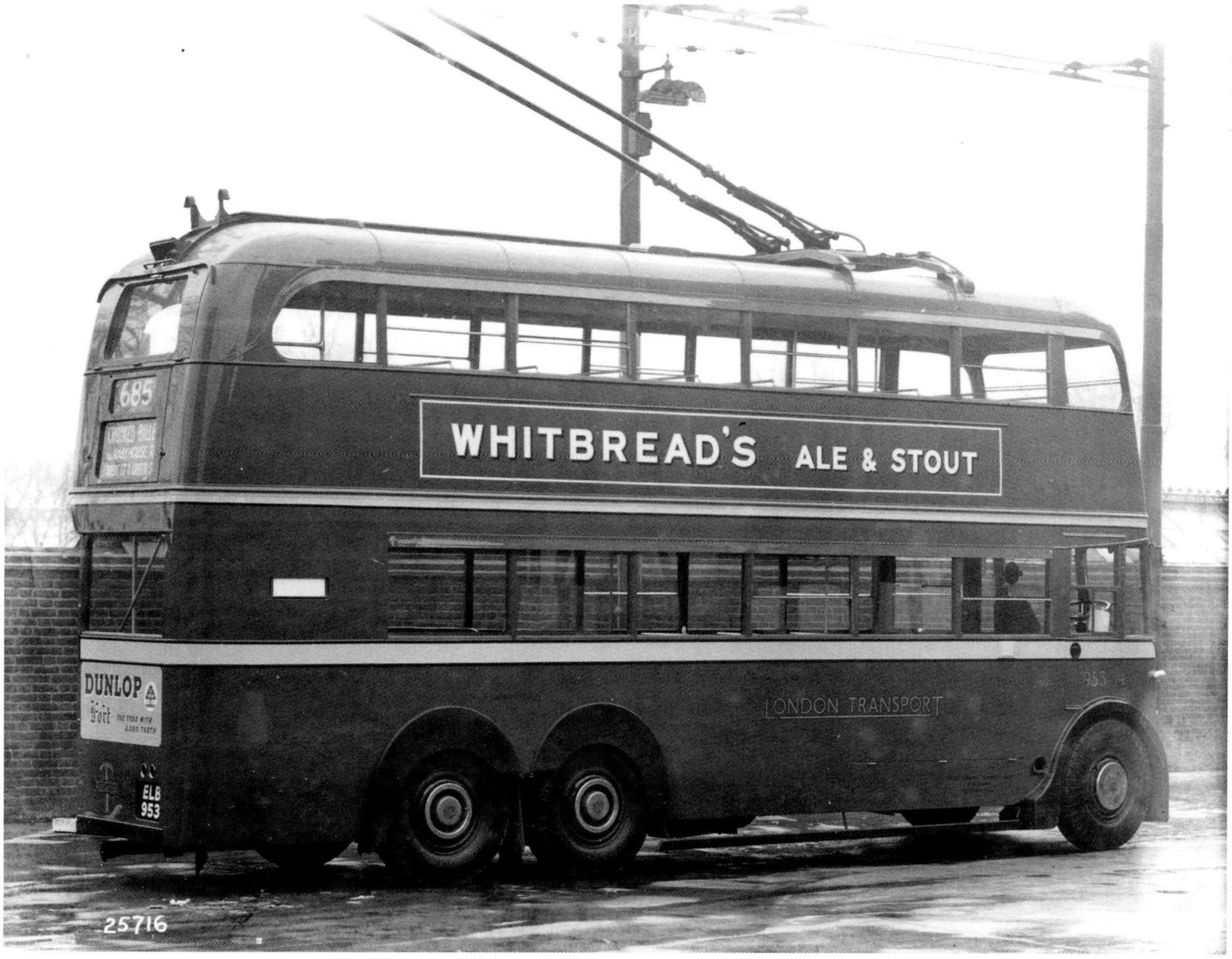

London Transport produced the first chassisless trolleybus in March 1937, numbered 754. This was followed by the first trolleybus of unit construction in February 1938, pre-production prototype M1 class 953. The bus was an AEC/Weymann product, and was allocated to West Ham, where it worked until destroyed in a fire in 1944. The trolleybus is seen here at that Depot in as delivered condition.
Mick Webber Collection

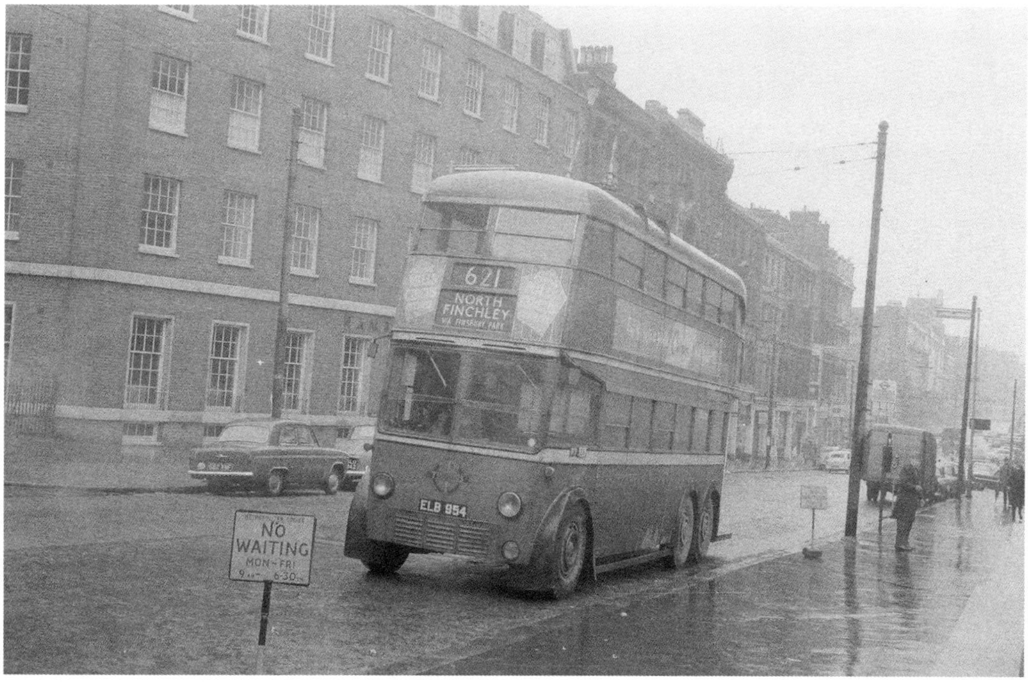

L2 class 954 is a preproduction prototype chassisless vehicle built by Metro Cammell with AEC running units that led to an order for 175 similar vehicles forming the L1, L2, L3 and X5 classes. 954 is seen at Holborn Circus on 28 January 1961. *John Shearman*

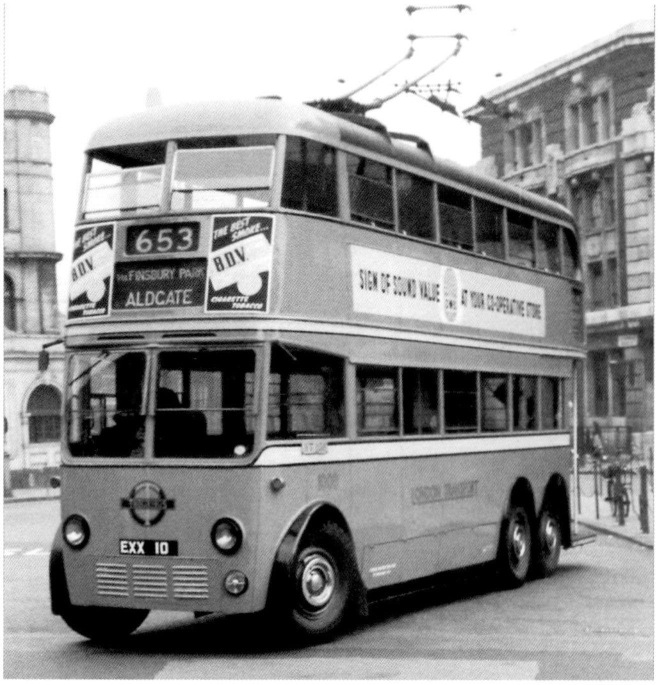

The only trolleybus with the EXX registration prefix, was J2 Class 1000. The vehicle is seen here working the 653 from Highgate Depot in the early 1950's.
Geoff Morant

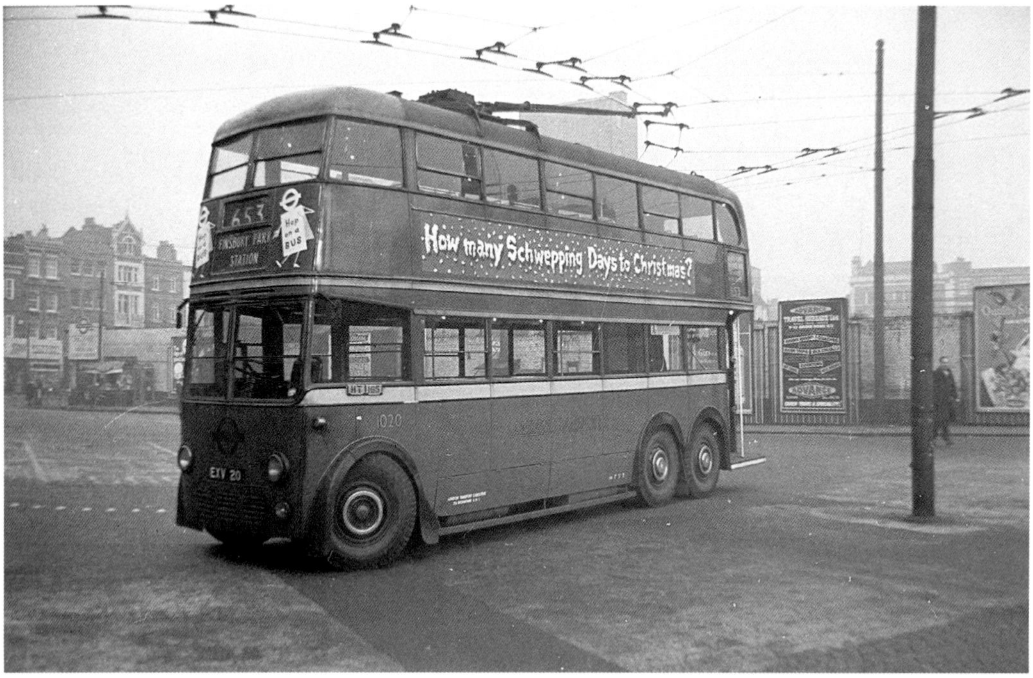

J2 class 1020 is seen at the Minories Bus Station, Aldgate in 1958.
John Shearman

Pentonville Road is the location, as J2 class 1022 heads for Moorgate on the 639, followed by an Austin saloon and an Atkinson lorry. BRCW were the bodybuilders of the J2 and J3 classes, which have AEC chassis. This trolleybus lasted until April 1960.
Mick Webber Collection

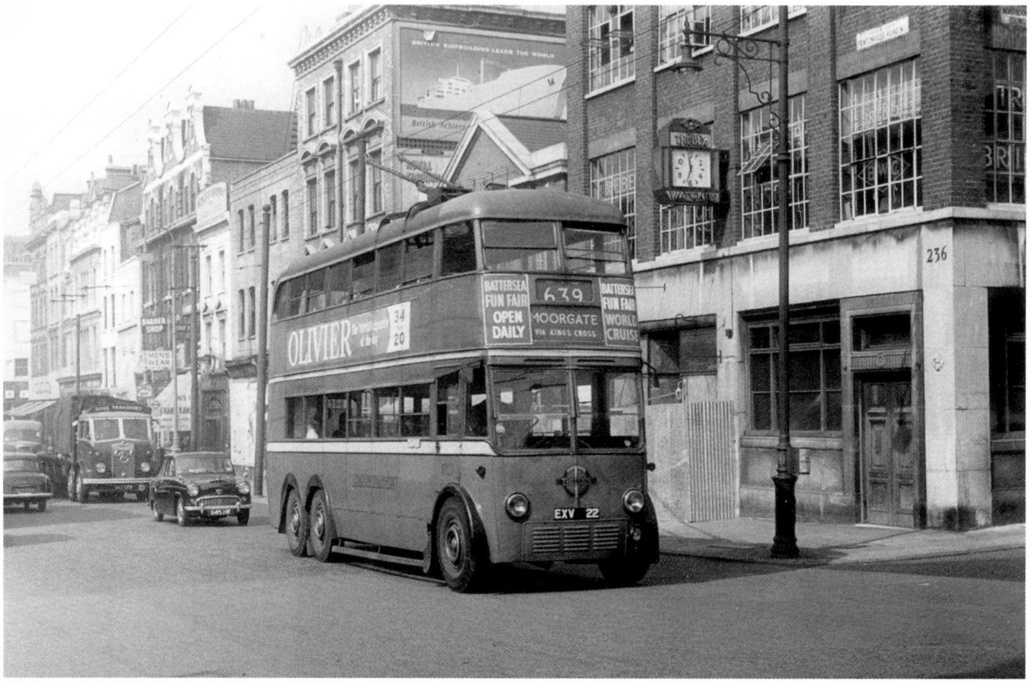

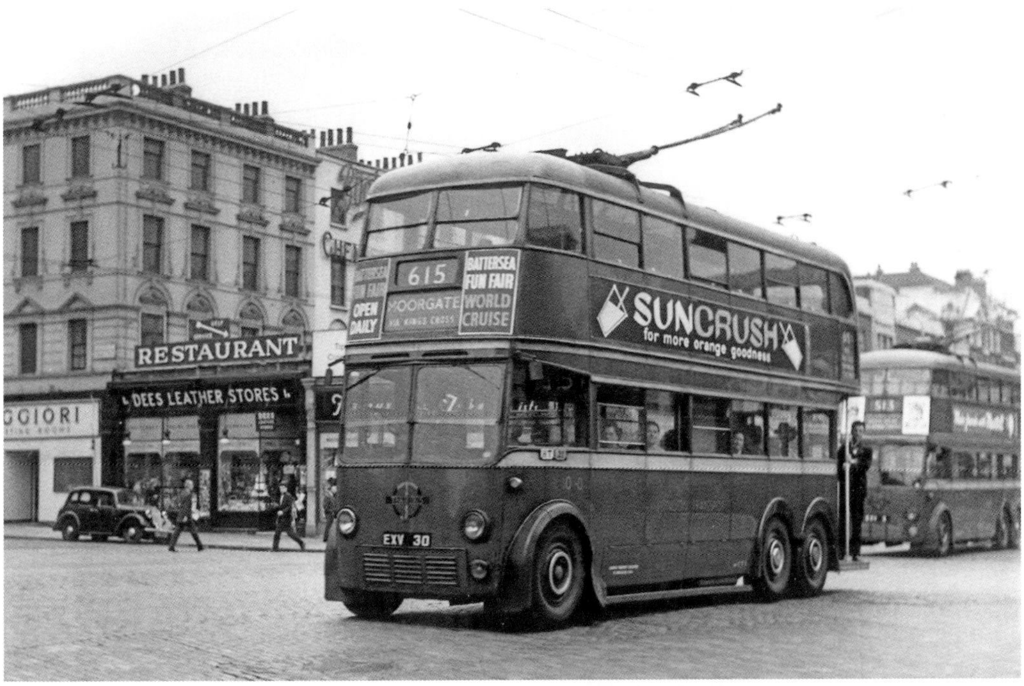

1030 was the first of the J3 class, and is seen here at Kings Cross operating from Highgate Depot on route 615.
Geoff Lumb

Highgate Village on 16 July 1960 is the location of 1052, a J3 class trolleybus fitted with coasting and run-back brakes required for the 611 route on Highgate Hill.
John Shearman

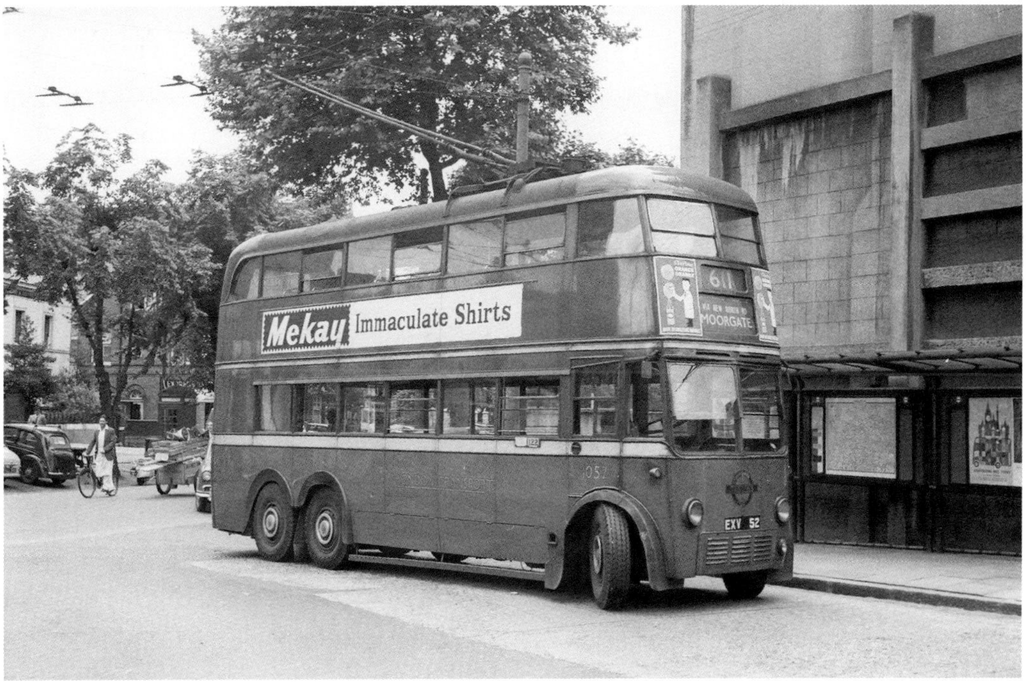

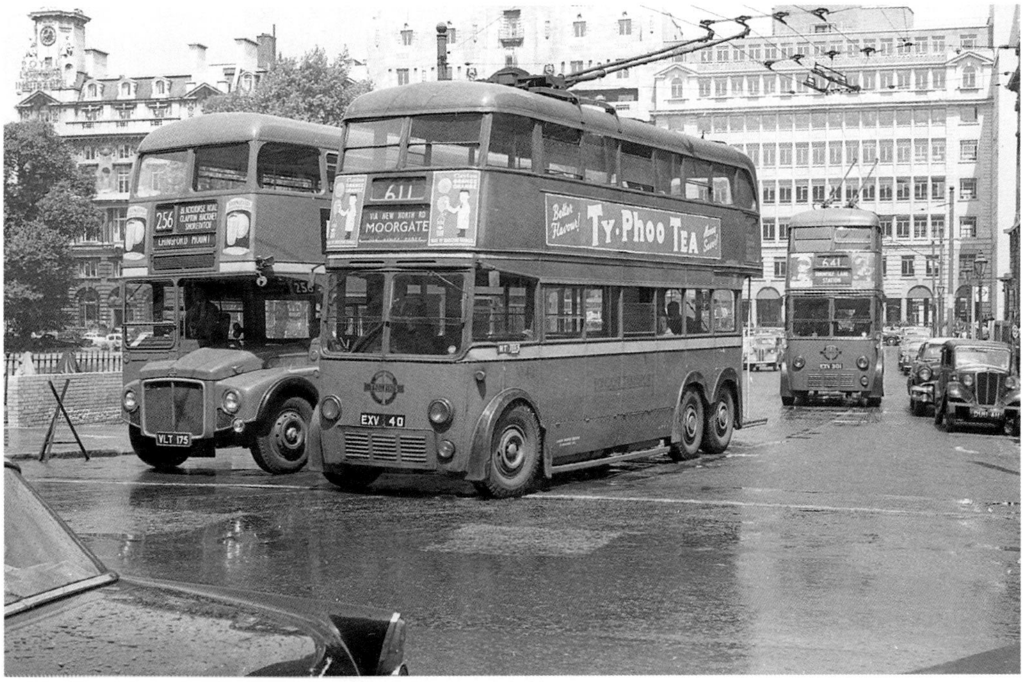

The old and new pass each other at Finsbury Square, Moorgate on 7 July 1960. In this photograph J3 class 1040 is alongside RM175 with K1 class 1301 following behind.
Brian Speller

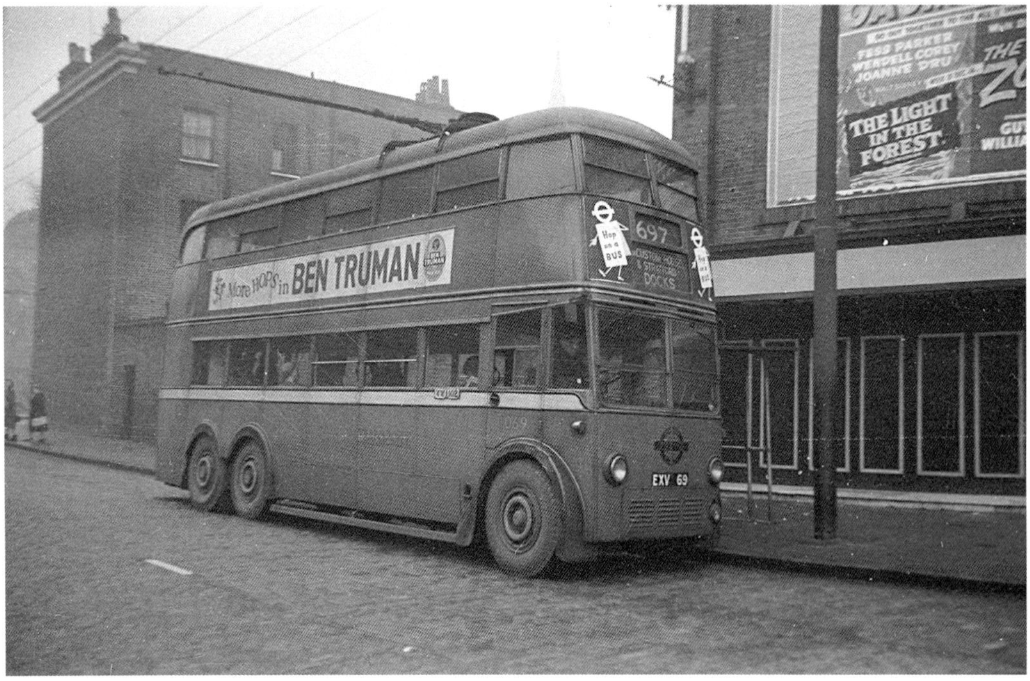

1069 is one of the 150 strong K1 class of all Leyland trolleybuses fitted with Metrovick control equipment. It is seen at Stratford Broadway in 1958. The K2 class also comprises all-Leyland trolleybuses, but these have English Electric controllers.

John Shearman

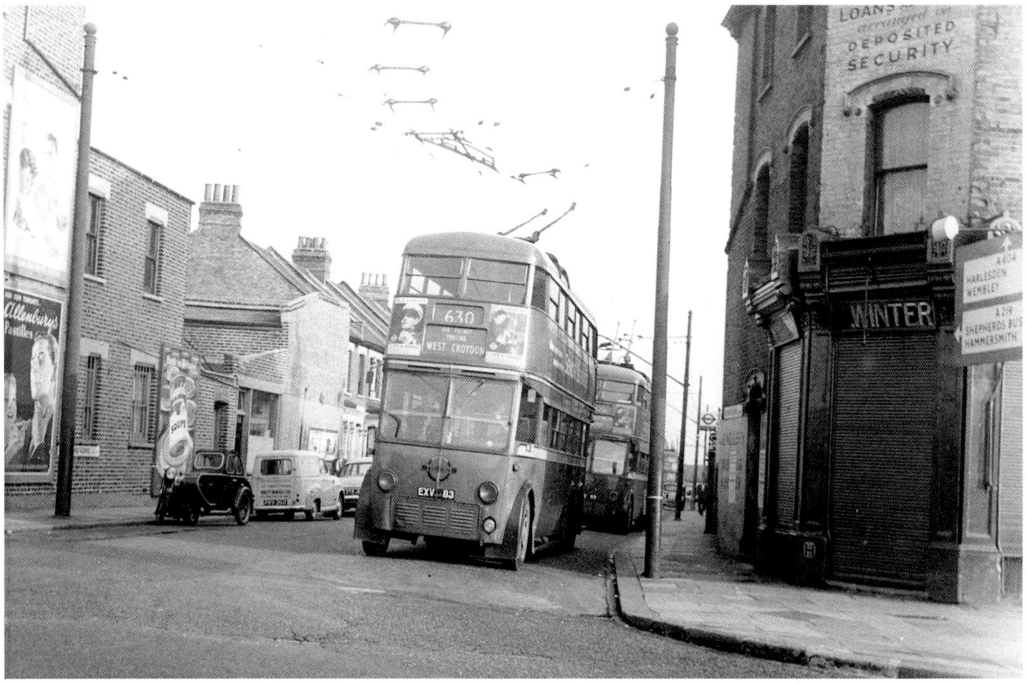

Letchford Gardens was the stand for trolleybuses turning on route 630, shown on the blinds as 'Nr Willesden Junction'. The terminus was a loop wired via Waldo Road, Harrow Road and back to Scrubs Lane, worked in an anti clockwise direction. K1 class 1083 waits for its long trip back to West Croydon in 1960.

Mick Webber Collection

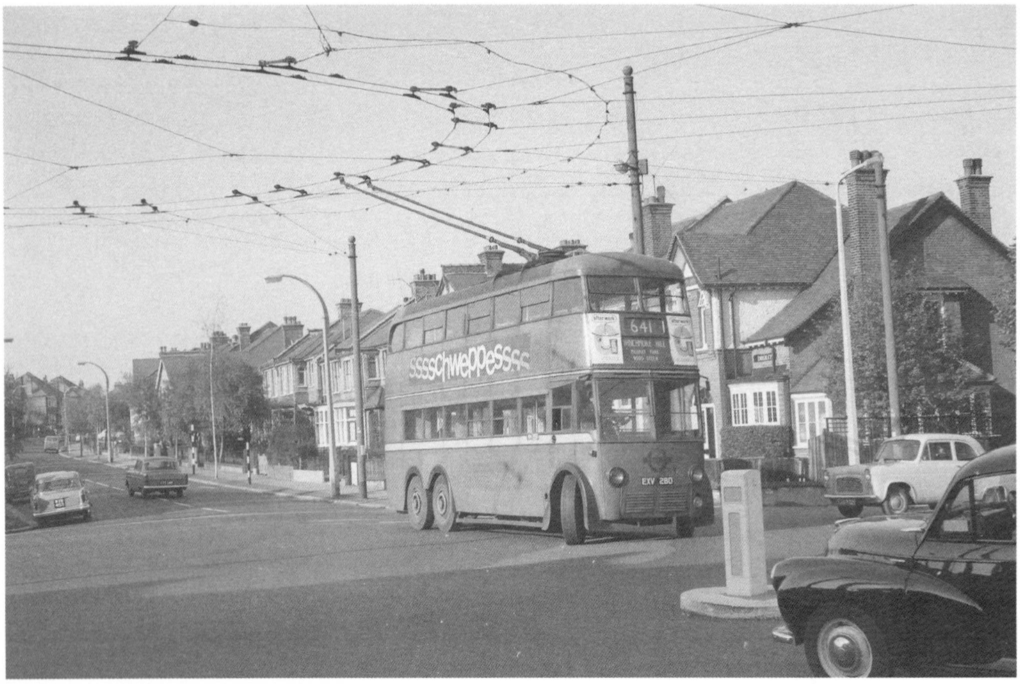

K1 class 1250 is seen turning at the 641's Winchmore Hill terminus on 4 November 1961. By this date route 629 to Enfield had been replaced by buses, so the onward wires had already been removed.

John Shearman

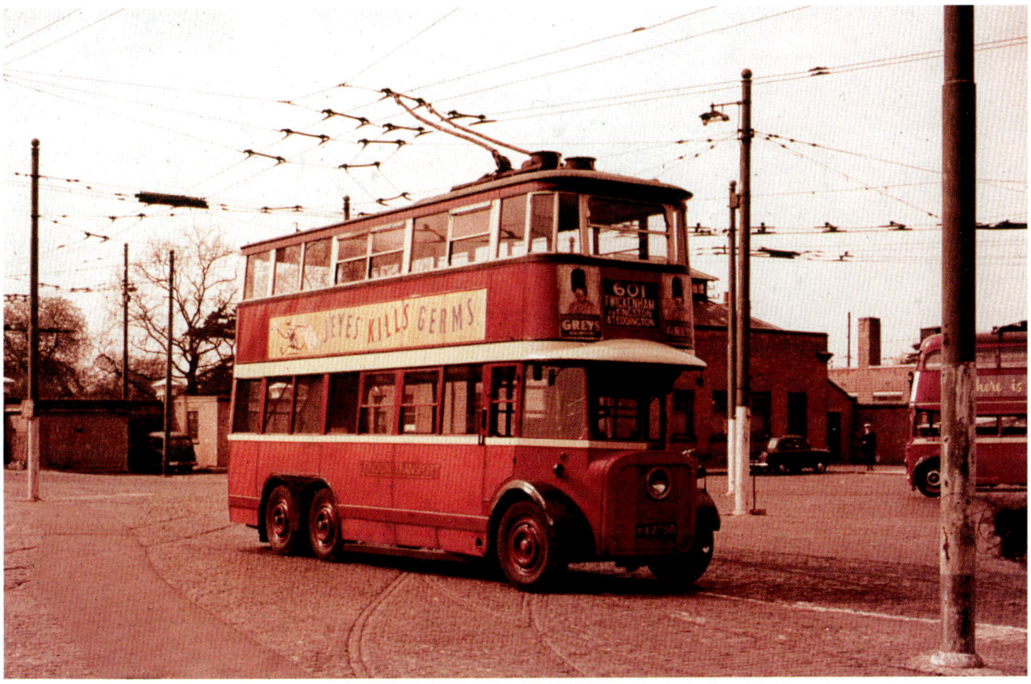

Diddler 1 (HX 2756) is seen at Fulwell Depot on 27 April 1962 carrying the 'Charlton' style of destination blinds. It is here in preparation for the final day of trolleybus service in London on 8 May 1962.
Brian Speller

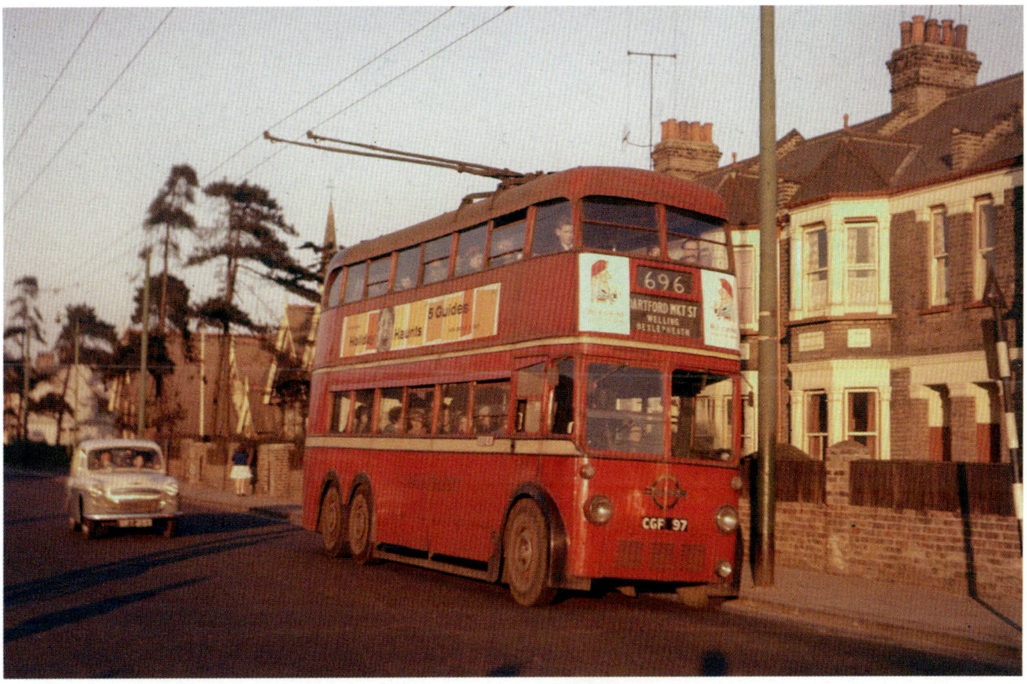

Rebodied and lengthened D2C class 97 is seen in Welling High Street heading towards Dartford.
Michael Dryhurst

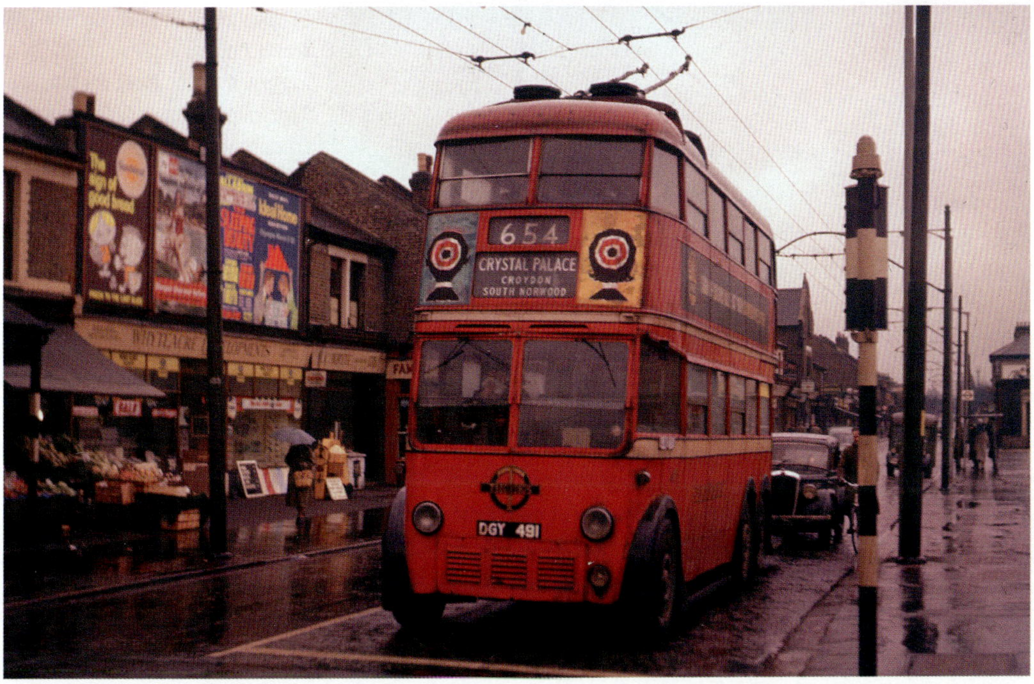

B1 class 491 spent the majority of its working life at Holloway Depot. It is seen here after transfer to Carshalton Depot working route 654 in Northcote Road, Selhurst. Because of the hills in the area the trolleybuses used were fitted with coasting and run back brakes.
Michael Dryhurst

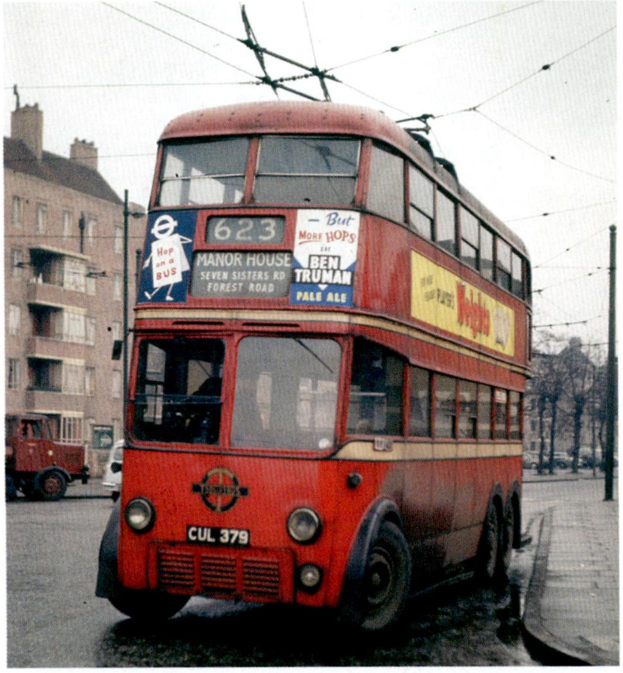

D2 class 379 is seen on lay over before its next duty in Seven Sisters Road, Manor House. The driver has yet to turn the destination blind for the return journey to the Napier Arms, Woodford.
Michael Dryhurst

Another D2 class trolleybus, this time 461 circling Hammersmith Broadway on its way to Clapham Junction. In the background can be seen the Hammersmith Trolleybus Depot that was subsequently used as a garage for the BEA airport service fleet of 4RF4 coaches. This view was taken before the building of the Hammersmith flyover had begun.
Michael Dryhurst

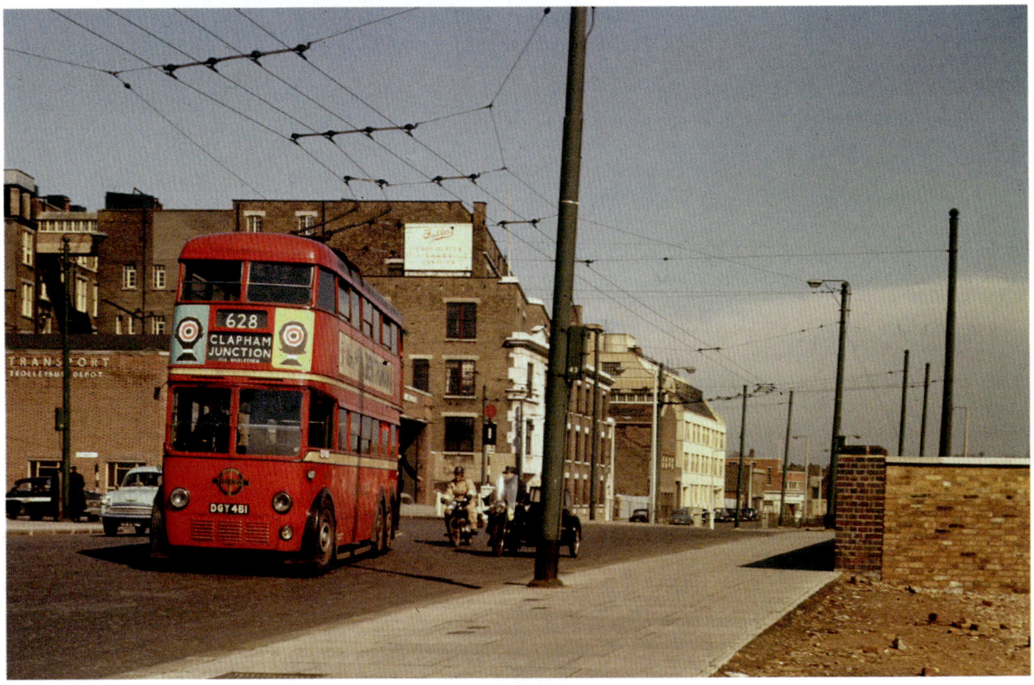

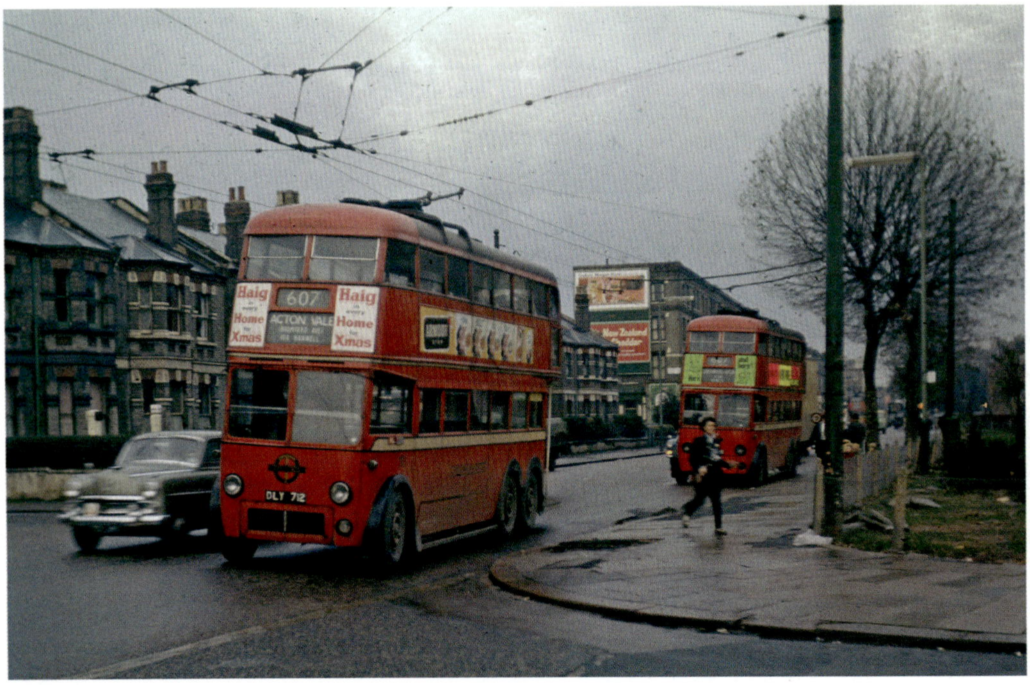

F1 class 712 is just about to complete a short working journey at Acton Vale. The 'clippie' is seen about to change the frog having leapt off the platform, with a further 607 vehicle continuing on its through journey to Shepherds Bush behind.
Michael Dryhurst

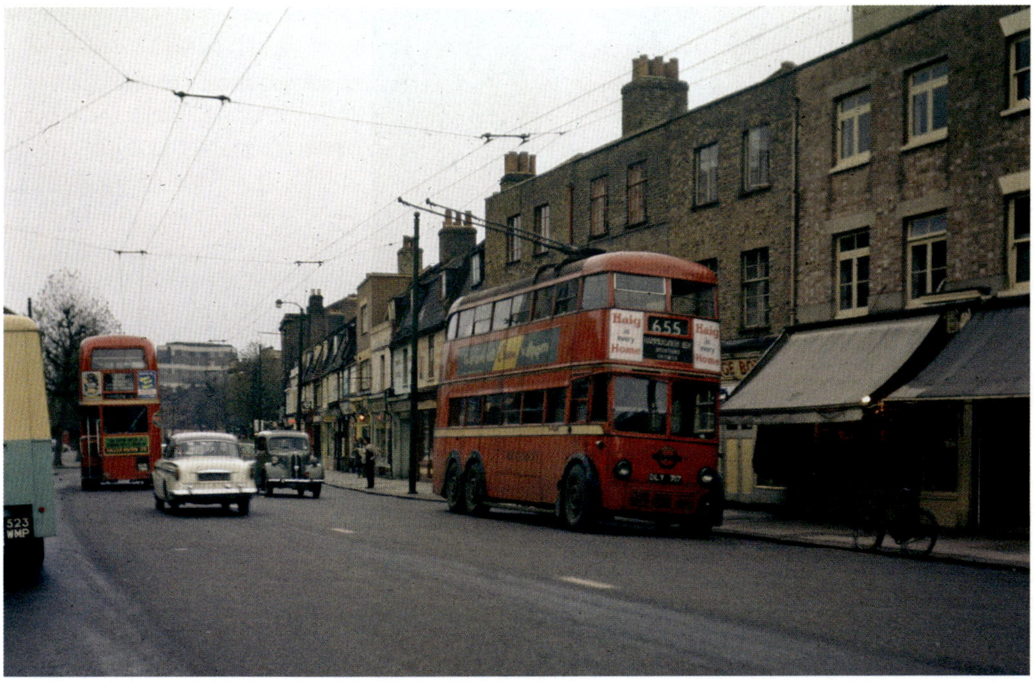

F1 class 717 heading towards Hammersmith Broadway along Chiswick High Road on route 655.
Michael Dryhurst

At Manor House, J1 class 945 awaits to turn into Seven Sisters Road from Green Lanes while H1 class 782 continues its southbound journey along Green Lanes towards Moorgate.
Michael Dryhurst

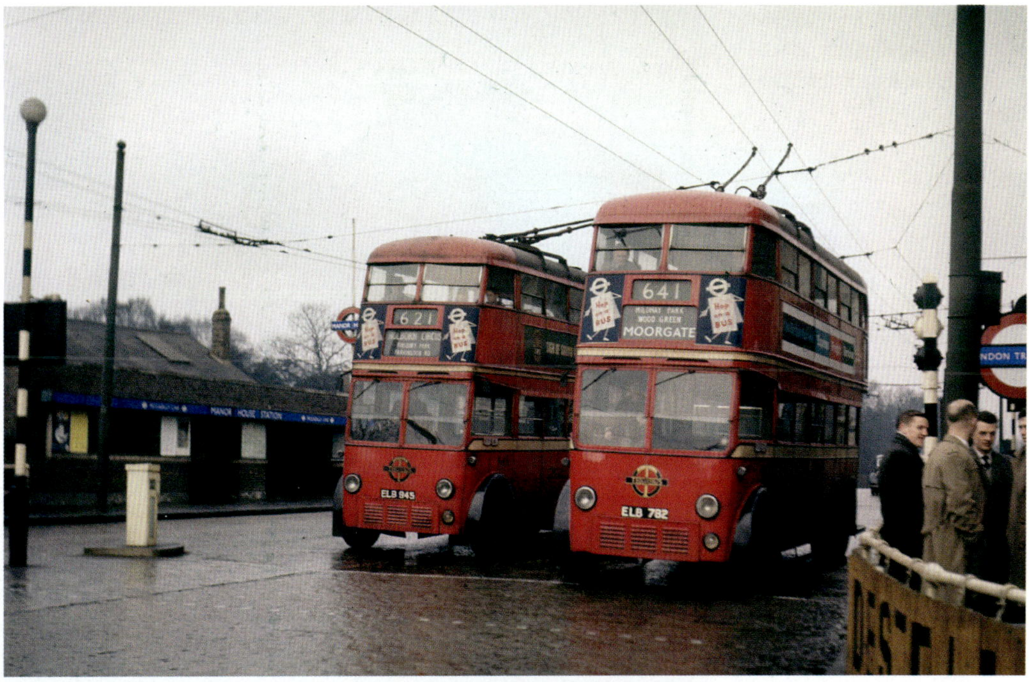

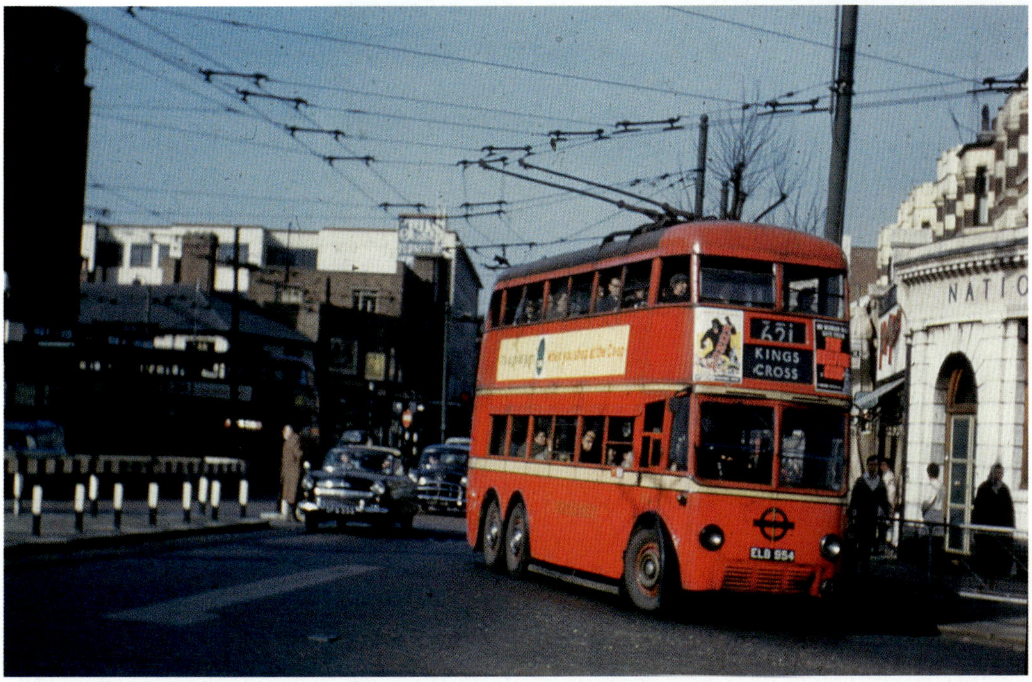

954 was a pre production Metro Cammell, AEC chassisless L2 vehicle. It was immediately recognisable by the cream band being extended beneath the windscreens around the front of the vehicle. It operated initially from Holloway Depot, but spent its later years working from Finchley. It is seen here on route 621 on a short working to Kings Cross.
Geoff Morant

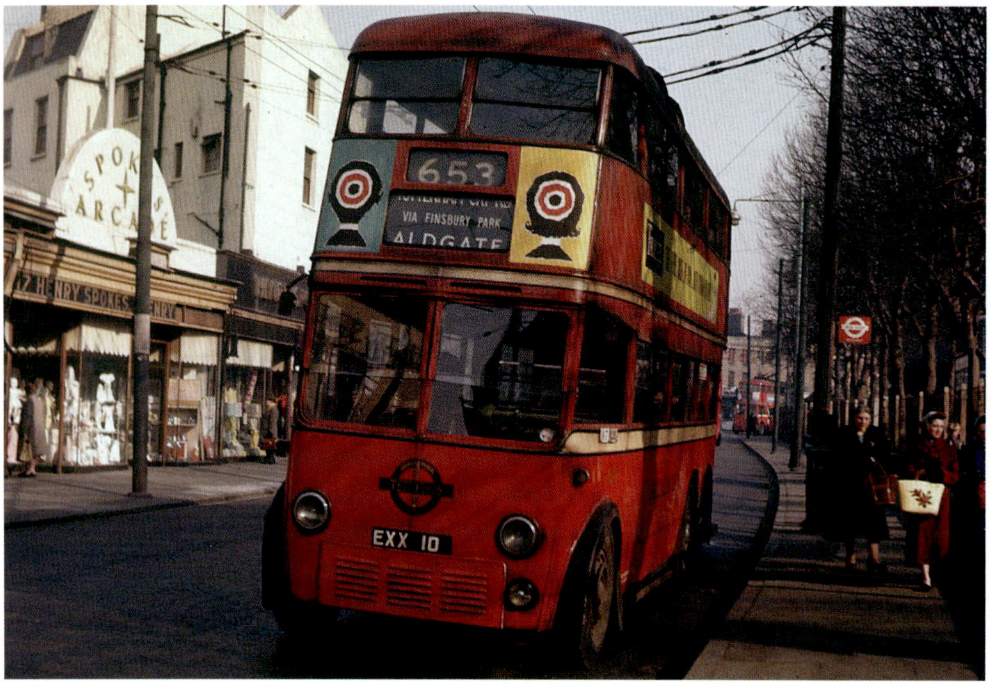

J2 class 1000 (EXX 10) is seen at Clapton Common heading towards Aldgate on the circuitous 653 route. Subject to three exceptions, and this is one, all London trolleybus registration numbers coincided with the fleet number.
Michael Dryhurst

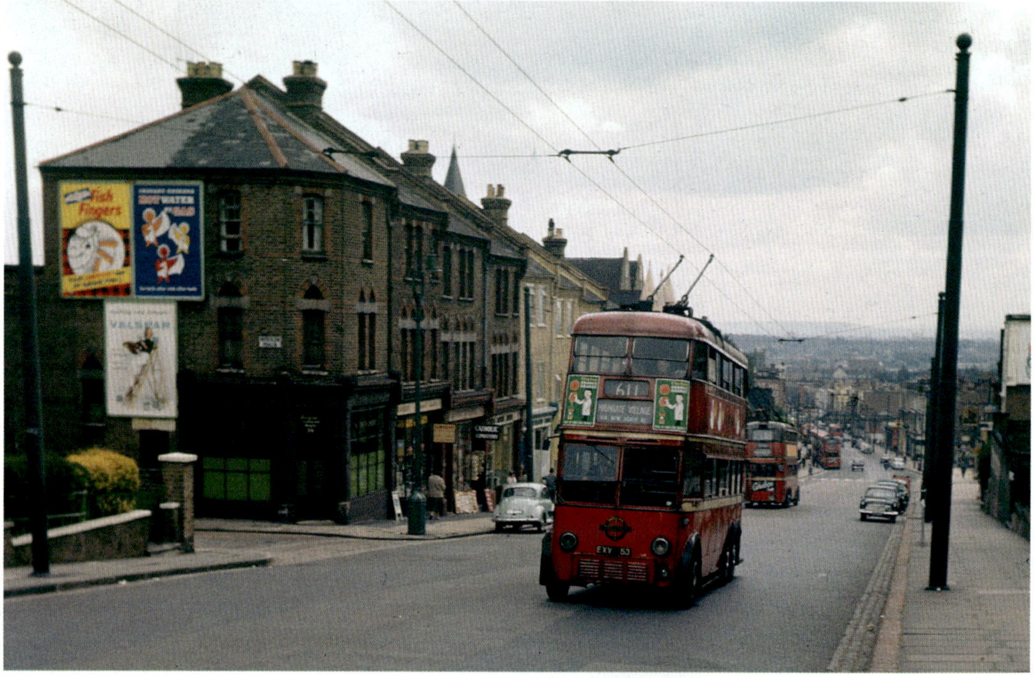

J3 class 1053 is seen ascending Highgate Hill effortlessly on its regular duty on route 611.
Michael Dryhurst

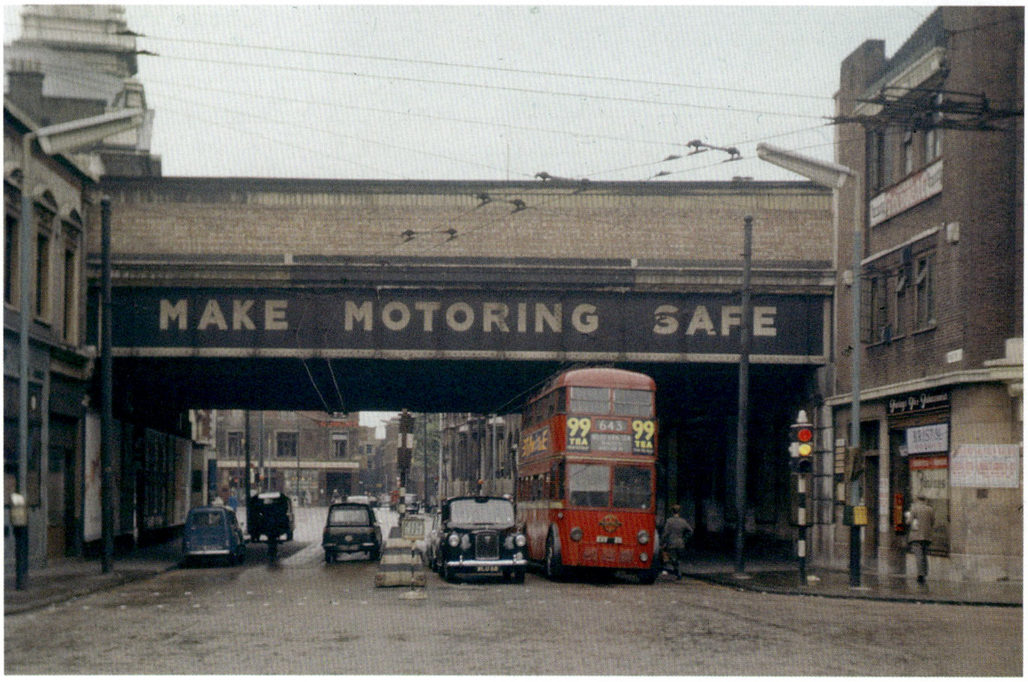

K1 class 1211 is seen in Kingsland Road, Shoreditch while operating out of Stamford Hill Depot.
Michael Dryhurst

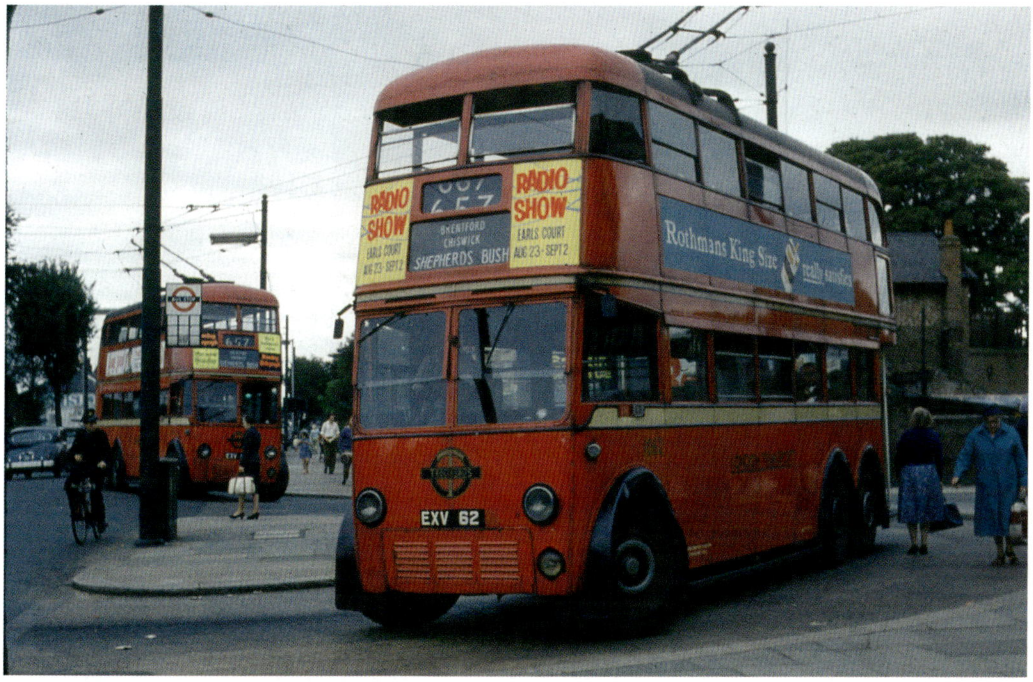

K1 class 1062 is seen at the Hounslow terminus of route 657.
Geoff Lumb

Two K1 class trolleybuses, 1116 and 1074 can be seen here on route 657, occupying the terminus at Hounslow, Wellington Road. They are operating from Isleworth Depot during the final months of trolleybus operation.
LCC Tramways Trust

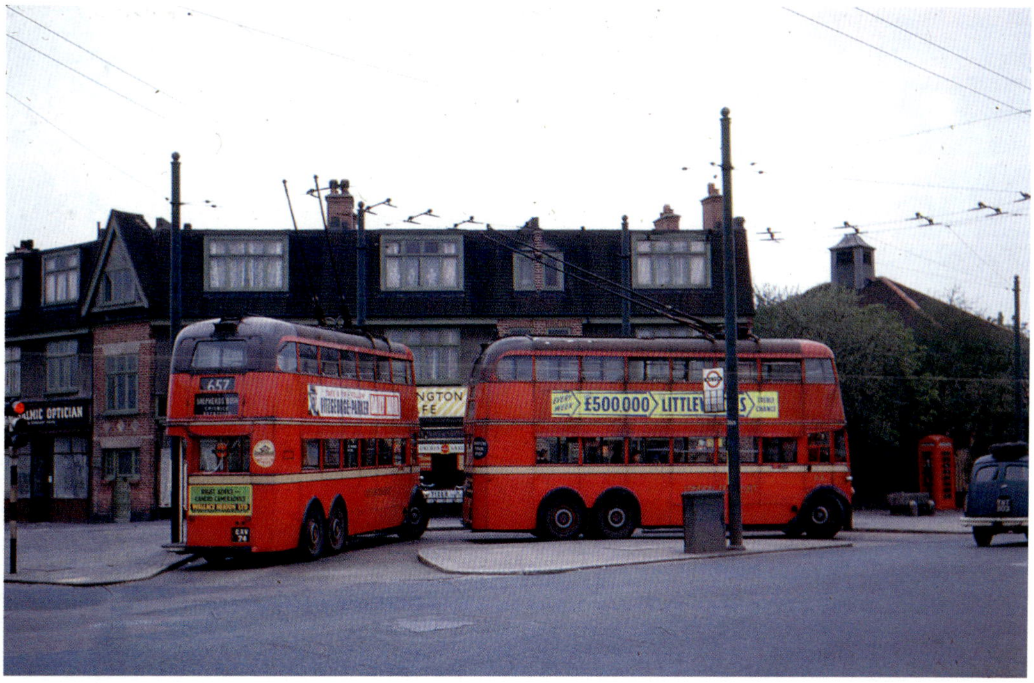

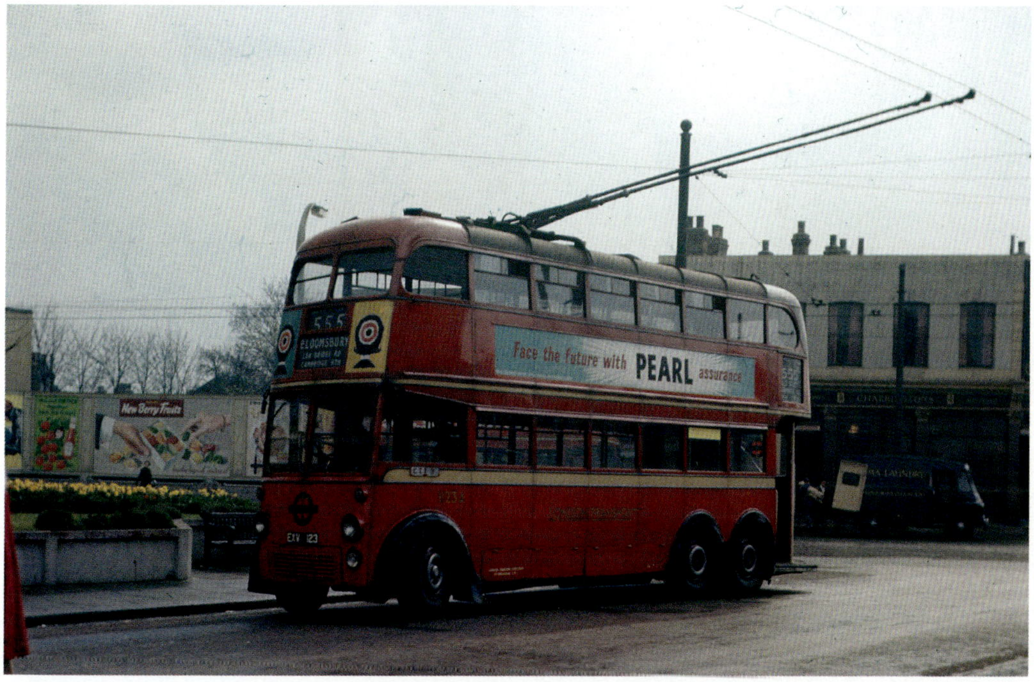

Of the wartime casualties, the first London trolleybuses to be rebodied were by Weymann. This was denoted by the addition of an 'A' suffix to the fleet number. K1 class 1123A lays over at 'Leyton Green', immediately outside Leyton (T) bus garage.
Michael Dryhurst

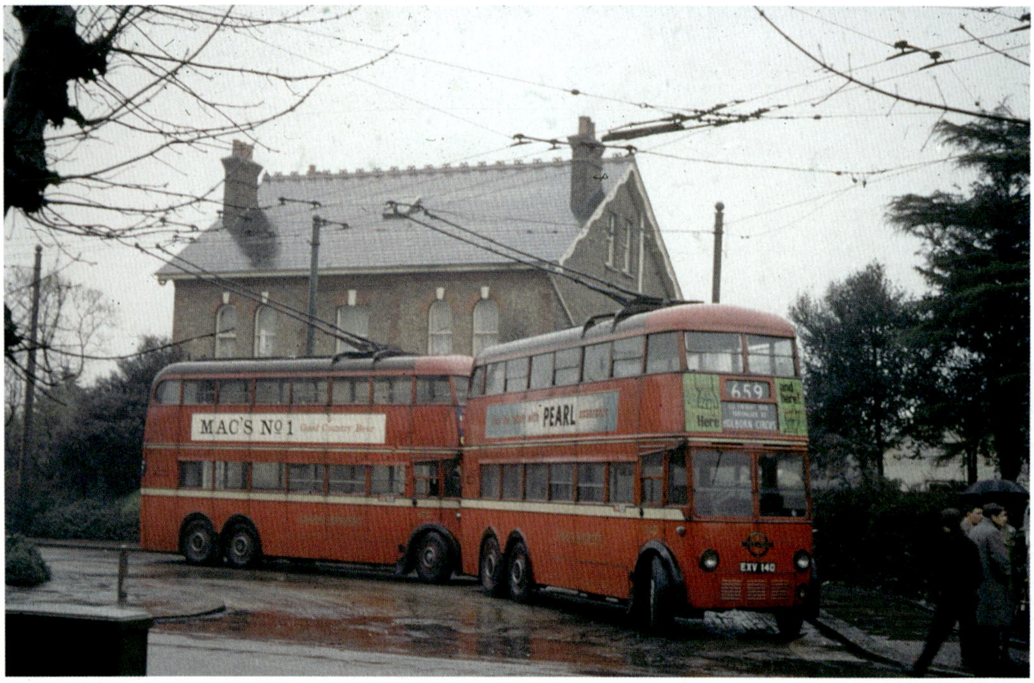

K1 class 1140 is seen at the Waltham Cross terminus of three trolleybus routes, namely the 649, 659 and 679.
Vic Nutton

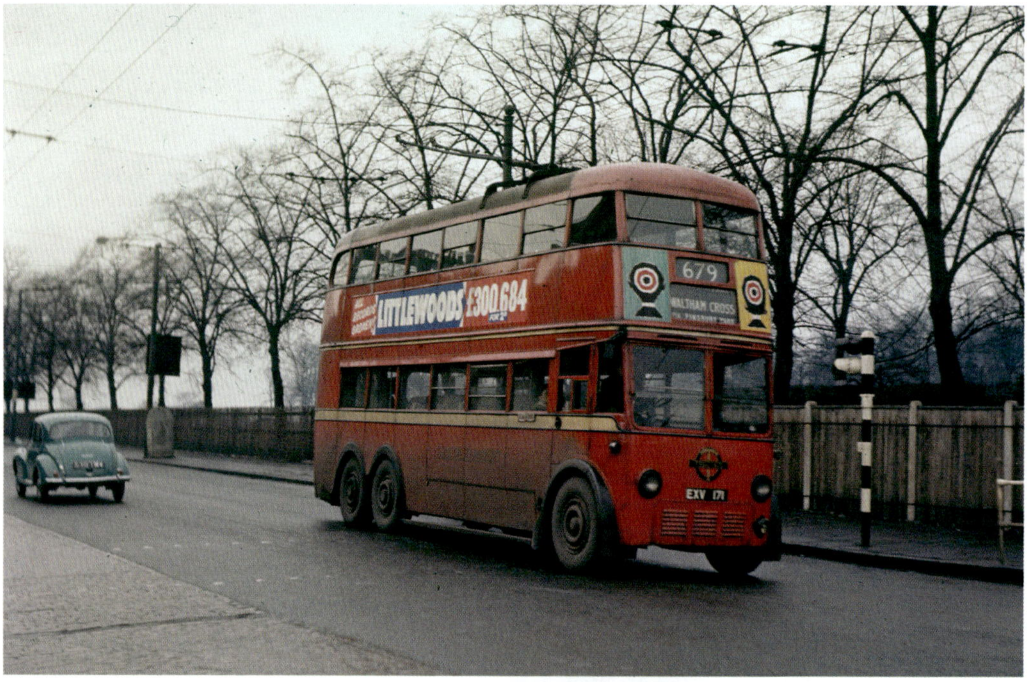

K2 class 1171 is seen speeding along Green Lanes towards Waltham Forest.
Michael Dryhurst

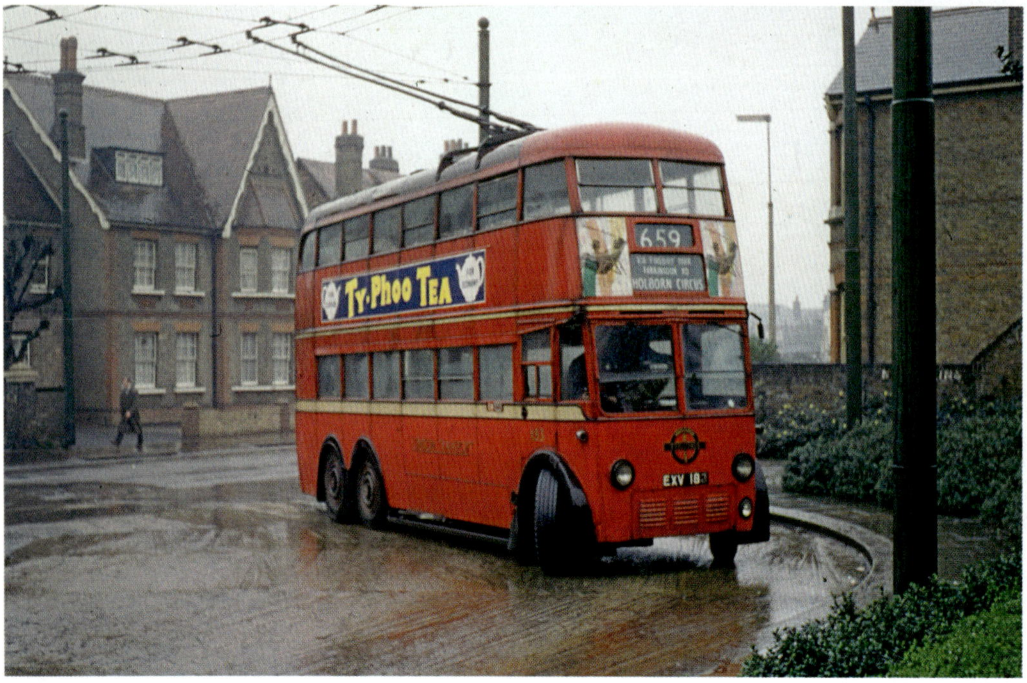

K2 class 1183 rests at the Waltham Cross terminus of the 659 before it makes a return journey to Holborn Circus.
Geoff Lumb

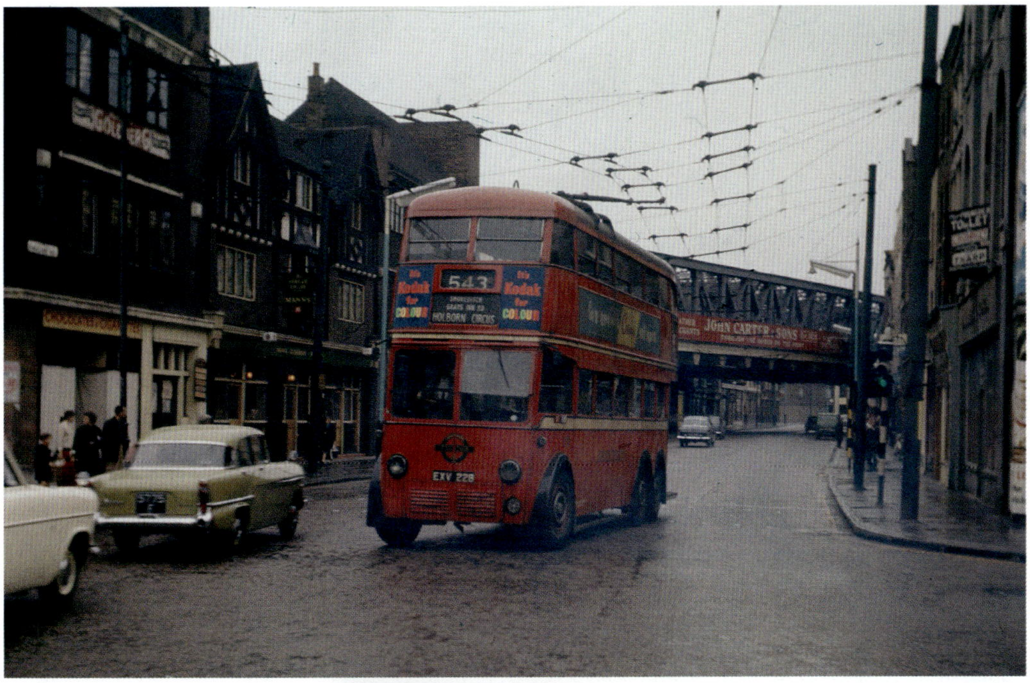

All Leyand K2 class 1228 is about to turn into Old Street from Kingsland Road.
Geoff Lumb

One of the second batch of the K2 class, 1305 is seen in Ball's Pond Road, the thoroughfare which was the butt of many a joke on 'The Goon Show'.
Michael Dryhurst

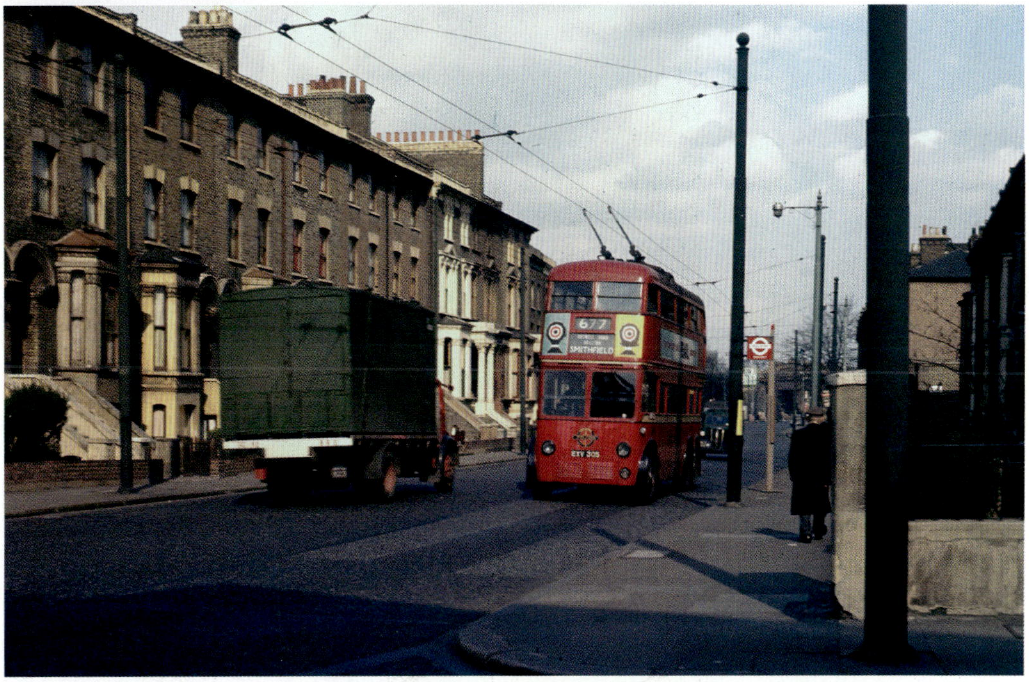

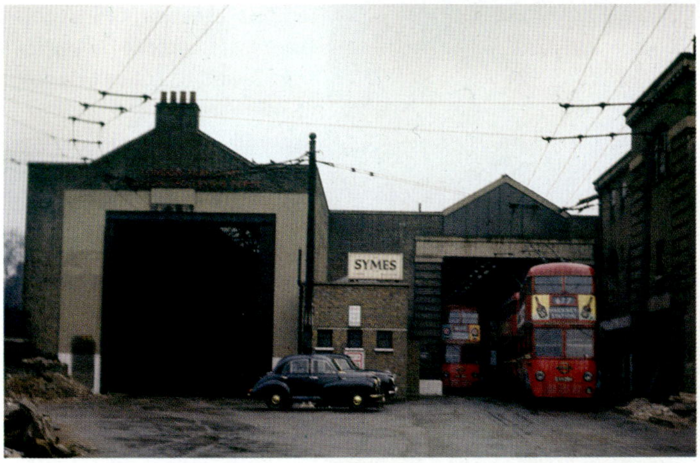

From the second batch of 50 K1 class trolleybuses, 1291 is seen on the forecourt of Clapton Depot. At this time, work was in progress converting and modifying the depot to make it suitable for motorbus operation, when it would become Clapton Garage.
Michael Dryhurst

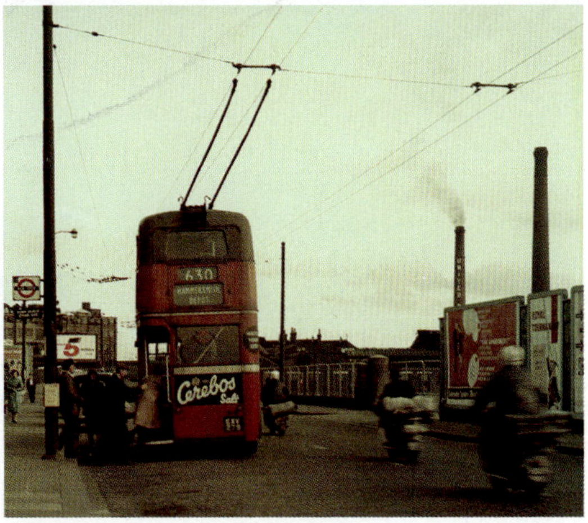

K1 class 1279 picks up passengers in Scrubs Lane on its way back to Hammersmith Depot. The wire leading to the terminal loop and stand in Letchford Gardens, can be seen just ahead of the trolleybus.
Mick Webber Collection

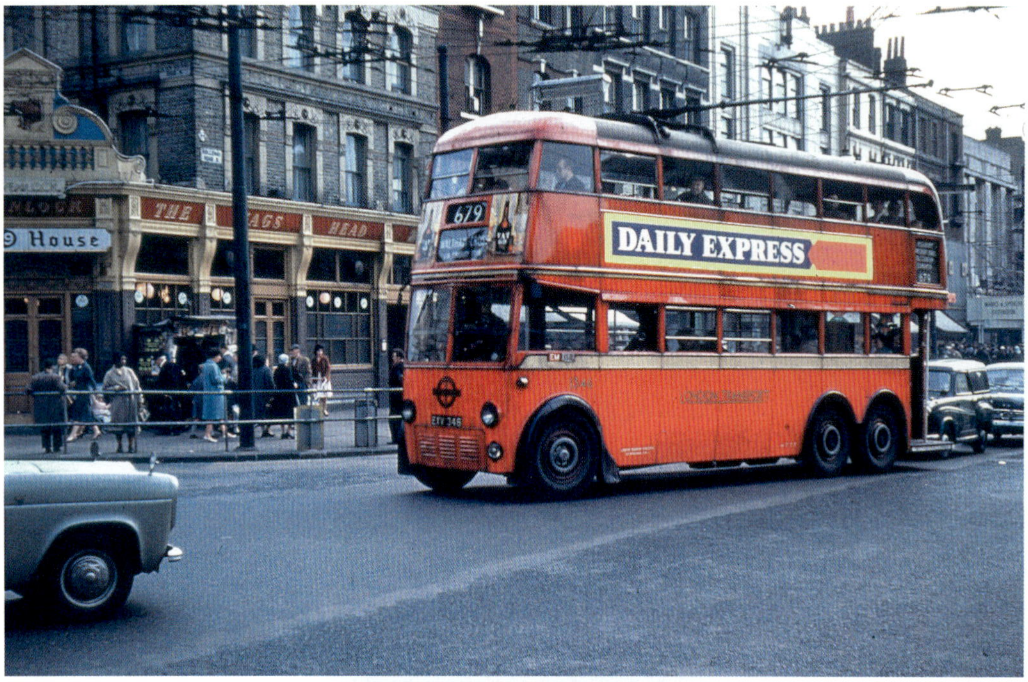

The Nags Head was one of the more complex junctions of trolleybus overhead in London, and K2 class 1346 is making the turn from Holloway Road into Seven Sisters Road, on its way north to Waltham Cross.
Mick Webber Collection

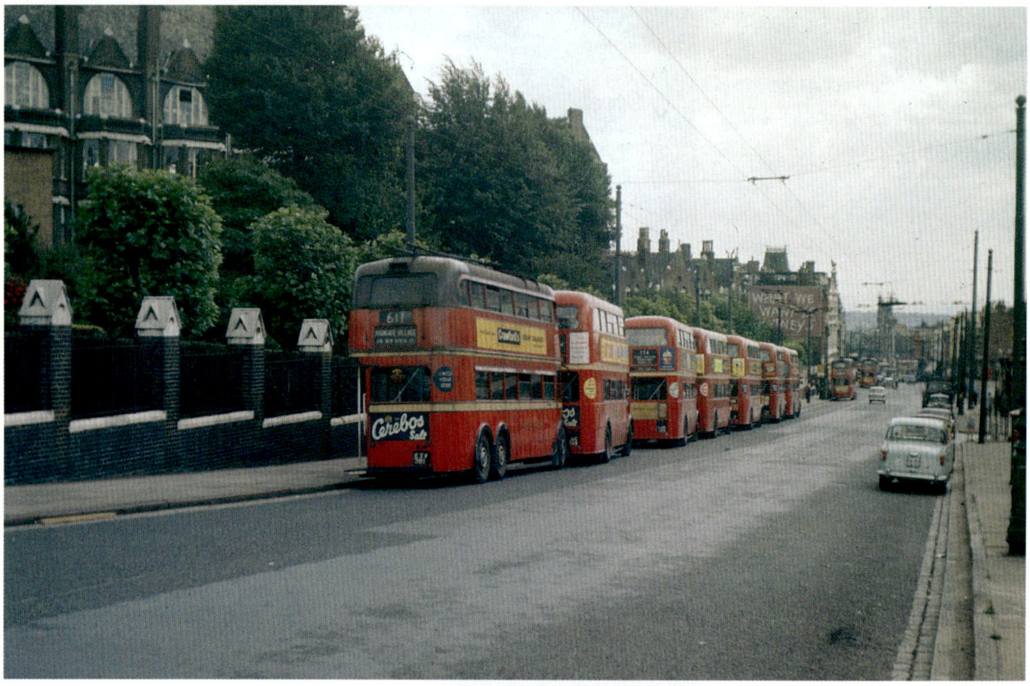

The small class of 15 L1s were always allocated to Highgate Depot for use on route 611. 1361 lays over at the tail end of a line of buses all awaiting their next duty above Archway.
Michael Dryhurst

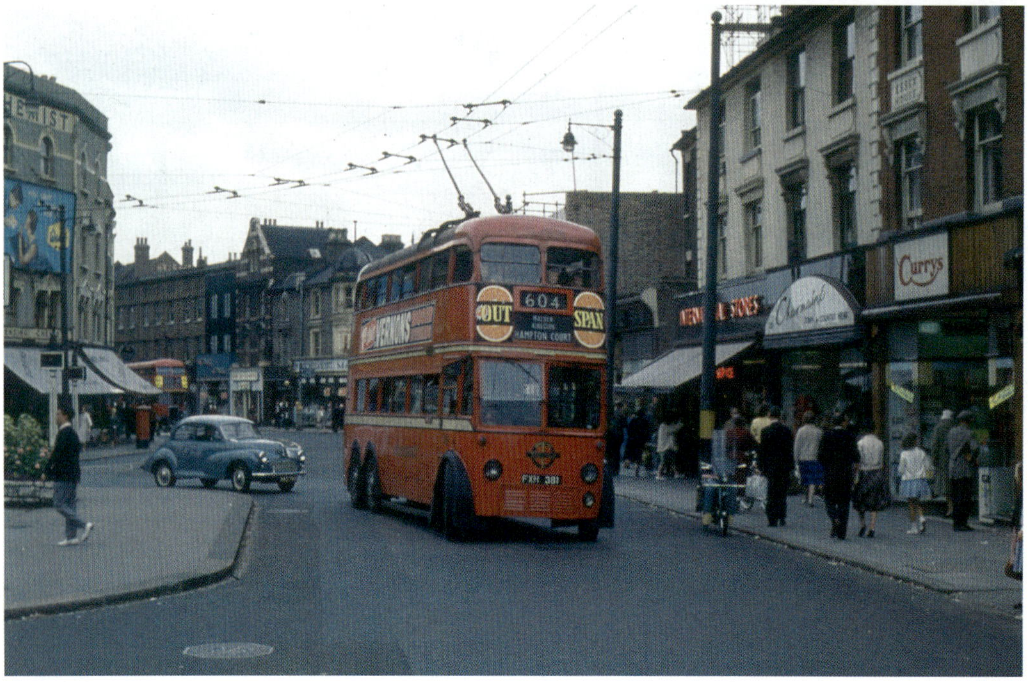

L3 class 1381 was one of this large class of trolleybuses transferred to Fulwell Depot in February 1960 to replace the sold Q1 trolleybuses. The L3 class was the sole allocation at Fulwell Depot at the close of trolleybus operation in May 1962.
Geoff Lumb

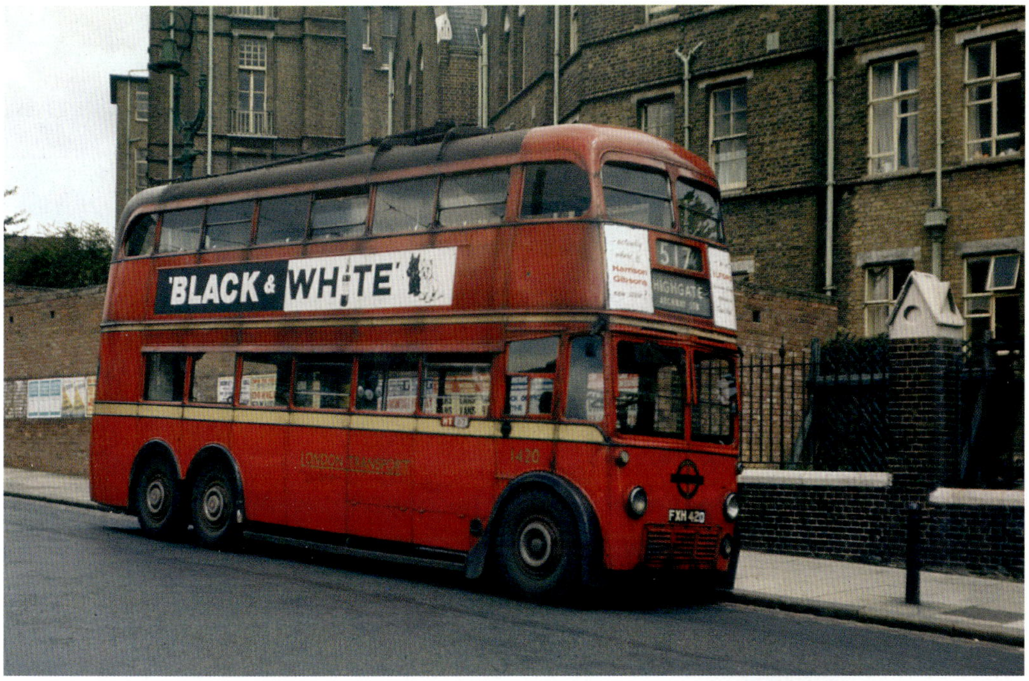

L3 class 1420 is seen while operating from Highgate Depot, resting at Archway. This trolleybus eventually ended its days at Fulwell Depot.

Michael Dryhurst

Easter Monday 1962, and L3 class 1426 waits for service at Fulwell Depot. It will be photographed no doubt, many more times in the next two weeks leading up to 8 May.

Mick Webber

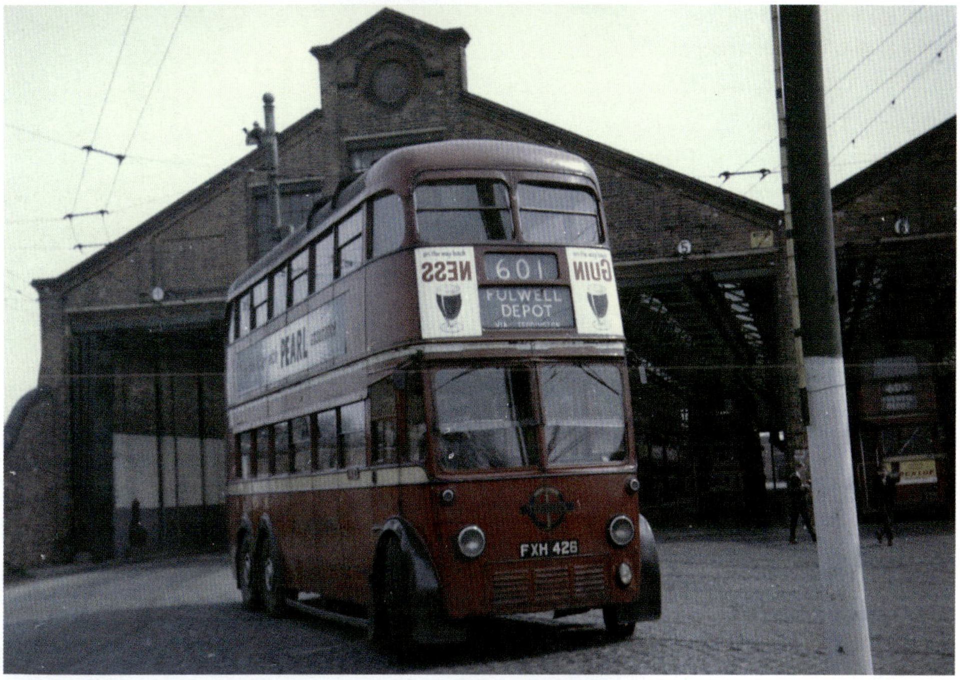

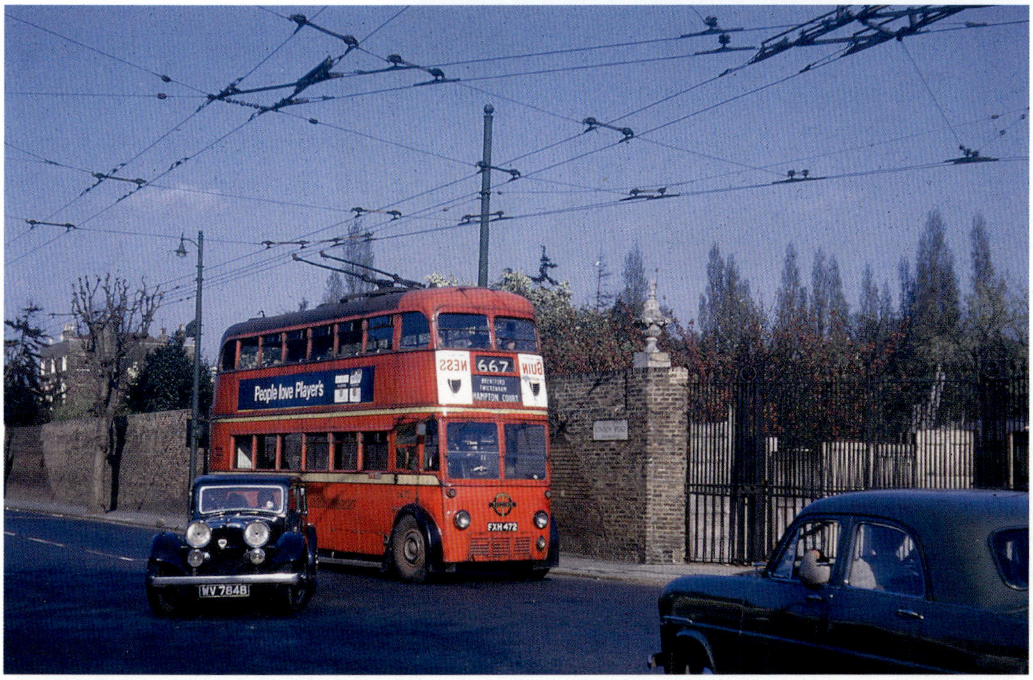

L3 class 1472 is turning into Twickenham Road from London Road, Isleworth on a southbound journey to Hampton Court. This trolleybus was one of five L3s fitted with sliding ventilators.

Julian Bowden Collection

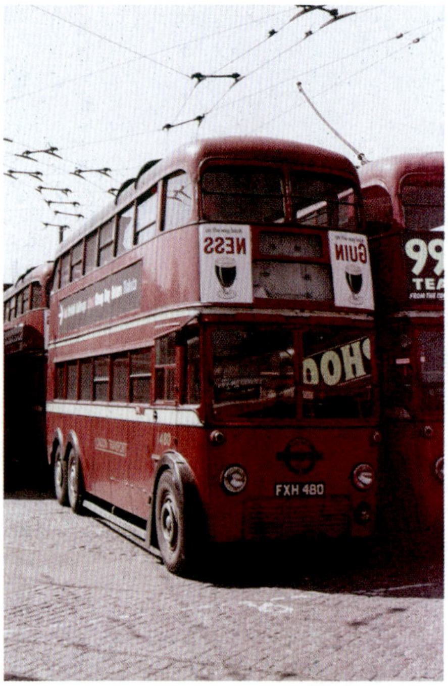

Withdrawn L3 class 1480 is seen in the yard at the back of Fulwell Depot on 7 June 1962, nearly a month after withdrawal from service.
Brian Speller

On 8 April 1962, 1490 is at Wimbledon Station, the eastern terminus of route 605.
Brian Speller

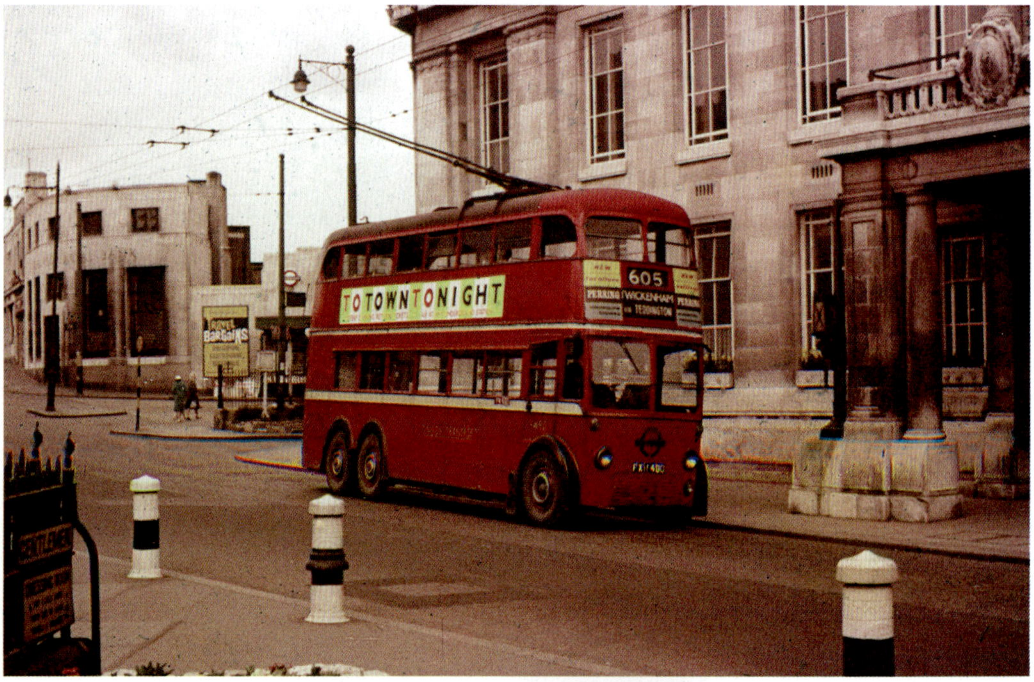

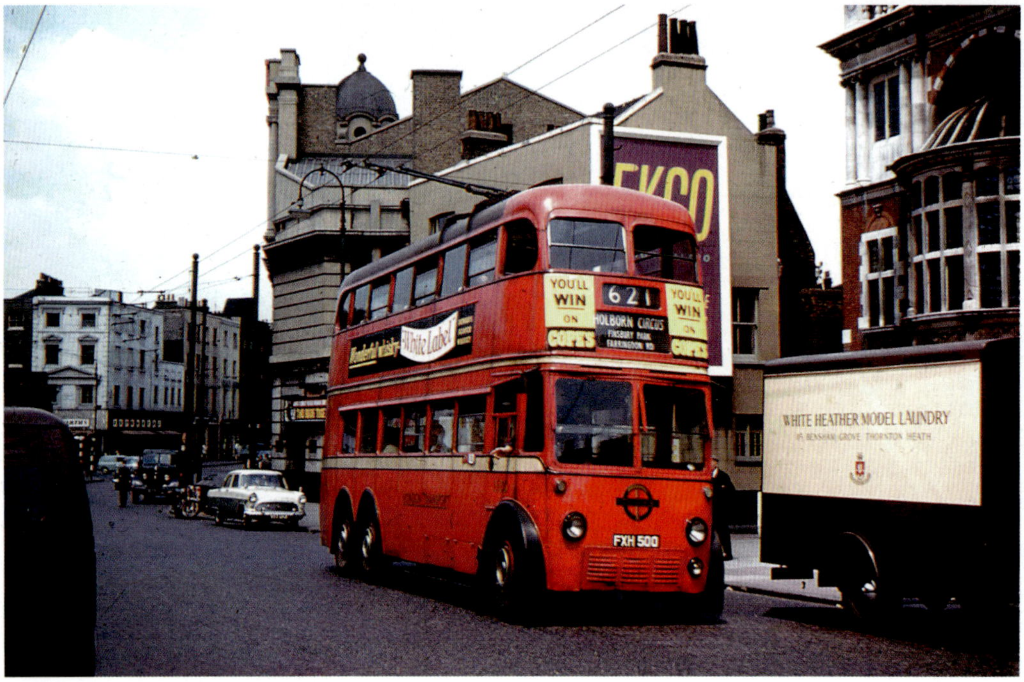

The driver signals to pull out on his way to Holborn Circus on route 621. L3 class 1500 from Finchley, has been well looked after, and it is hard to imagine it being delivered back in the dark days of 1940.
LCC Tramways Trust

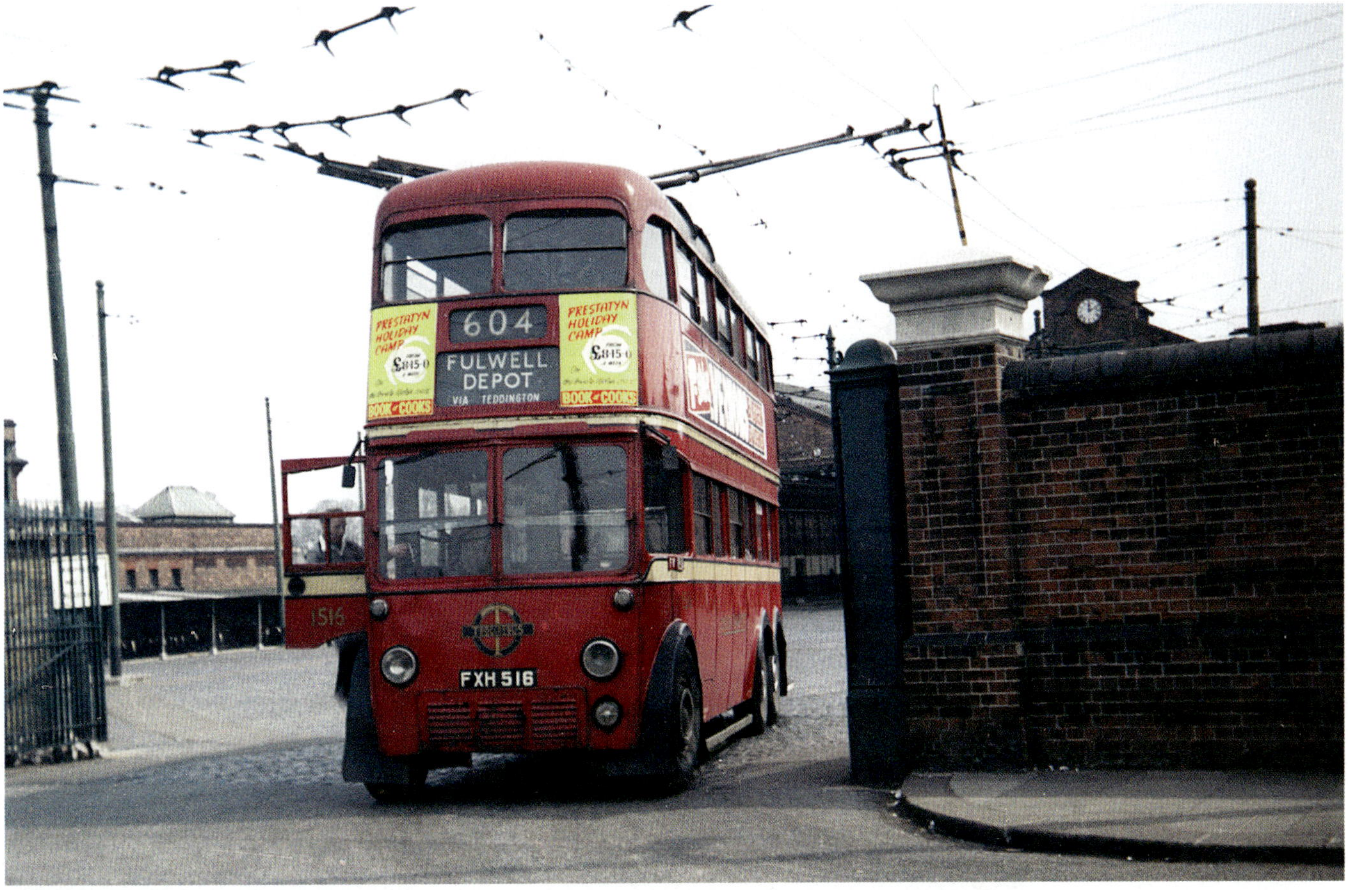

Fulwell Depot, and Easter Monday 1962 is once more the date for this view of L3 class 1516. The conductor has just put the booms up on the wires leading out to Hampton Court., and the driver is about to climb in to set off, and take up service on route 604. *Mick Webber*

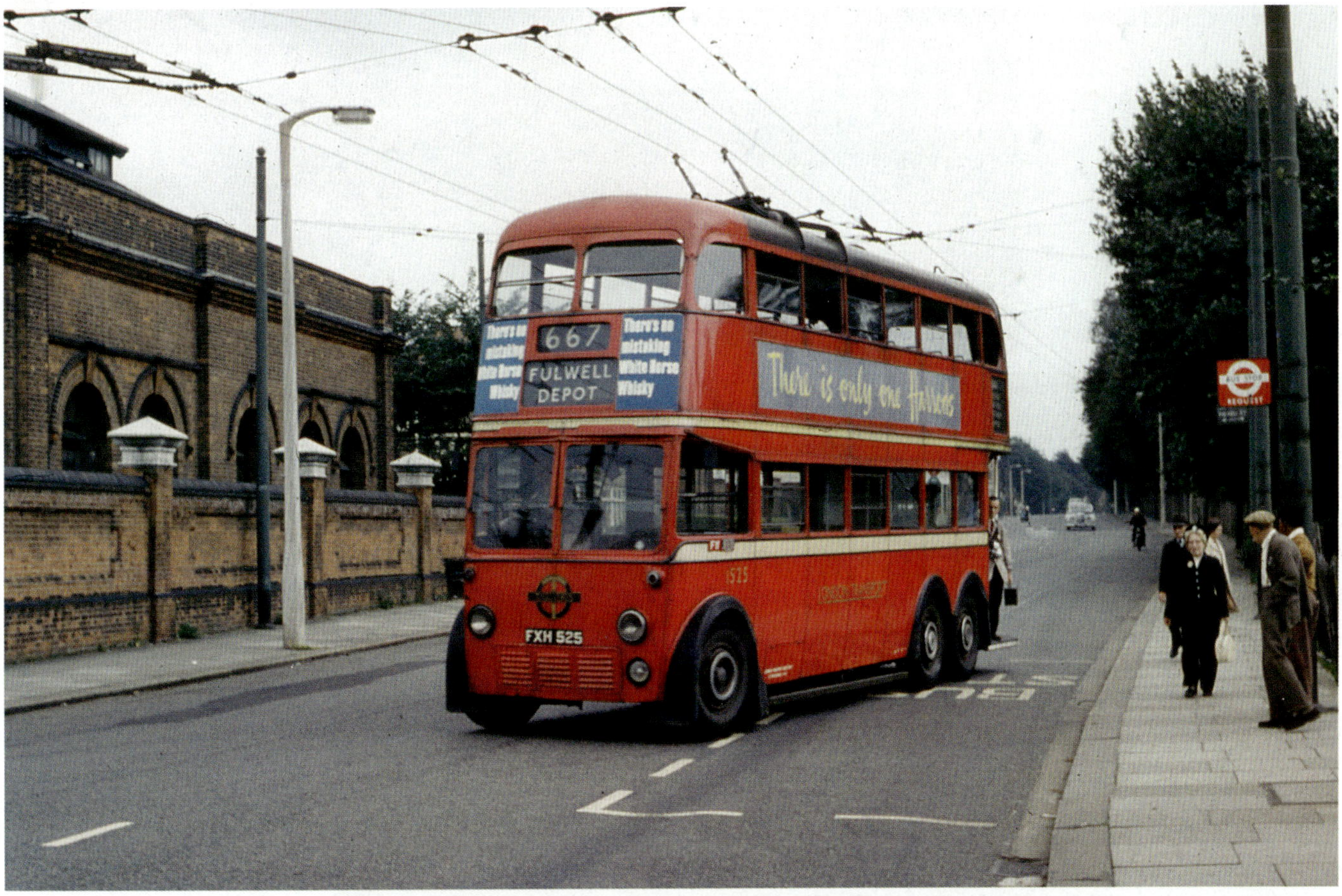

L3 class 1525 is seen turning into Fulwell Depot from Stanley Road with the conductor set to leap off the platform once the trolleybus has entered the front yard at this depot. *Geoff Lumb*

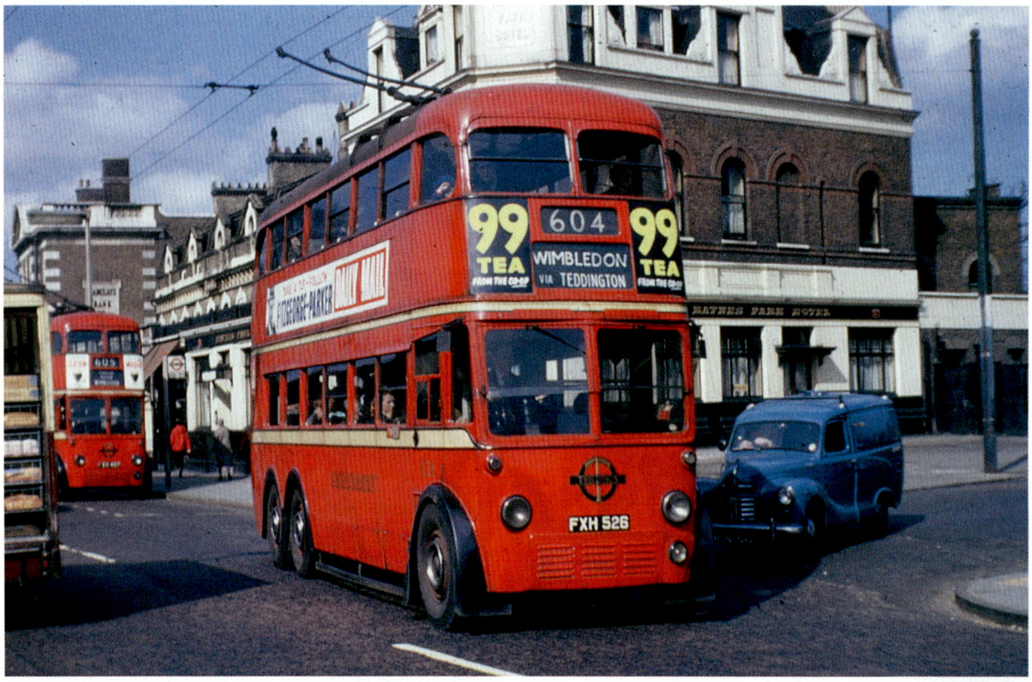

Is it a 604 with a 605 blind display, or a 605 with the wrong route number? We will never know, but L3 class 1526 shows the 605 Sunday display as it passes through Raynes Park in the sunshine. The vehicle looks very smart, and is a credit to the staff at Fulwell Depot.
Mick Webber Collection

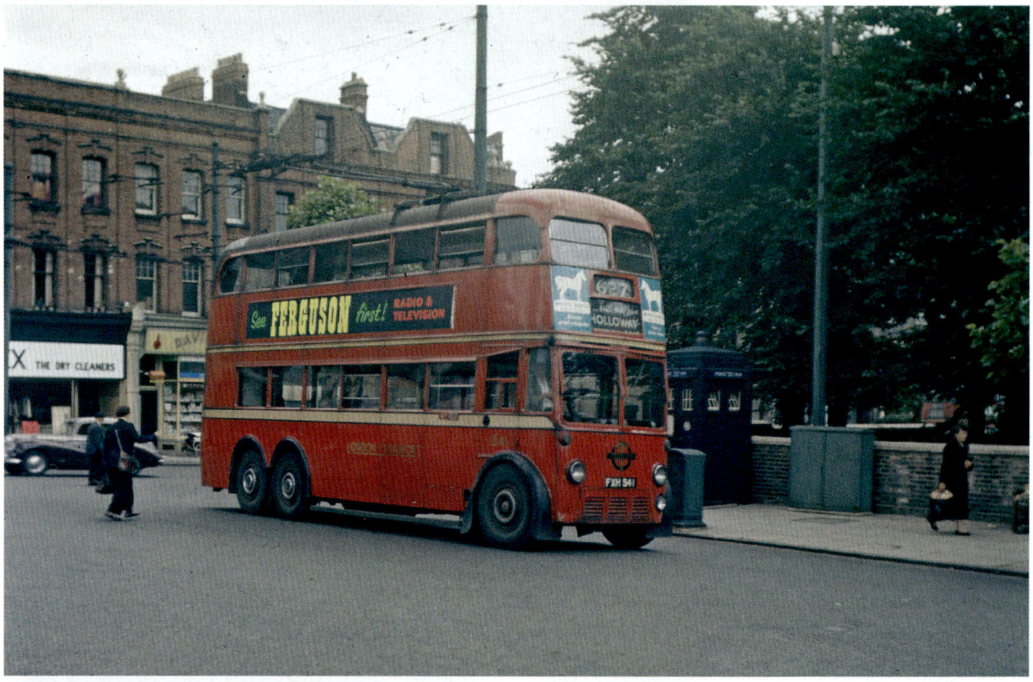

M 1 class 1541 makes its way home to Highgate Depot, and has just turned into Pemberton Gardens. It is passing a "Doctor Who" police box on the right, and a section box can also be seen. The 627 was shared with Edmonton and Wood Green Depots, although Highgate had the majority of workings.
Michael Dryhurst

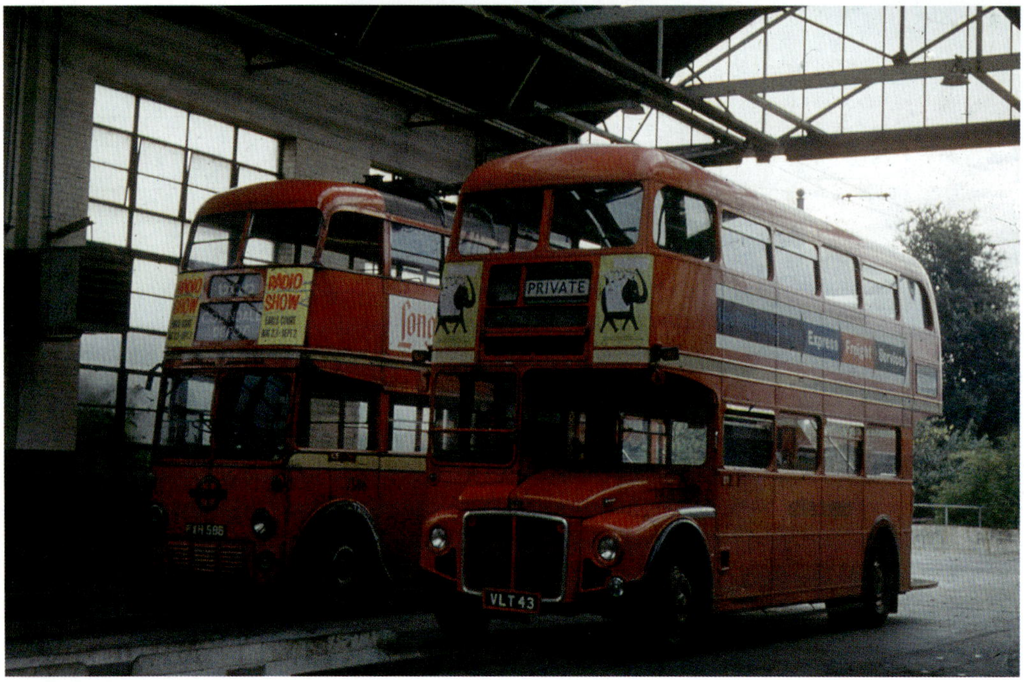

The AEC Routemaster bus, seen here in the form of RM 43, was built as the trolleybus replacement vehicle. Alongside RM 43 is N1 class 1586 at Colindale Depot.
Vic Nutton

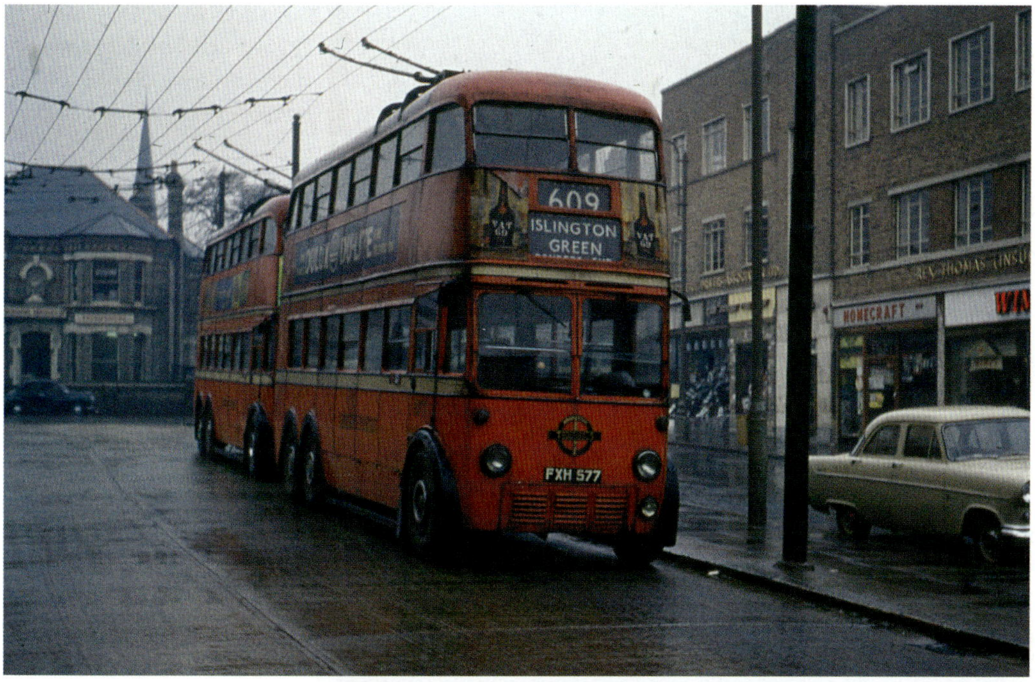

N1 class 1577 is seen on a dull wet day at North Finchley, Tally Ho Corner before it operates a short working as far as Islington Green rather than the final city terminus of Finsbury Square, Moorgate.
Geoff Lumb

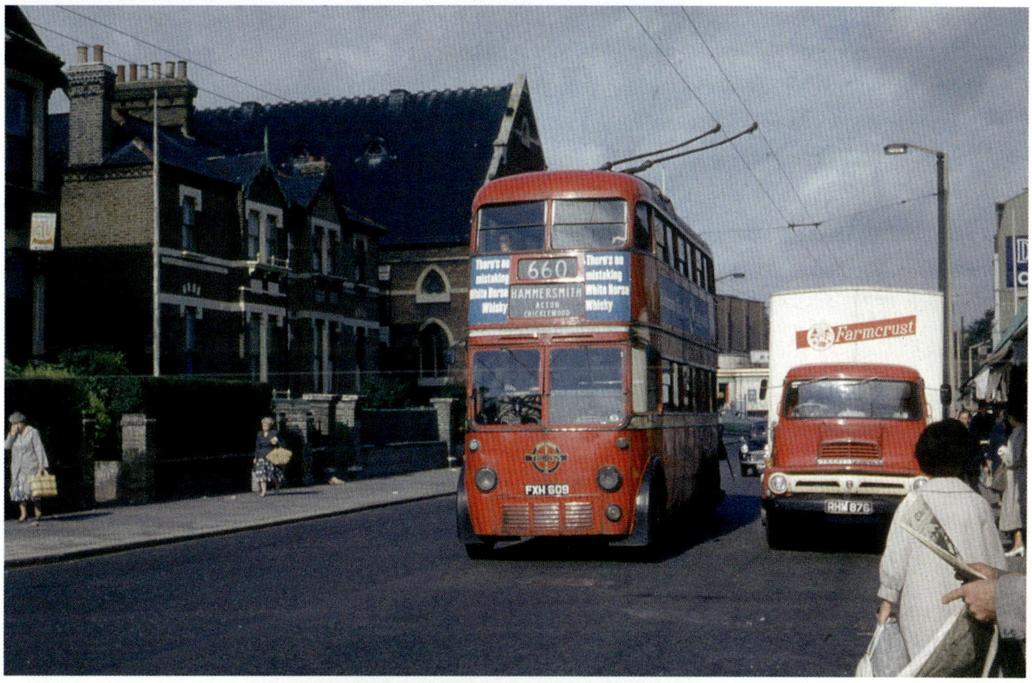

N1 class 1609 is pulling up at a bus stop to pick up further passengers while heading towards Hammersmith on route 660 from North Finchley.
Geoff Lumb

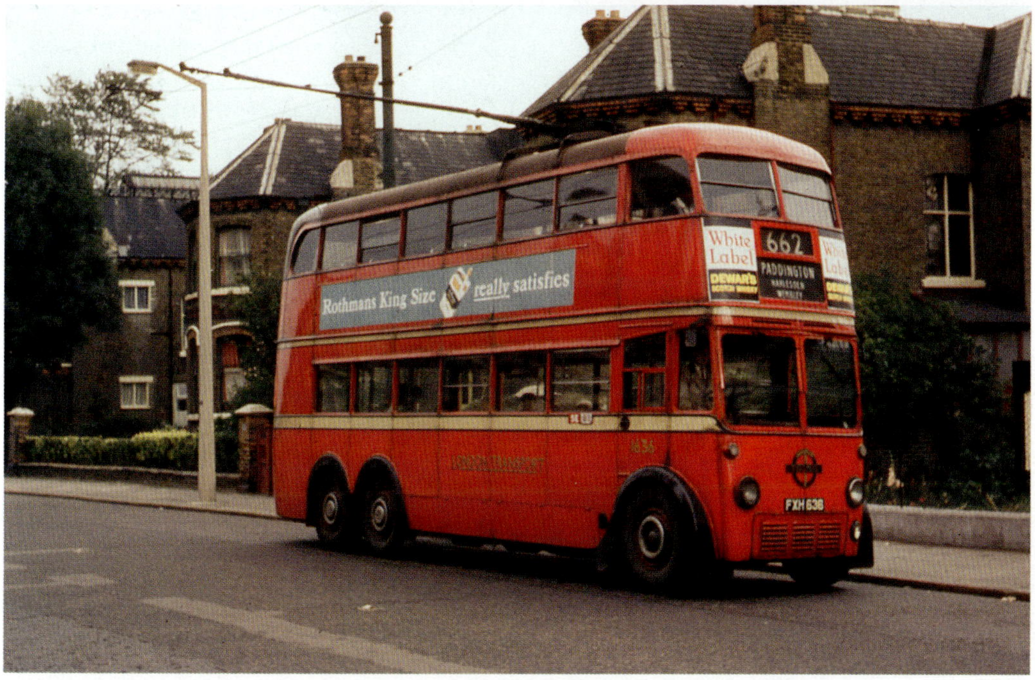

N1 class 1636 has been reallocated from its original east London depot at Bow to Stonebridge Depot and it is seen at Craven Park waiting for its next duty on the 662.
Geoff Lumb

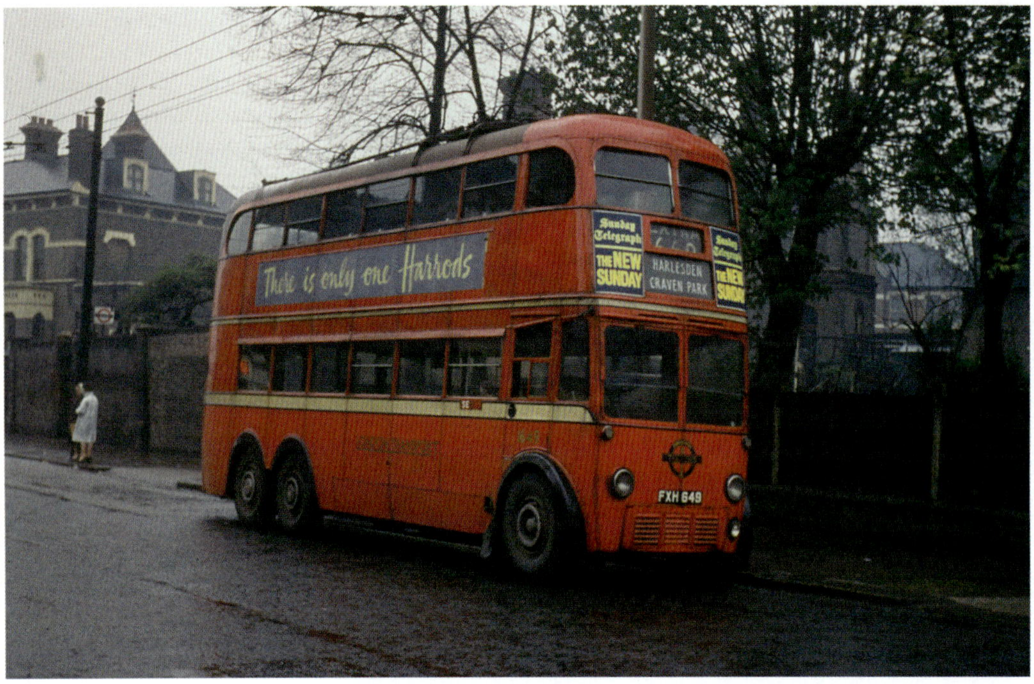

N2 class 1649 is seen at Craven Park resting between duties. The N2 class trolleybuses carried Park Royal bodies on AEC chassis.
Geoff Lumb

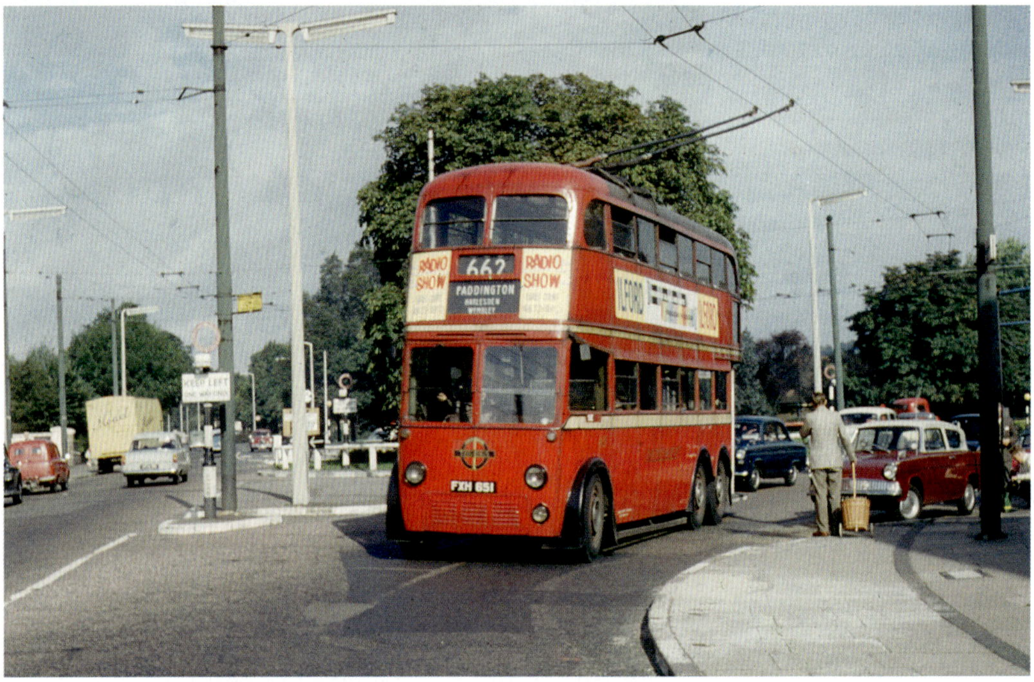

N2 class 1651 is seen at Sudbury Town, the western terminus of the 662, beginning its journey back to Paddington Green.
Geoff Lumb

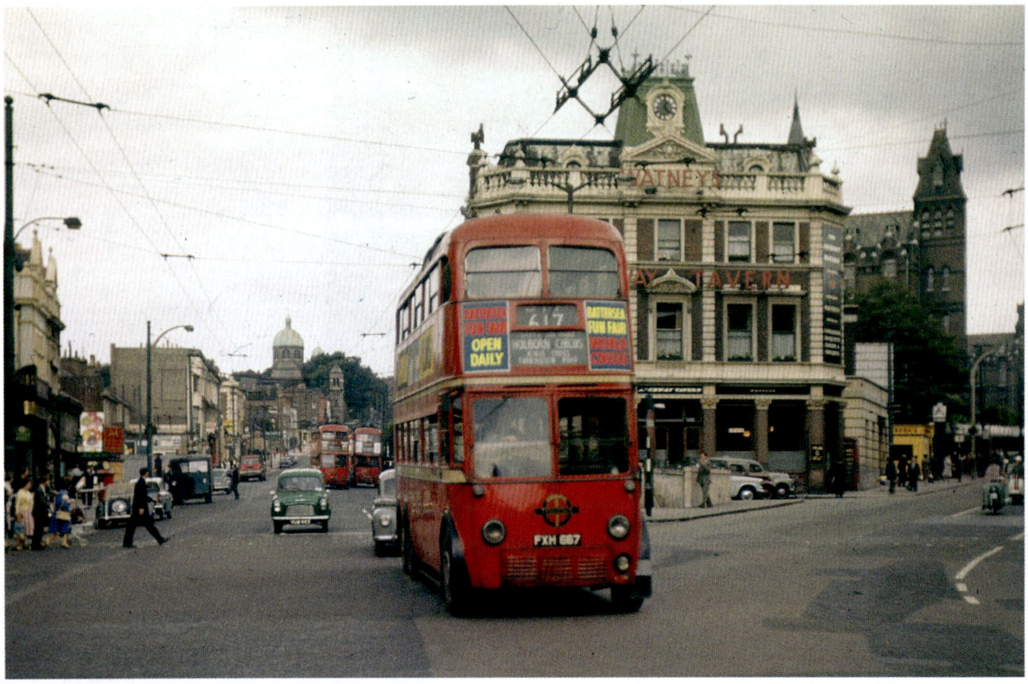

Some of the most distinguishable London Transport trolleybuses were the N2 class. The Park Royal bodies incorporated thicker than usual upper deck front pillars with much contoured metalwork. 1667 is one of these vehicles passing the imposing Archway Tavern at the start of its journey to Holborn Circus.
Michael Dryhurst

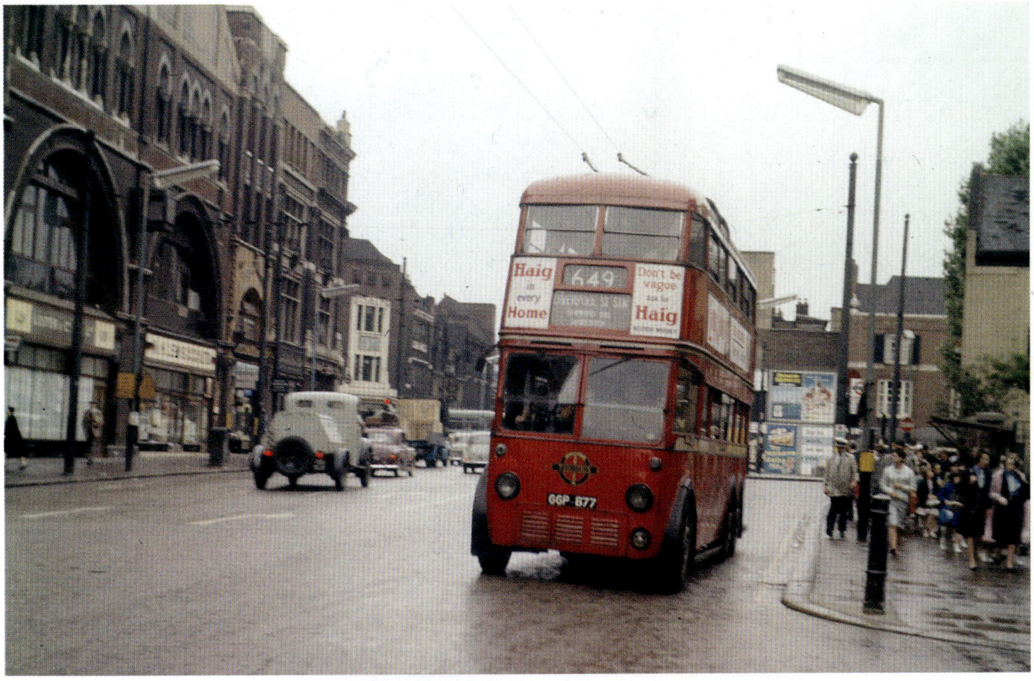

The last all Leyland trolleybuses for London Transport were the 25 strong K3 class. 1677 has just about reached its destination at Liverpool Street, being seen in Bishopsgate.
Michael Dryhurst

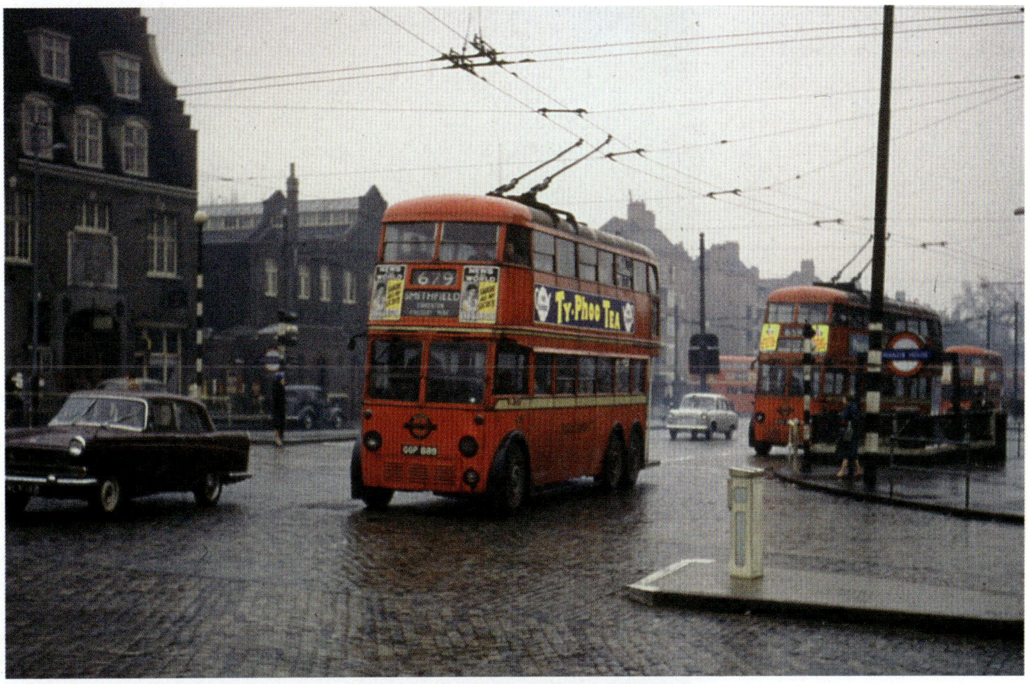

K3 class 1689 is crossing the busy intersection at Manor House heading towards Smithfield having started its journey from Waltham Cross.
Geoff Lumb

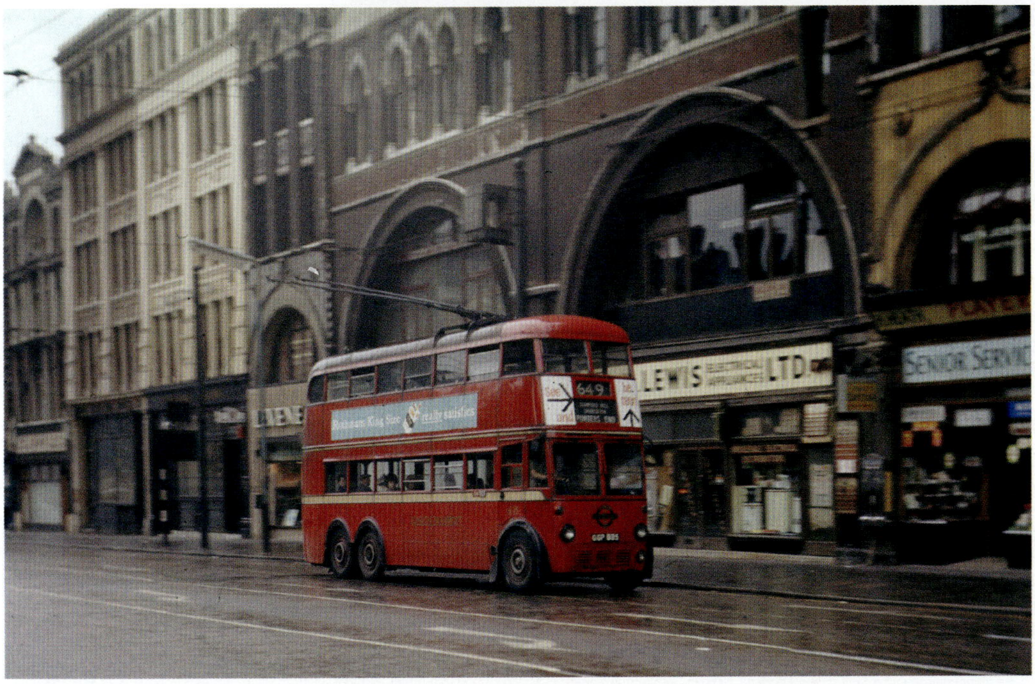

The penultimate K3 class 1695, heads north on a short working of the 649 to 'Ponders End' where the terminus was the forecourt of Enfield Bus Garage.
Michael Dryhurst

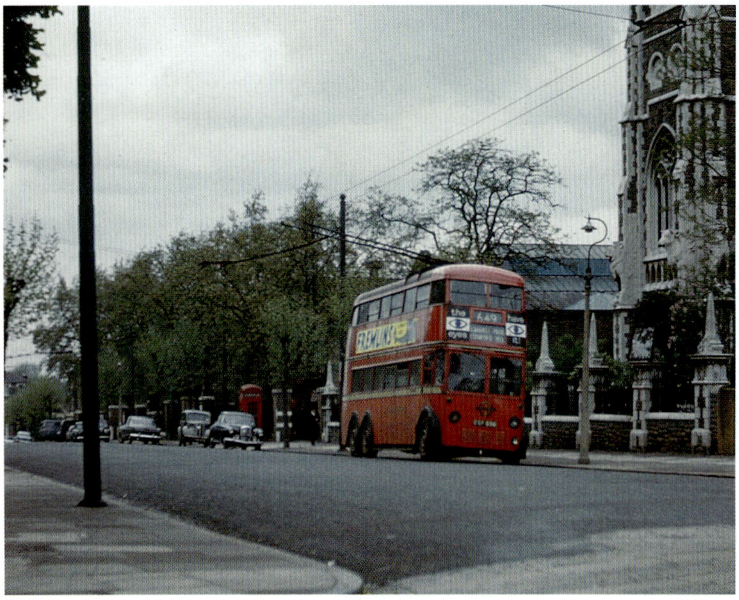

K3 class 1696 is seen on a 649 short working in Rookwood Road outside Stamford Hill Depot. The K3 class of 25 vehicles were all allocated to Edmonton Depot where most spent their whole working lives.
Julian Bowden Collection

SA3 class 1753 waits for trade at Barkingside before returning to Barking Broadway. This view clearly shows the front doors of the vehicle, which were always panelled over during London service.
Mick Webber Collection

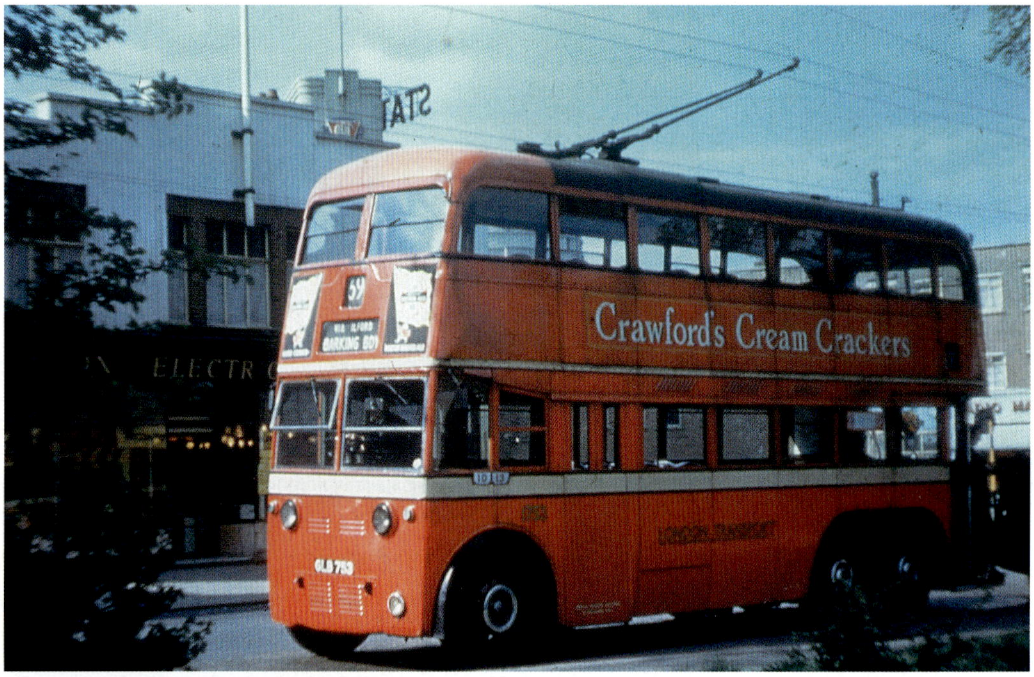

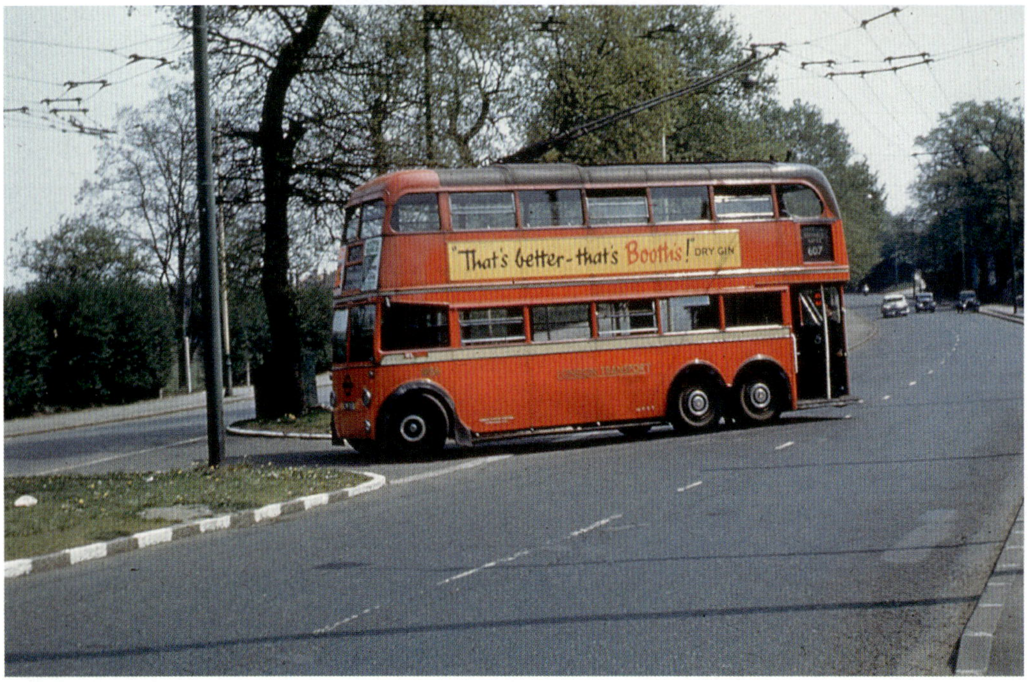

Q1 class 1856 is seen turning short along the Uxbridge Road. The vehicle has no running number and is therefore probably not in service.
Julian Bowden Collection

K2 class all-Leyland 1201, had a more eventful life than most other London trolleybuses. When withdrawn from Stamford Hill Depot, it was purchased by a secondhand car business in Shepherds Bush, where it was parked against a wall, painted white, and used as a store. It was eventually bought for preservation, and is now operating again at the East Anglia Transport Museum. It appears here when working from Stamford Hill Depot on route 647.
Mick Webber Collection

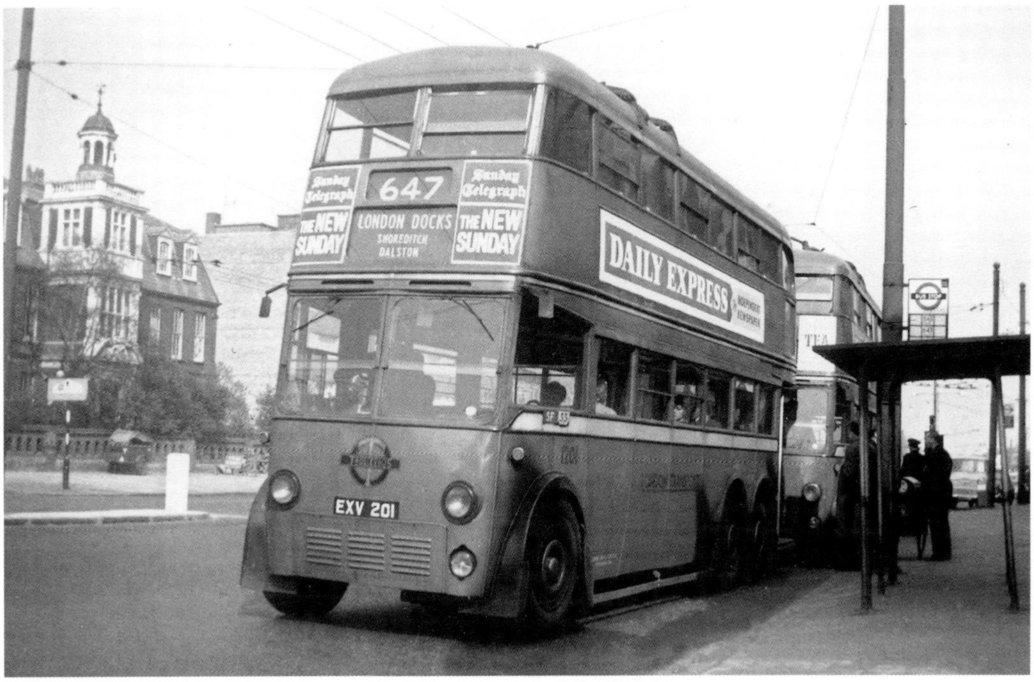

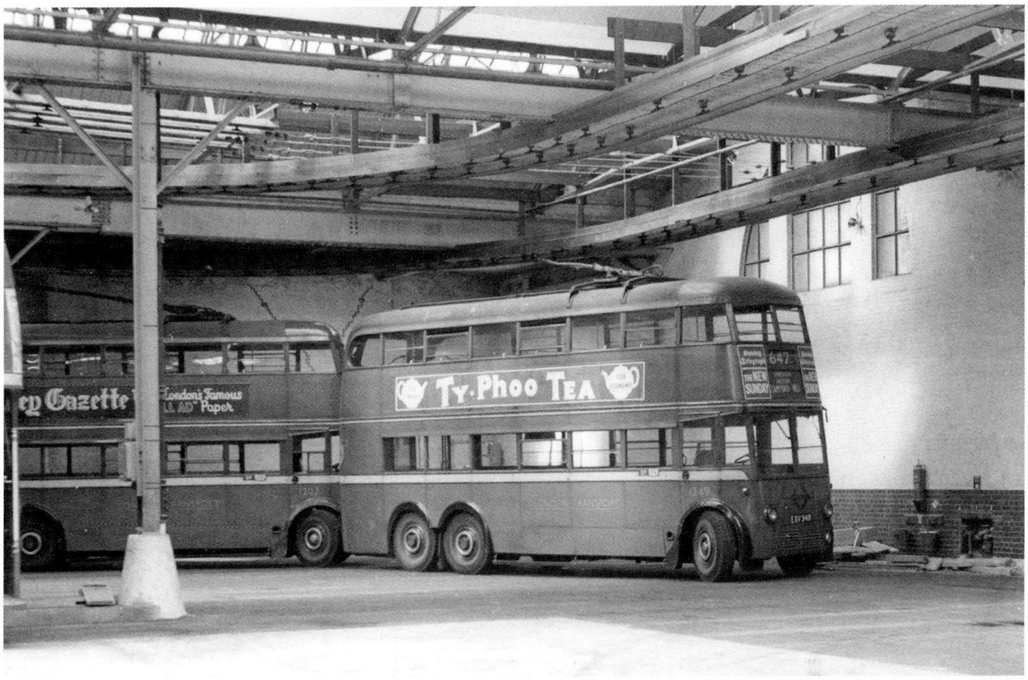

1349 is a K2 class trolleybus seen here in Stamford Hill Depot near the end of its service in 1961.
John Aldridge collection

Another trolleybus to have led an eventful life, is K2 class 1348. When withdrawn in 1961, it went to a historic transport collection near Dublin for preservation. After many years of deterioration in the open, it was brought back to England, and is now at the Sandtoft Trolleybus Museum.
Geoff Lumb

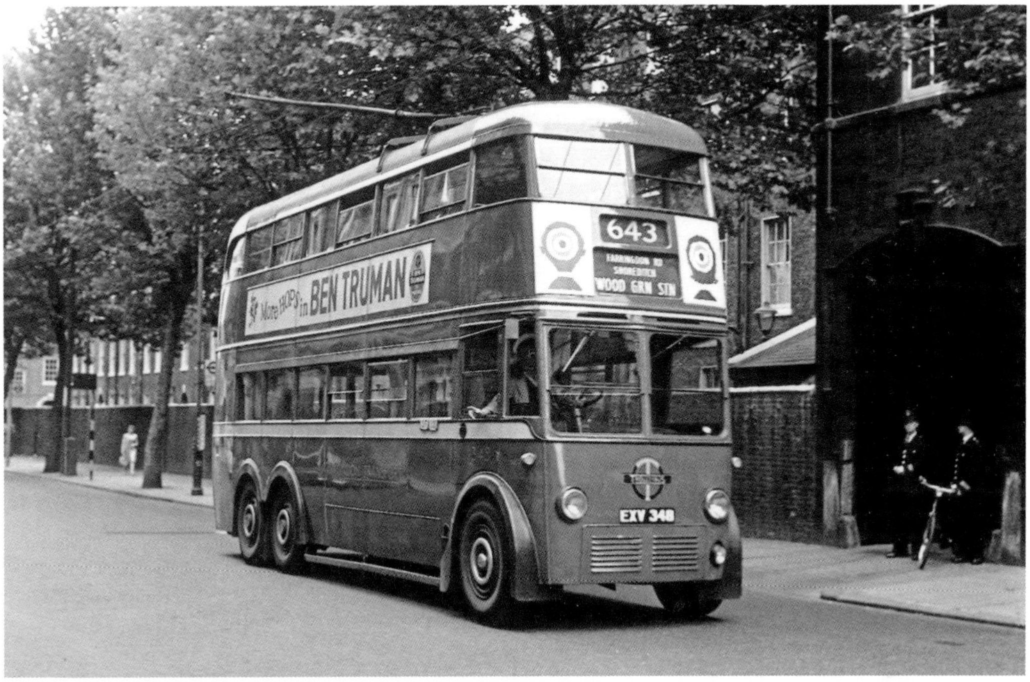

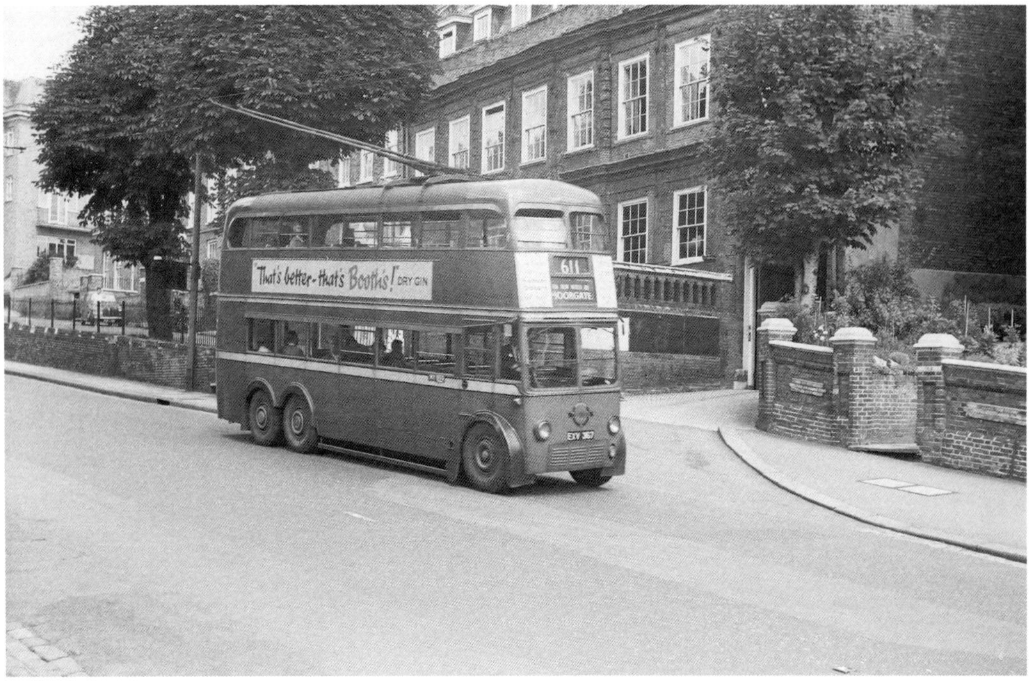

The L classes are chassisless vehicles produced by AEC and Metro Cammell. There were 15 L1s delivered in 1939, which always worked from Holloway (later Highgate) Depot. 1367 is shown here descending Highgate Hill on 16 July 1960.
John Shearman

At Highgate Village on 2 May 1959 is L1 class 1368, waiting for its return to Moorgate.
John Shearman

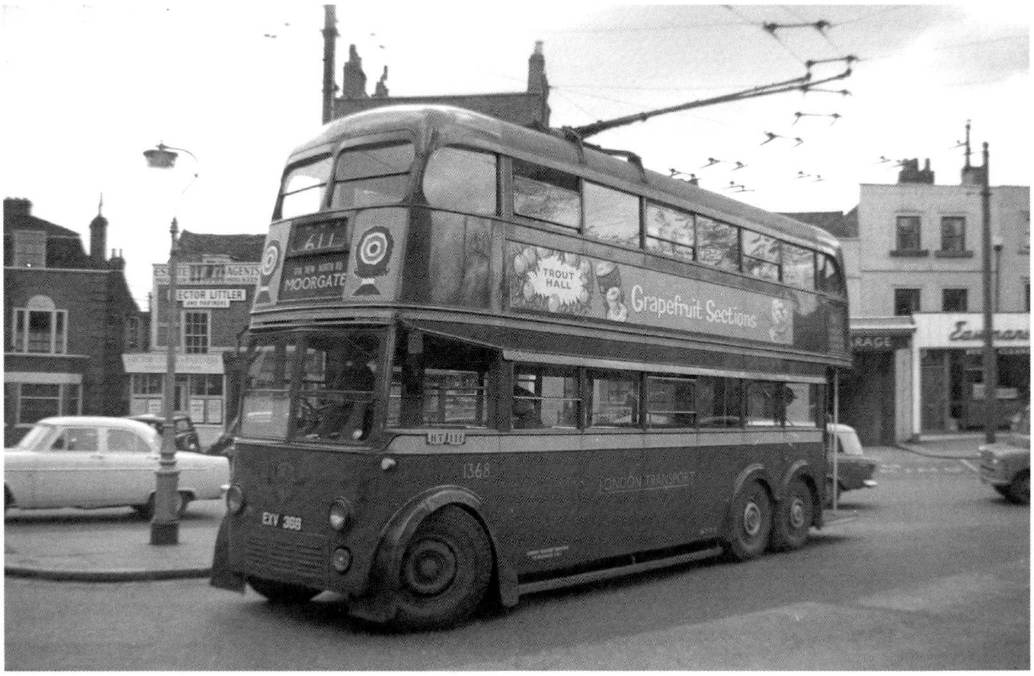

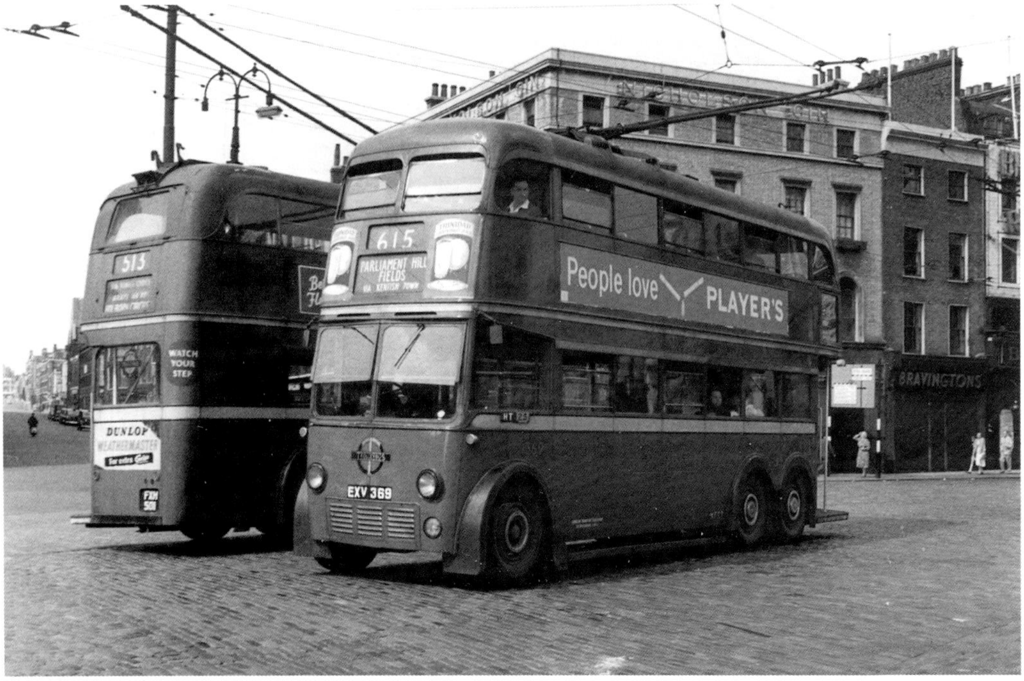

The L1 class is represented here by 1369 operating on the 615 from Highgate Depot, and it is passing L3 class 1501. The L1s are fitted with coasting and runback brakes for use on the 611, which traversed Highgate Hill.
Mick Webber Collection

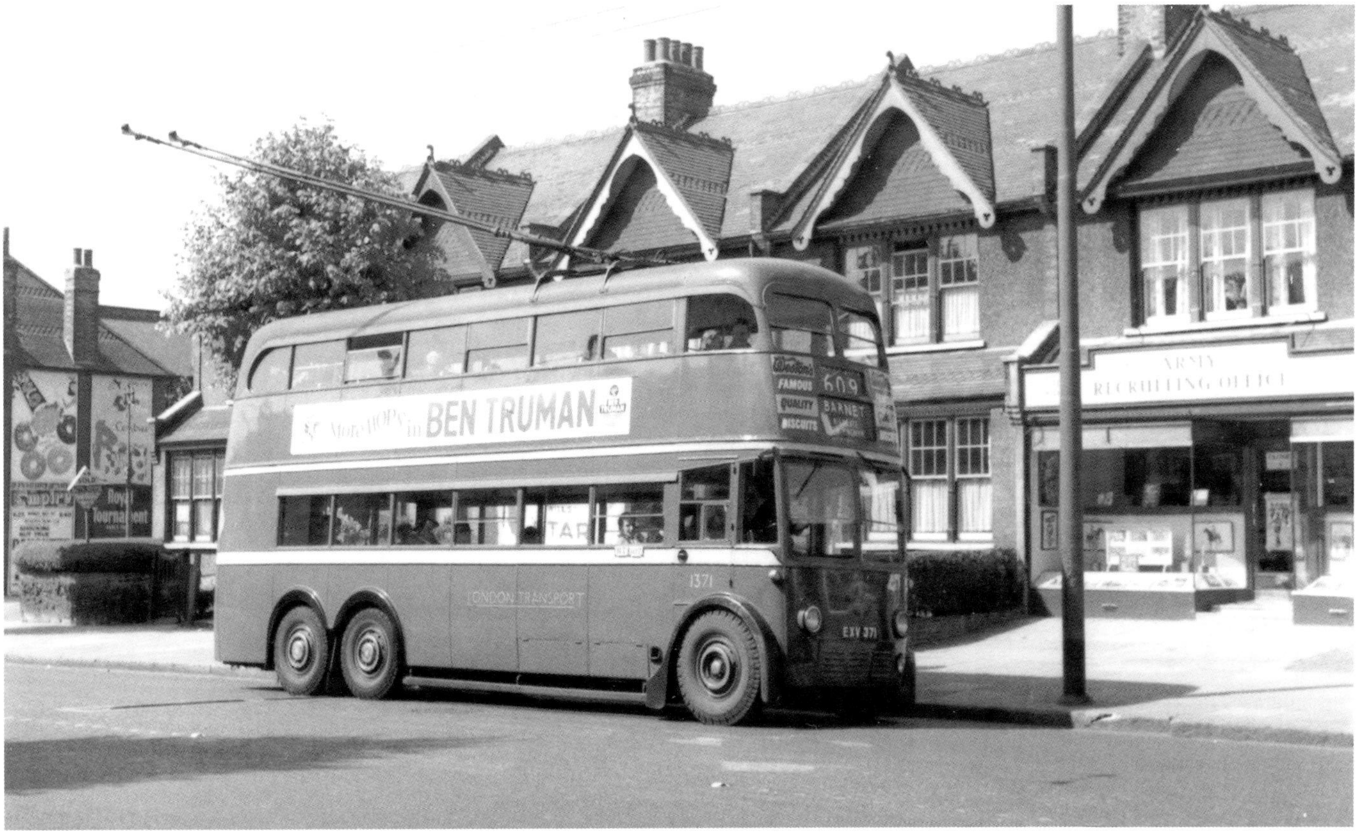

The L2 class was delivered in 1939. Most spent their entire lives at Holloway Depot (later Highgate), from which 1371 can be seen operating on the 609. *R.Kingdon/LCC Tramway Trust*

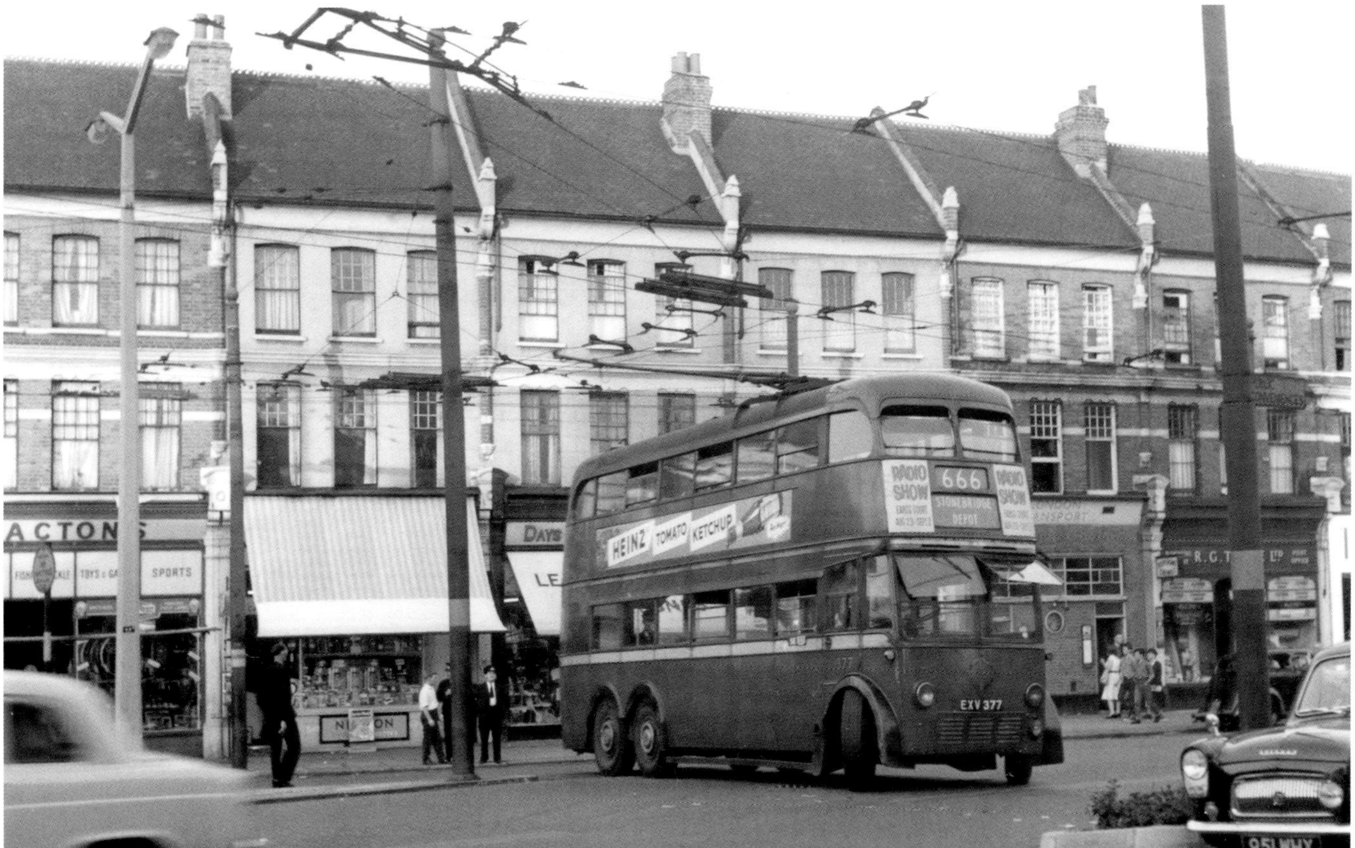

L2 class 1377 was a June 1939 delivery, and is making the tight turn at Craven Park, to run in to Stonebridge Depot. It would appear to be a rather hot day, as the driver has both windscreens wide open. There were only nine of the class, and some of them spent their last months in west London. *Mick Webber Collection*

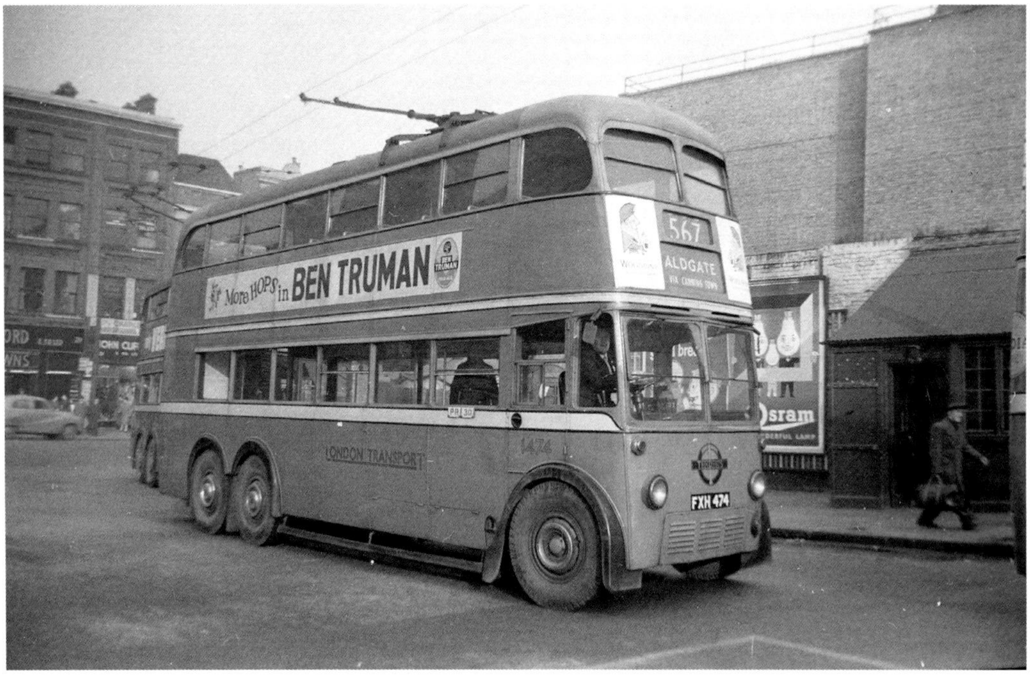

1474 is one of 150 trolleybuses of the L3 class and is seen at the Minories Bus Station, Aldgate in 1958. This class are also chassisless AEC, Metro Cammell vehicles.
John Shearman

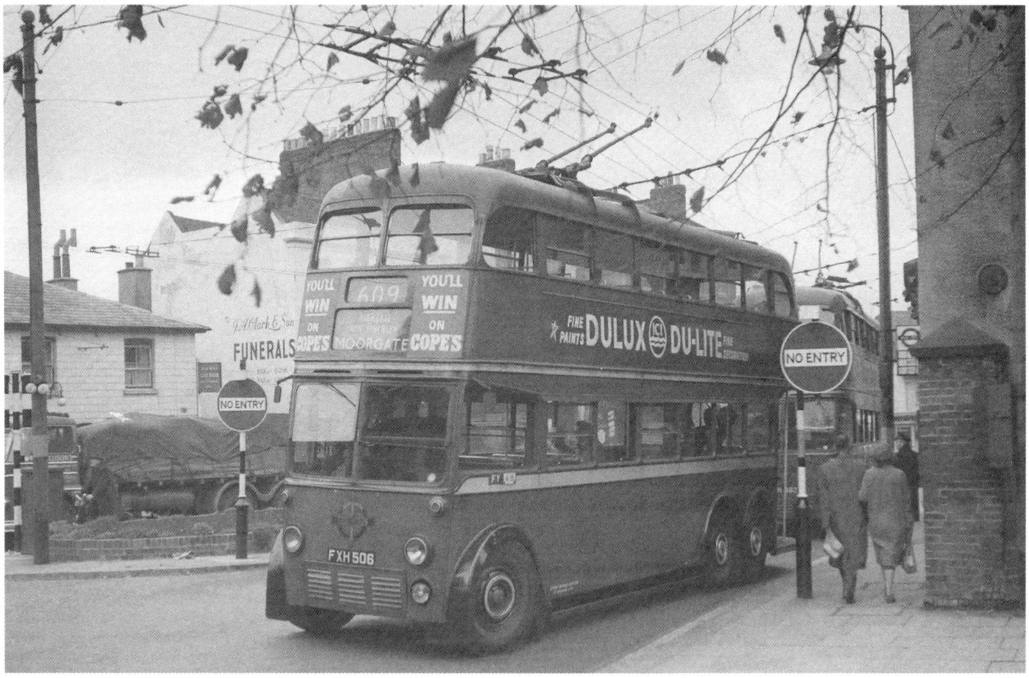

Another L3 class trolleybus, 1506, is seen at Barnet on 21 September 1961. Within two months the 609 was converted to bus operation using the first of the 30 feet long RML Routemaster buses.
John Shearman

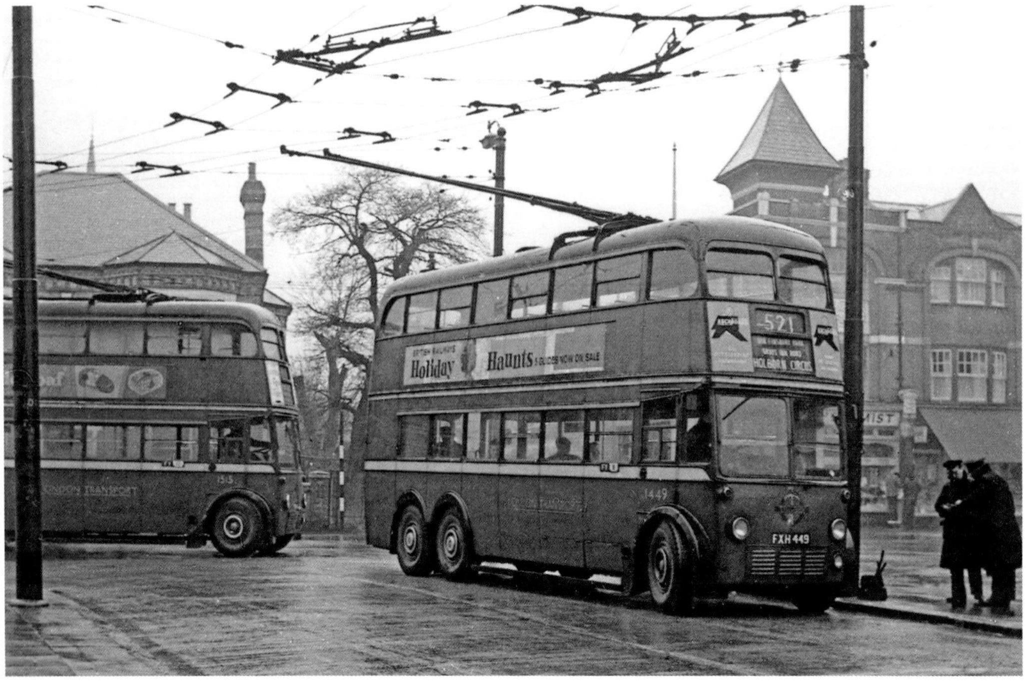

North Finchley was a very busy trolleybus terminus, and two L3s, 1449 and 1515, are seen here, the former on the 521.
Travel Lens Photographic

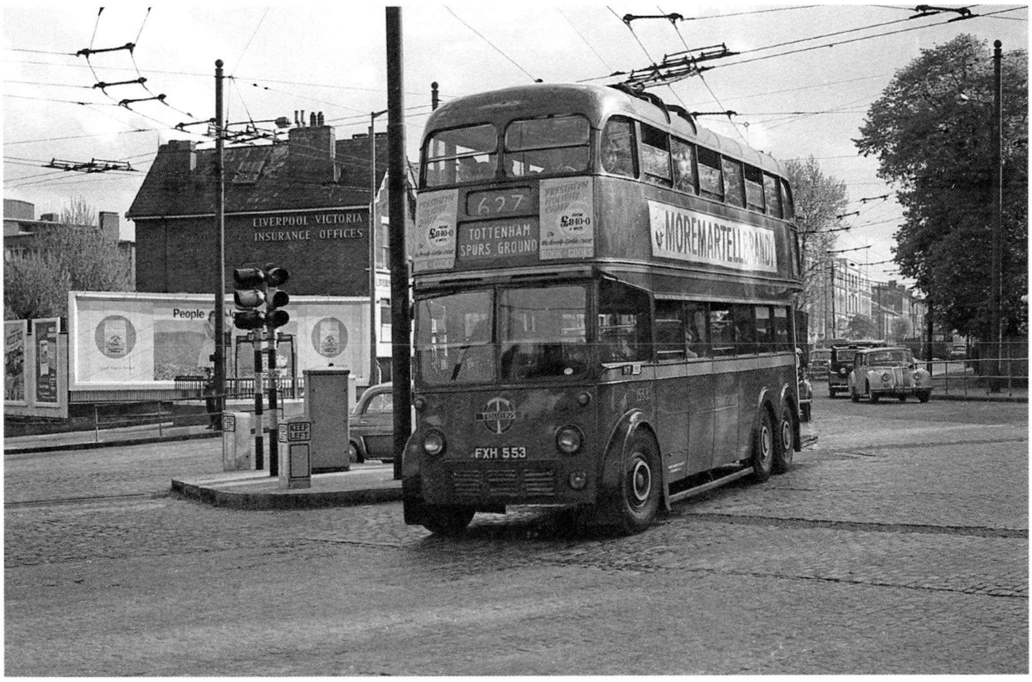

1553 is seen at Manor House on 24 April 1961. This is one of 25 vehicles that comprised the M1 class. The AEC design of lightweight chassis, and with Weymann bodywork built at Addlestone, produced an overall weight less than that of trolleybuses with a conventional chassis.
Brian Speller

M1 class 1552 is seen in the High Road, East Finchley two days before the end of service on route 517.
Brian Speller

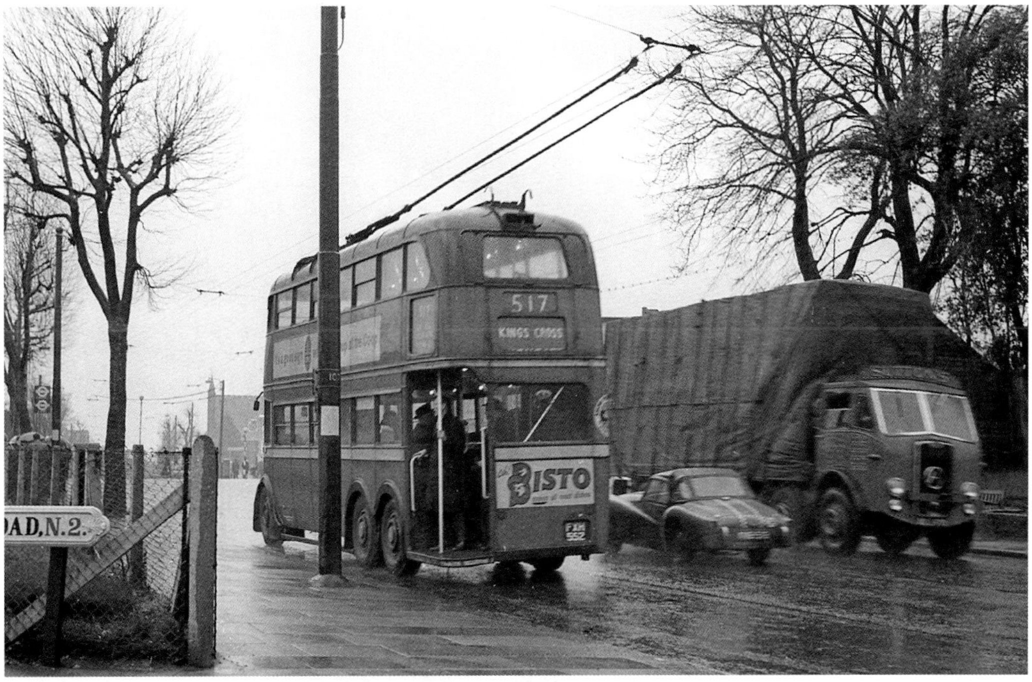

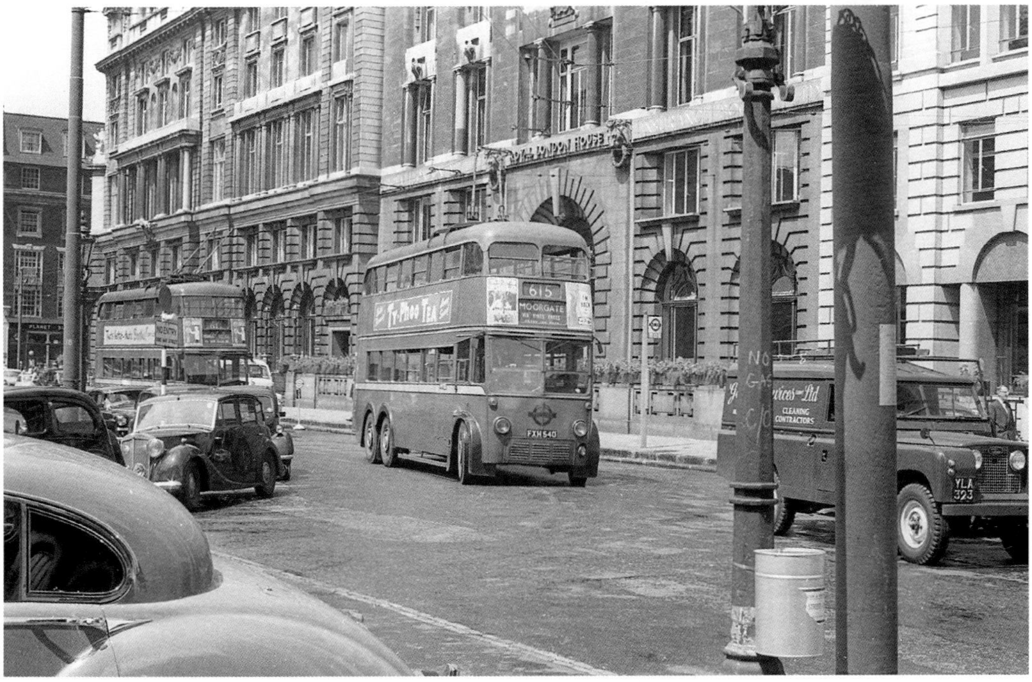

Route 615 terminated at Finsbury Square, Moorgate where M1 class 1540 was photographed on 7 July 1960. This route was operated by Holloway Depot (later Highgate) which was the largest capacity depot on the London trolleybus system.
Brian Speller

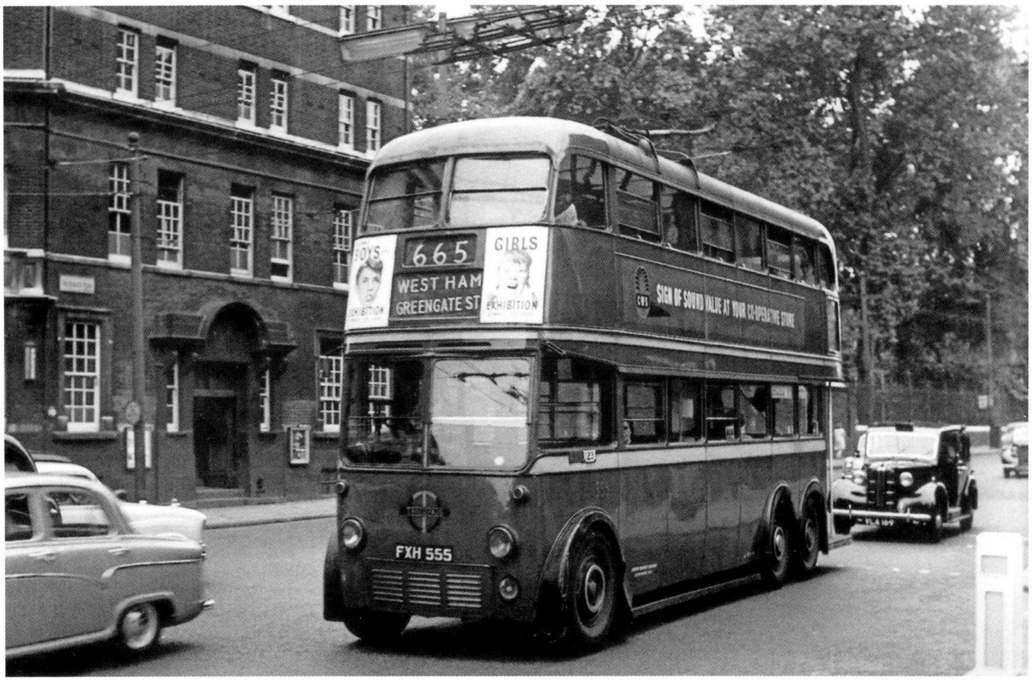

Theobalds Road, Bloomsbury is the location, where N1 class 1555, makes its way back to West Ham Depot on route 665.
Geoff Lumb

By 1958 total service levels were being reduced which resulted in some re-allocations of newer trolleybuses. 1644 was the highest numbered N1 and was an early transfer from east London to Stonebridge Depot to replace older trolleybuses in west London. 1644 is seen at Hammersmith in 1958.
John Shearman

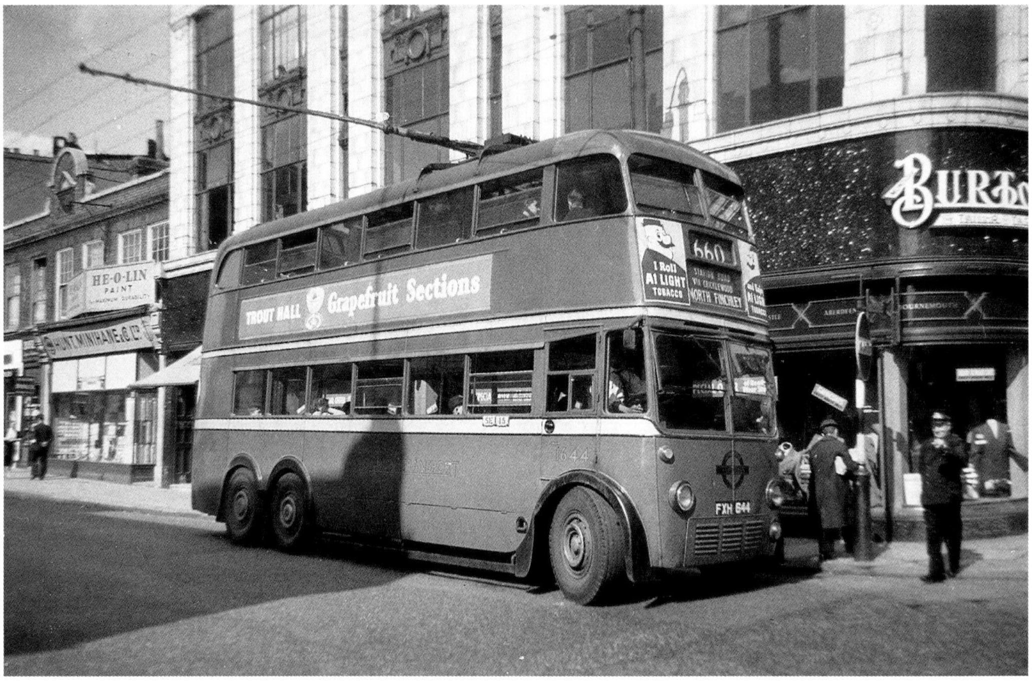

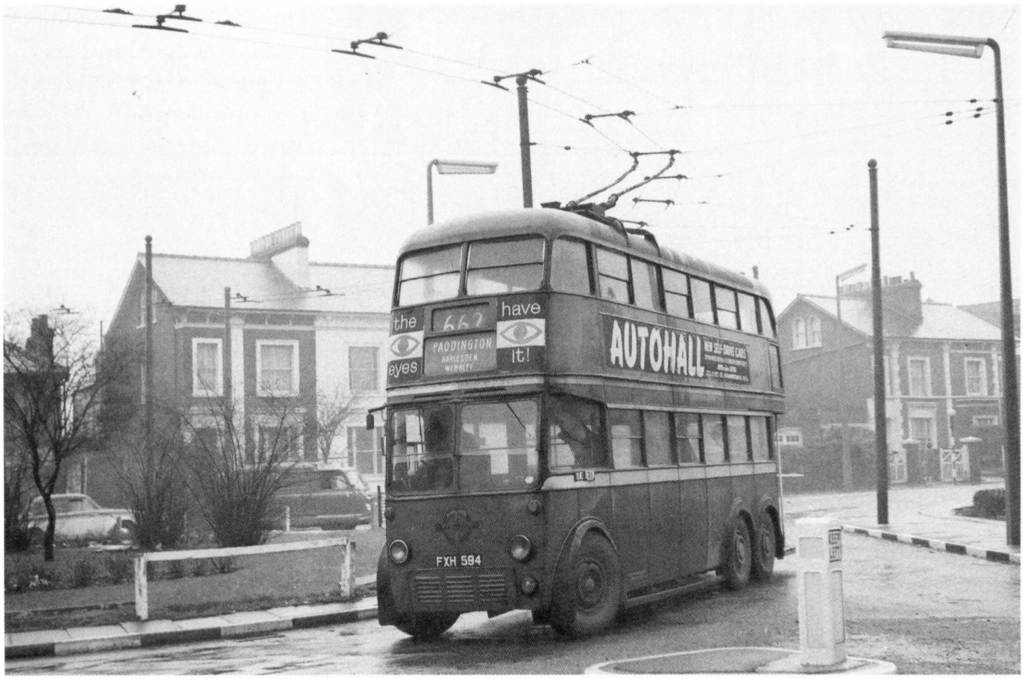

The N1 class comprised BRCW bodied AECs. 1594 is seen at Sudbury on 30 December 1961.
John Shearman

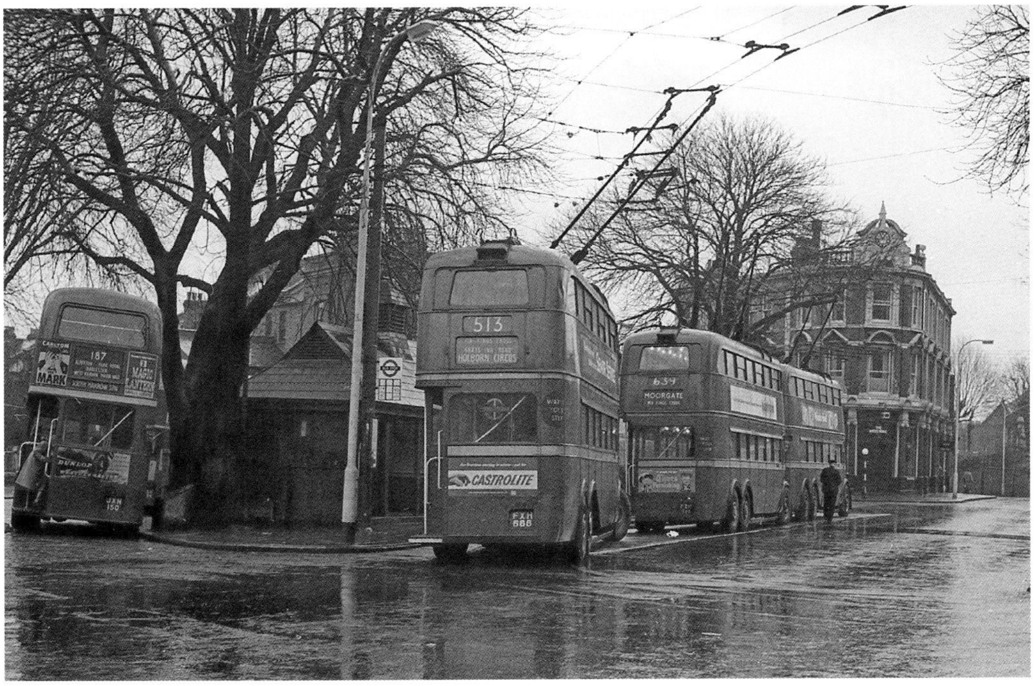

The N2 class is Park Royal bodied. 1668 is seen on the last Sunday of operation of trolleybus route 513 at South End Green, Hampstead Heath. This route ceased two days later on 31 January 1961 and was replaced by two bus routes, the 45 and 63.
Brian Speller

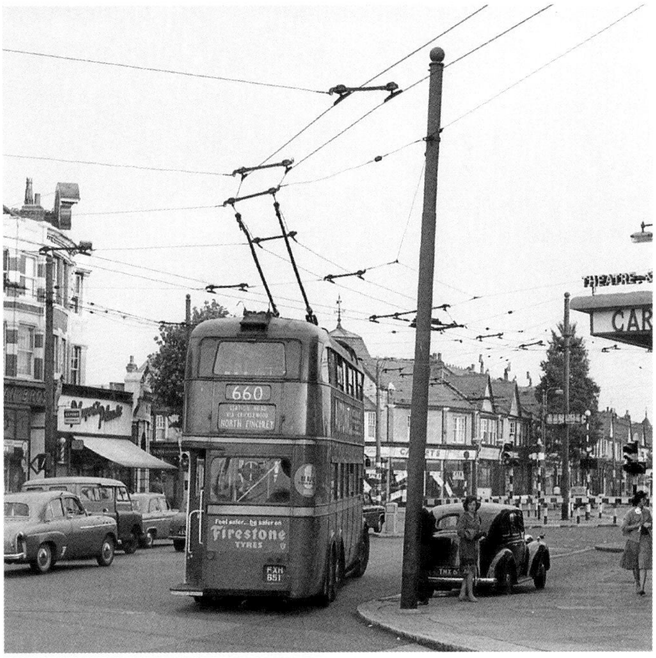

The High Road in North Finchley is the location where N2 class 1651 was photographed on 29 July 1961.
Brian Speller

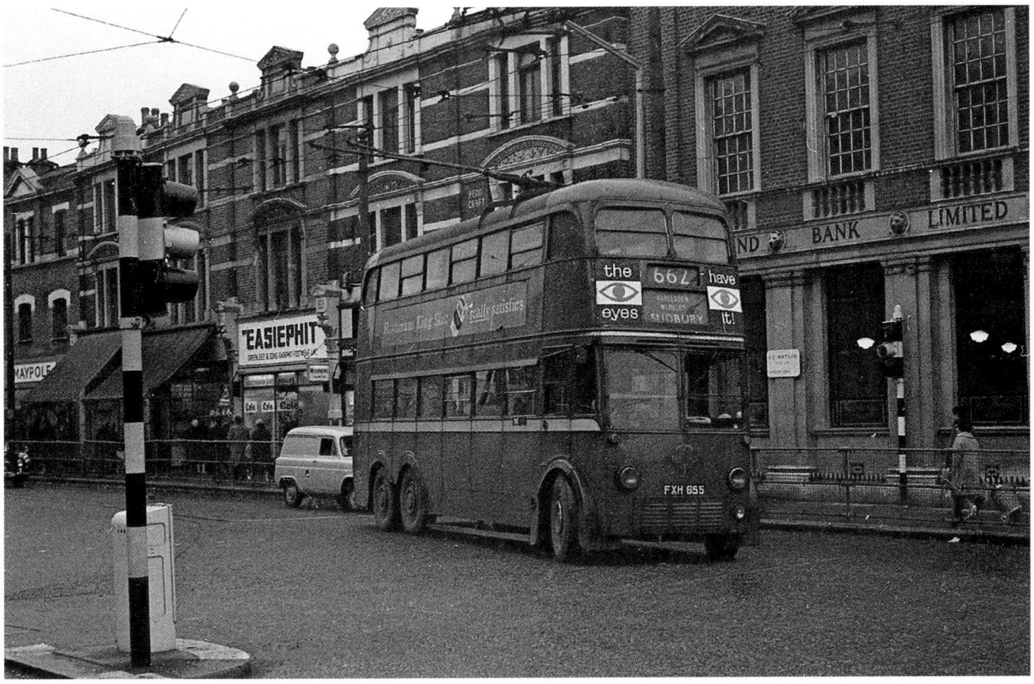

N2 class 1655 heading for Sudbury on route 662 is seen in Harlesden High Street on 30 December 1961.
Brian Speller

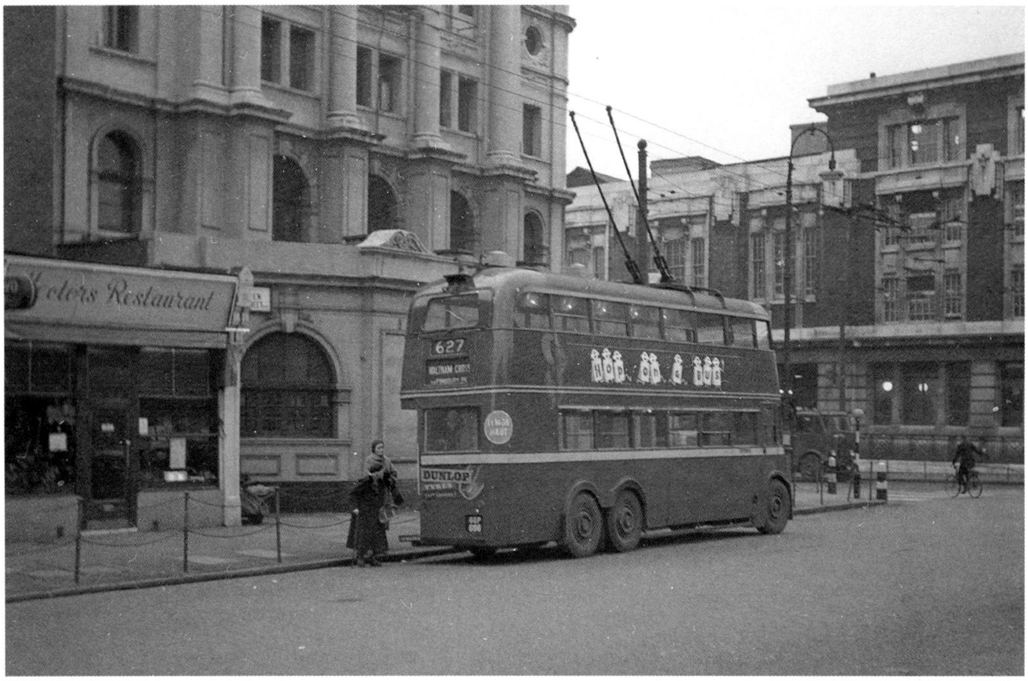

Leyland supplied 427 trolleybus bodies to London Transport, of which some of the last were the 25 members of the K3 class, delivered in late 1940. 1696 is seen at Mornington Crescent Station on a short worked 627 journey.
Michael Dryhurst

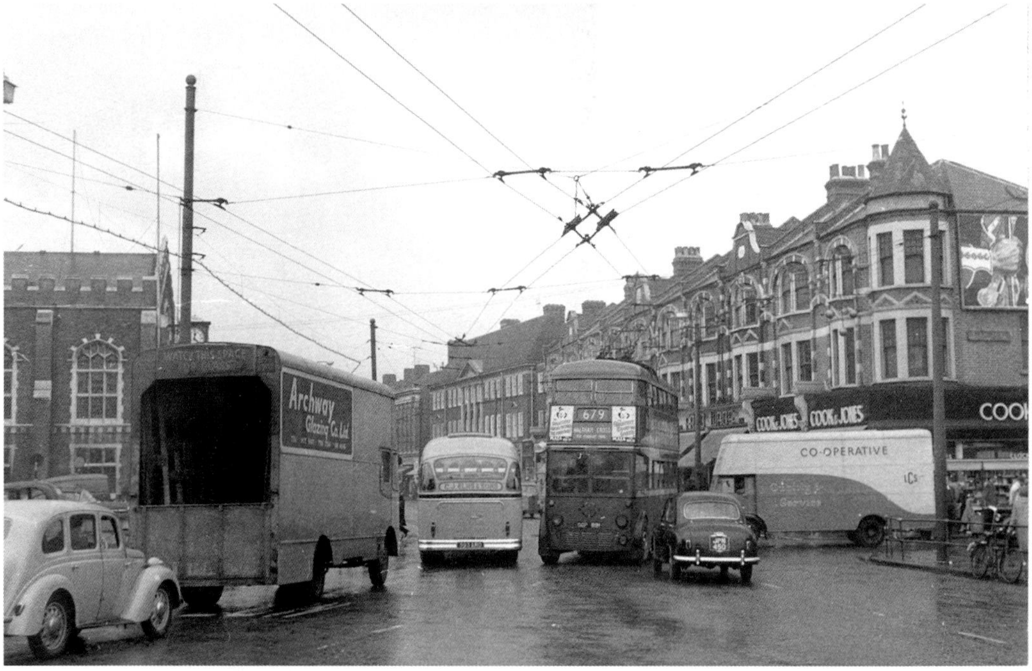

The K3 class was always associated with Edmonton Depot. 1691 is working the 679 to Waltham Cross, and passes a Bedford/Duple coach of C.J.Elms, as it makes its way through Lower Edmonton on a gloomy day.
Mick Webber Collection

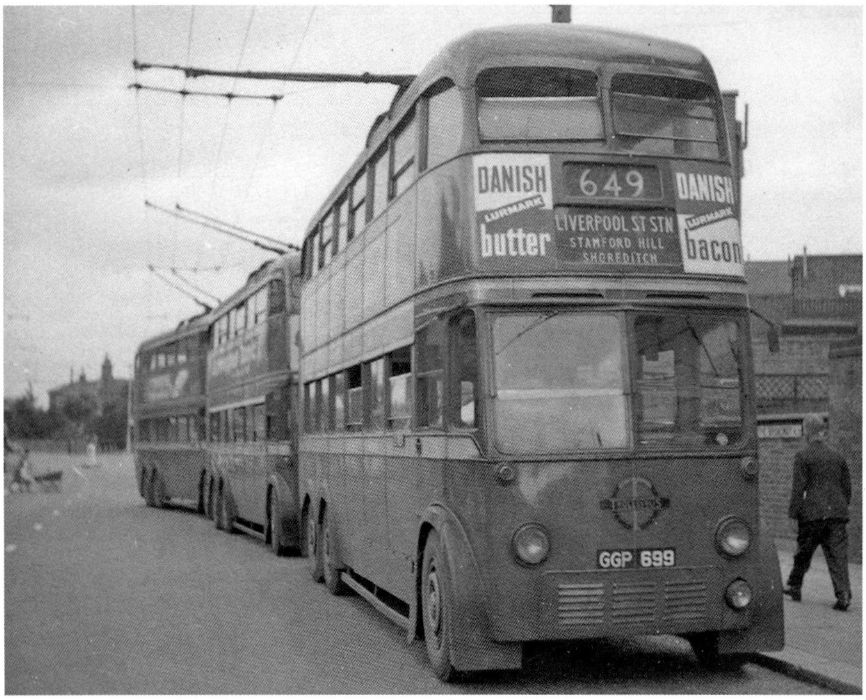

Although the P1 class only totalled 25 trolleybuses, they served at a number of depots, but most notably Hammersmith and Edmonton. 1699 was operated from the latter when seen on-stand at 'Edmonton Town Hall'.
Michael Dryhurst

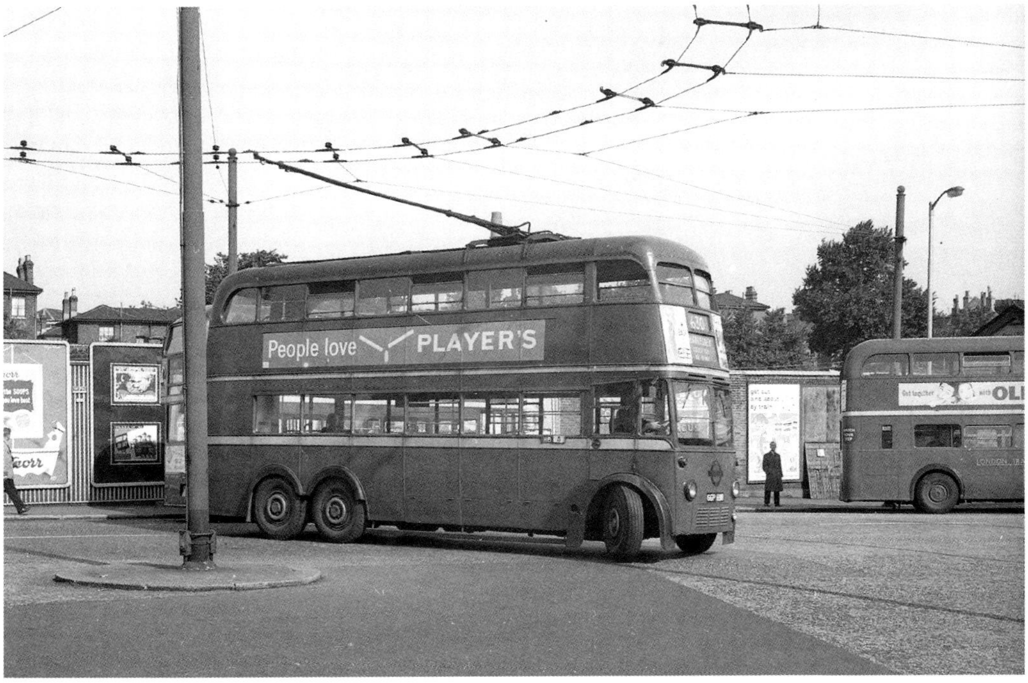

The last Leyland trolleybuses ordered by London Transport were 1697-1721, the 25 members of the P1 class. They have Metro Cammell bodies identical to those of the chassisless L3 trolleybuses. 1698 is turning at West Croydon where the wires have already been removed for route 654.
Michael Dryhurst

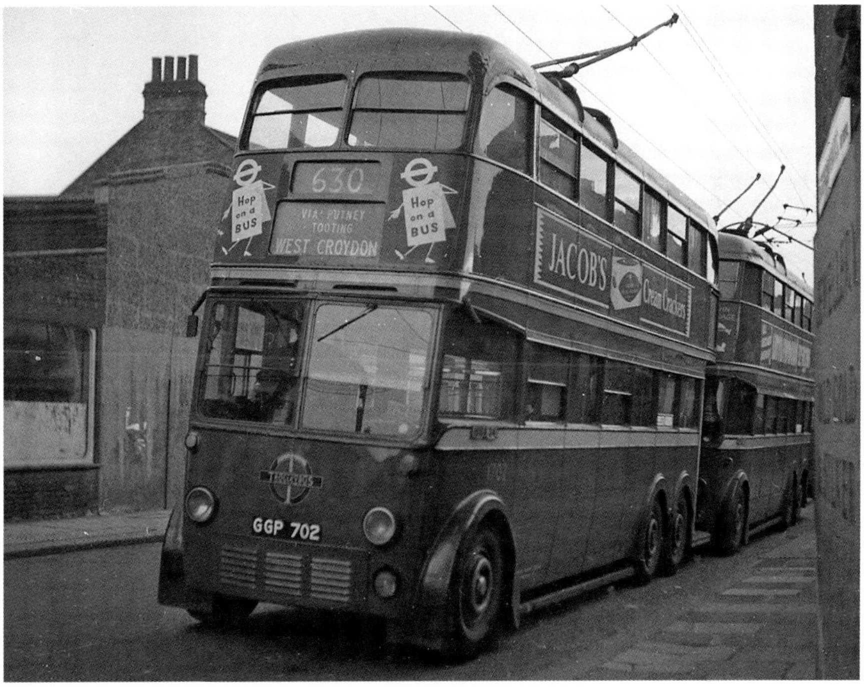

P1 class 1702, stands at the terminus known as "Nr Willesden Junc" on route 630.
Michael Dryhurst

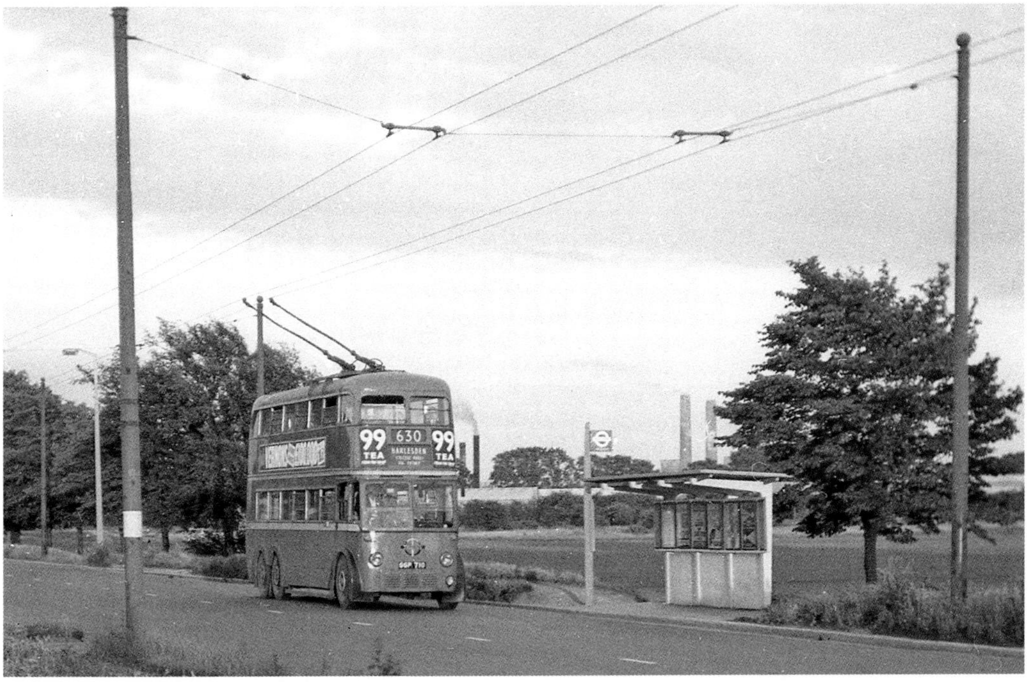

This scenic view is of the 'country section' of the lengthy 630 route, that ran across the verdant terrain of Mitcham Common.
Michael Dryhurst

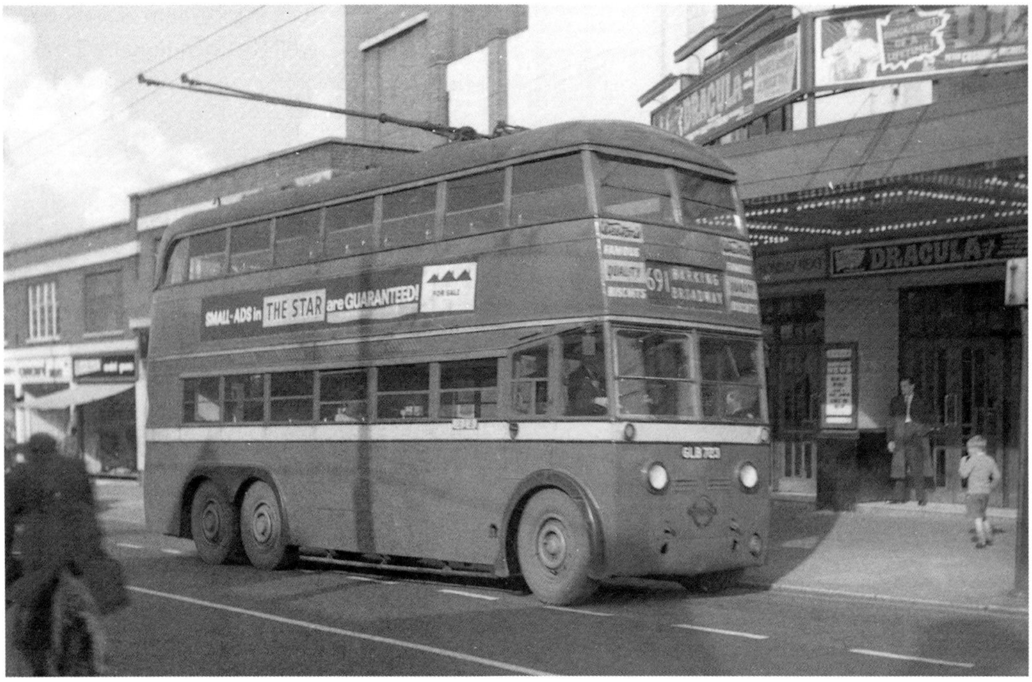

By 1941 wartime U boat activity precluded the shipment of trolleybuses ordered and being built for export. These included Leylands for Durban and AECs for Johannesburg, all with Metro Cammell bodies. London Transport secured 25 of the former and 18 of the latter. SA1 class 1723 is seen at work in Barking.
Michael Dryhurst

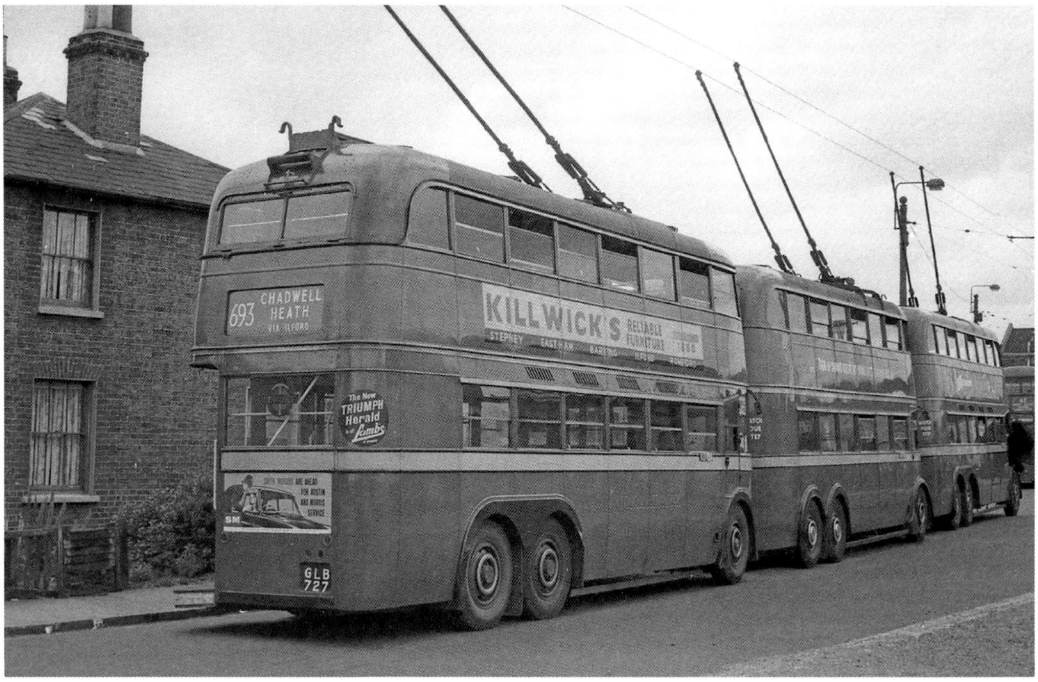

The South African trolleybuses became London Transport SA classes and its first 8 feet wide vehicles. All 43 were only ever allocated to Ilford Depot. SA1 class 1727, a Leyland for Durban, is seen working route 693 at the Wangey Road, Chadwell Heath terminus on 6 June 1959.
Brian Speller

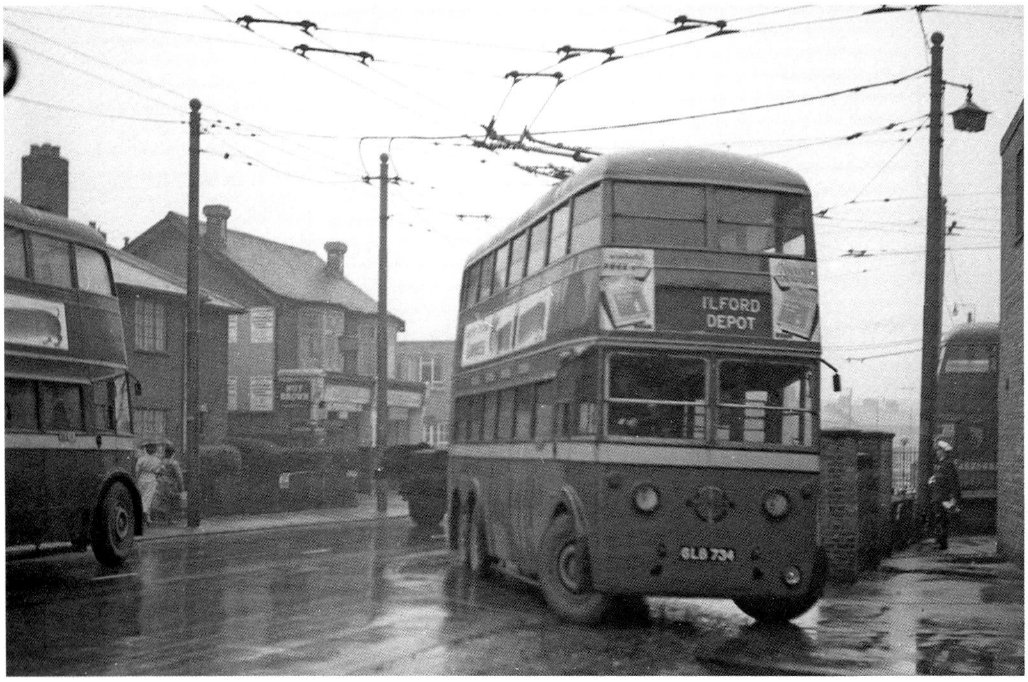

SA2 class 1734, turning into Ilford Depot, illustrates the narrower width of the rear axles compared with the front. The only difference in the SA1 and SA2 classes is the electrical equipment fitted, as originally ordered by Durban.
Michael Dryhurst

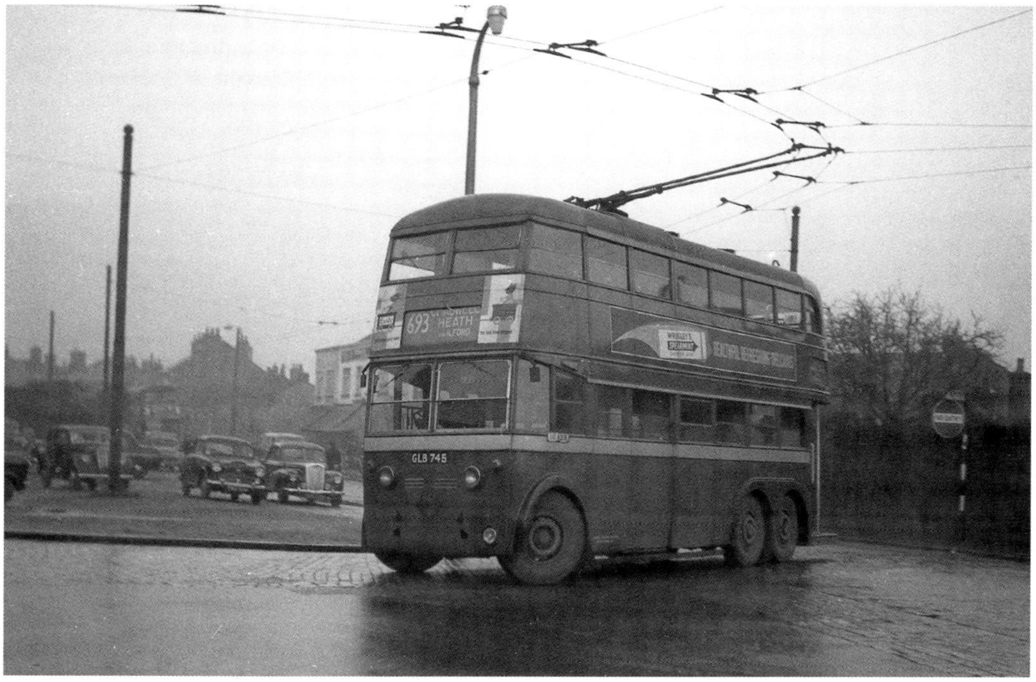

SA2 class 1745 turns at Chadwell Heath in January 1959.
Michael Dryhurst

Wangey Road in Chadwell Heath was the eastern terminus of the 693 route. At this location SA2 class 1746 illustrates the sealed front door that was never used in London service.
Brian Speller

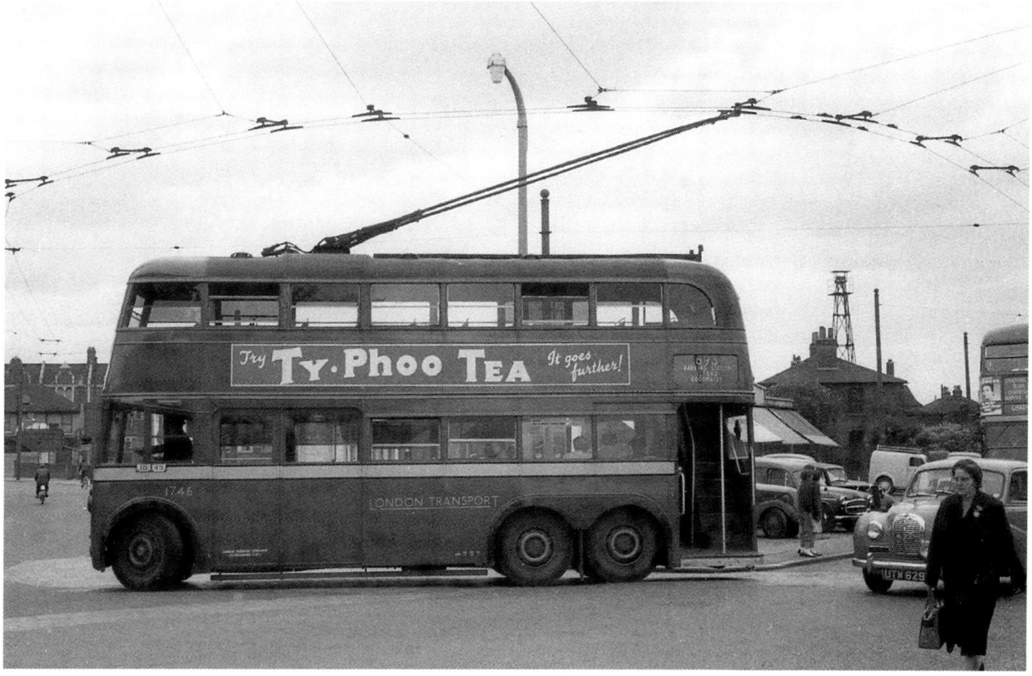

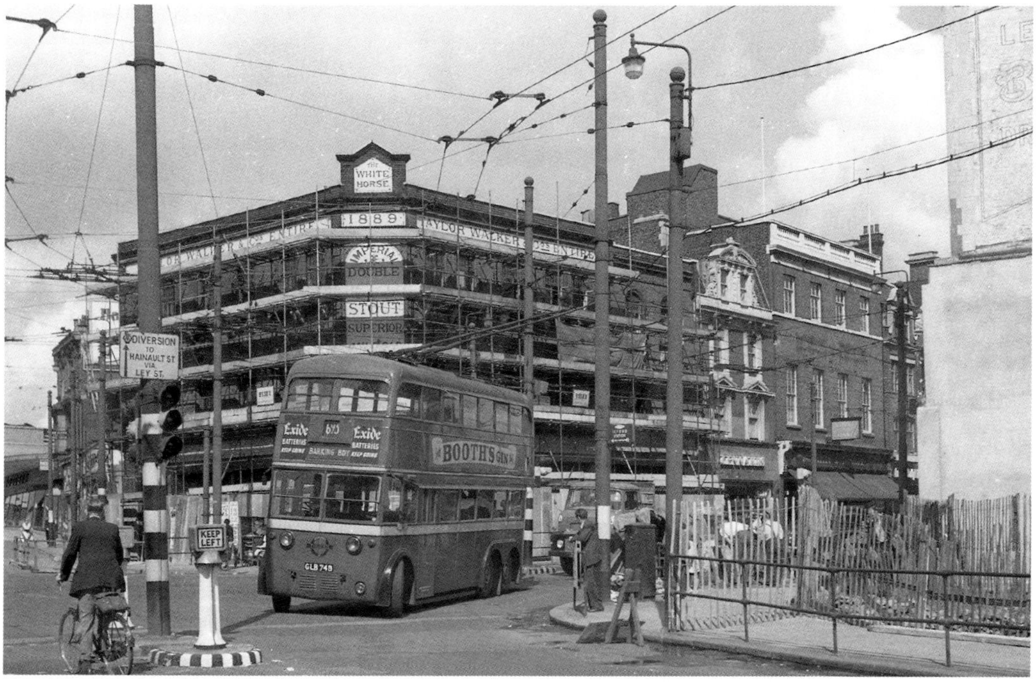

SA 3 class 1749 is seen on the 693 at Ilford. The SA3s were built with folding front passenger doors that like the SA1 and SA2 classes were sealed out of use for London service.
Michael Dryhurst

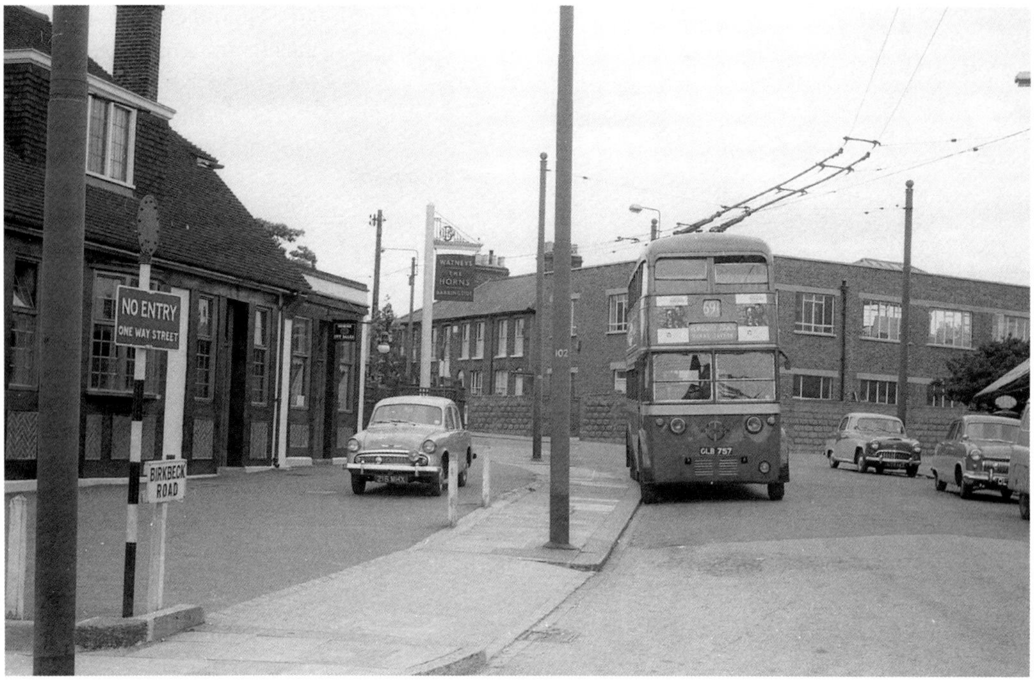

'The Horns' at Newbury Park is the location of this SA3, 1757, on a short working of route 691. The photograph was taken on 6 June 1959.
Brian Speller

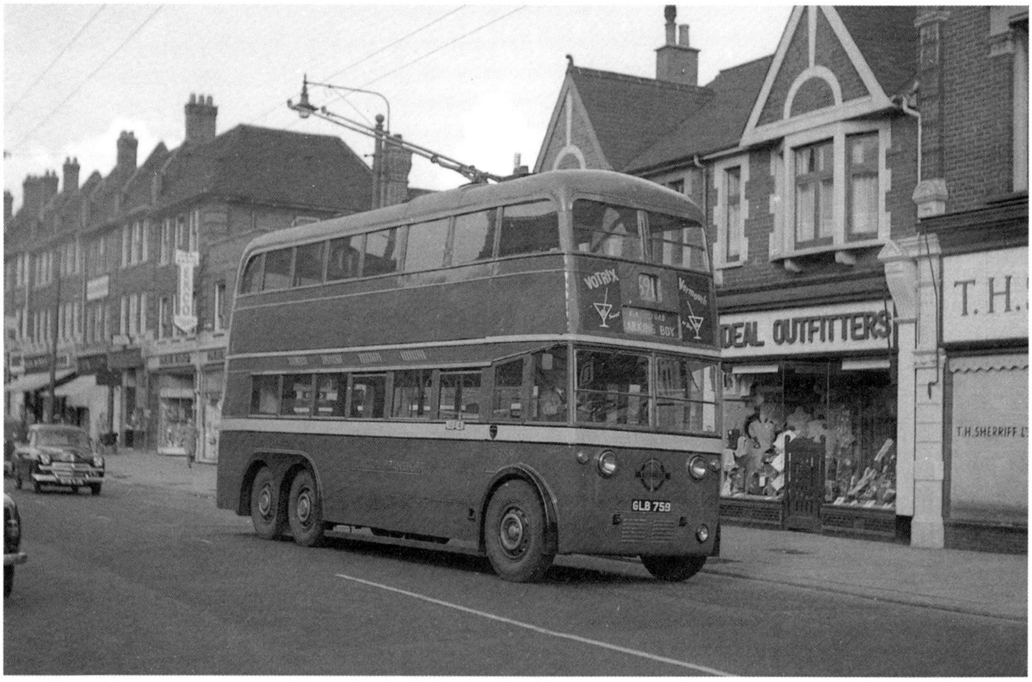

SA3 class 1759, an AEC ordered for service in Johannesburg, illustrates that, apart from L2 class 954, the SA classes were the only London trolleybuses to have the cream waistband continuing beneath the windscreens. 1759 is seen at Ilford Broadway.
Michael Dryhurst

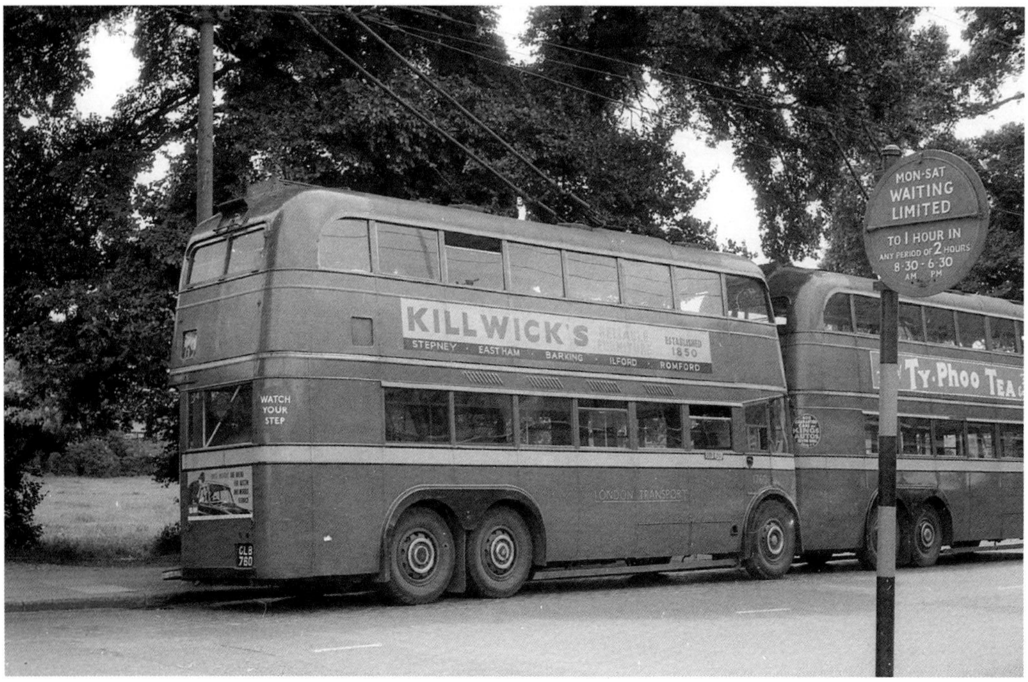

This view of SA3 class 1760 illustrates the route number box located on the offside stair panel that was never used in London service.
Brian Speller

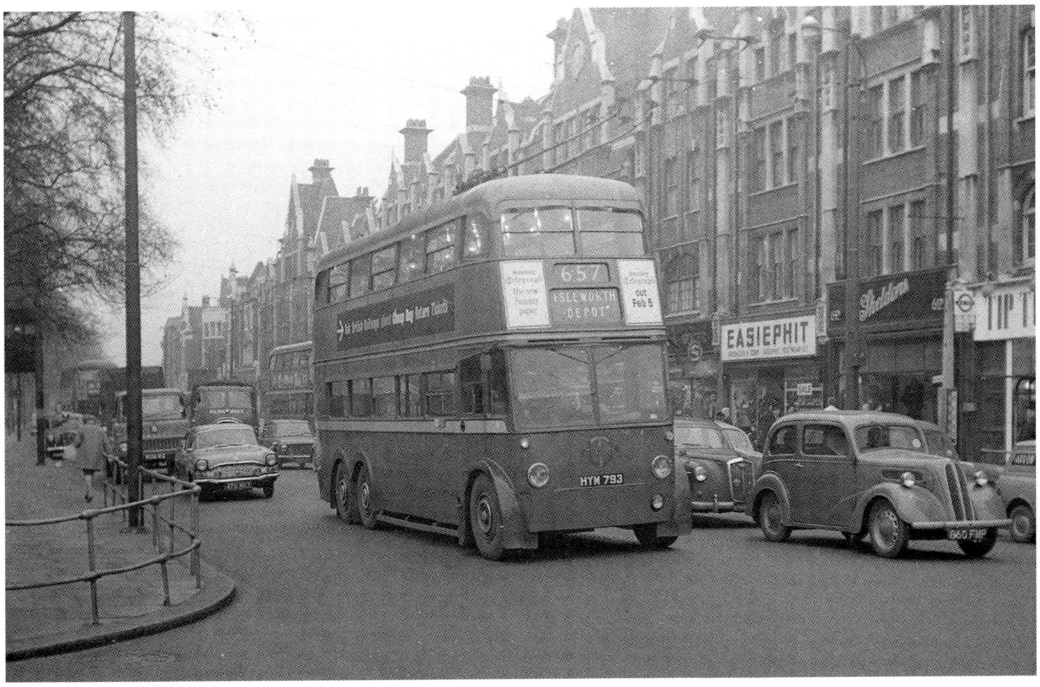

In 1946 the decision was taken not to use trolleybuses to replace the south London trams, thus somewhat frugal were postwar deliveries to London of such vehicles. With AEC and Leyland having pooled their trolleybus manufacturing resources into the newly created British United Traction Co., 77 BUT 9641Ts with Metro Cammell bodies of 8 feet width were received in 1948, that were known as the Q1 class. 1793 is seen at Shepherds Bush Green.
Michael Dryhurst

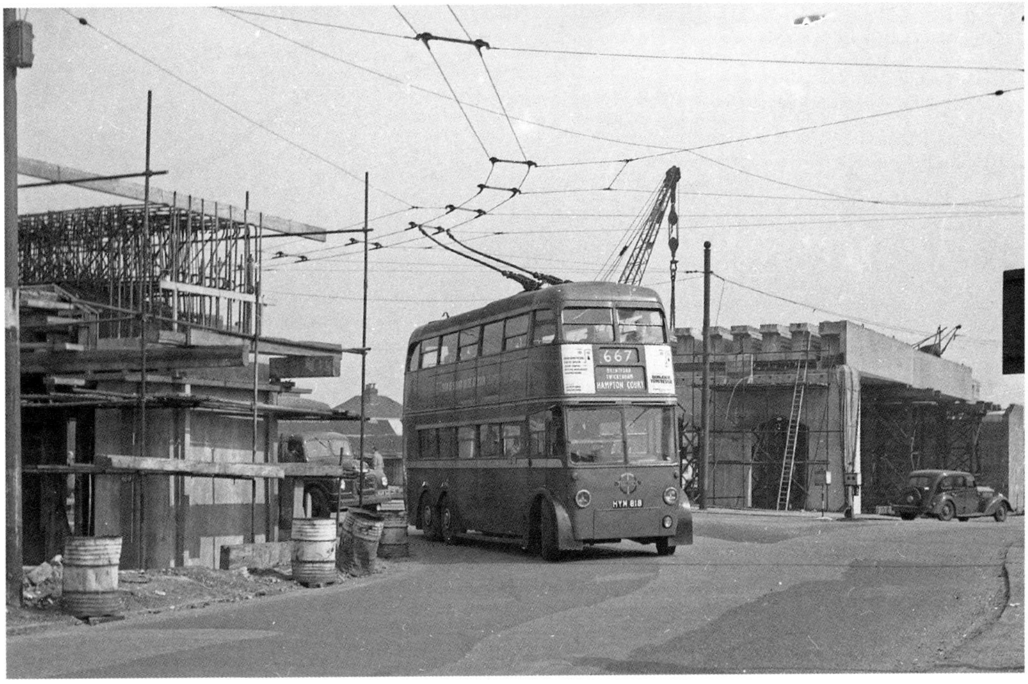

The odd total of 77 arose to replace the 60 Diddlers and 17 trolleybuses written off due to wartime losses. In 1958 the construction of the Chiswick Flyover (now part of the M4) caused the trolleybus overhead to be repeatedly realigned. Q1 1818 threads its way through the works.
Michael Dryhurst

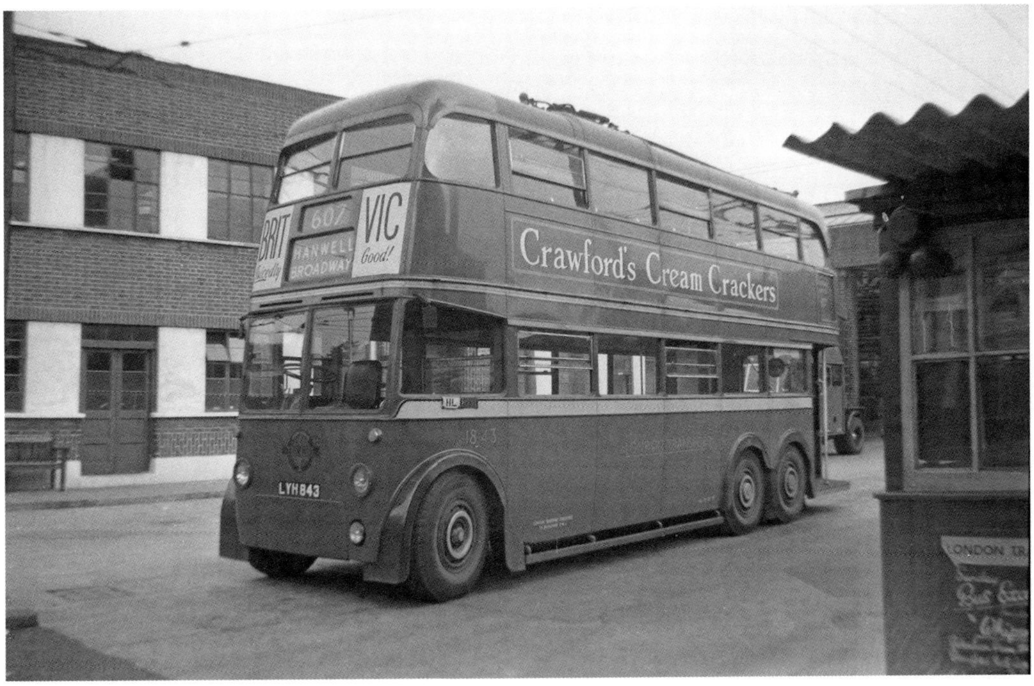

In 1952/53 came the last trolleybuses for London Transport – another batch of Metro Cammell bodied BUT 9641Ts totaling 50 that were also classed as Q1. Both batches of Q1s were all withdrawn prematurely and 125 of the 127 were sold for further service in Spain, although not all entered service there. 1843 from the second batch is seen on Hanwell Depot forecourt in 1958.
John Shearman

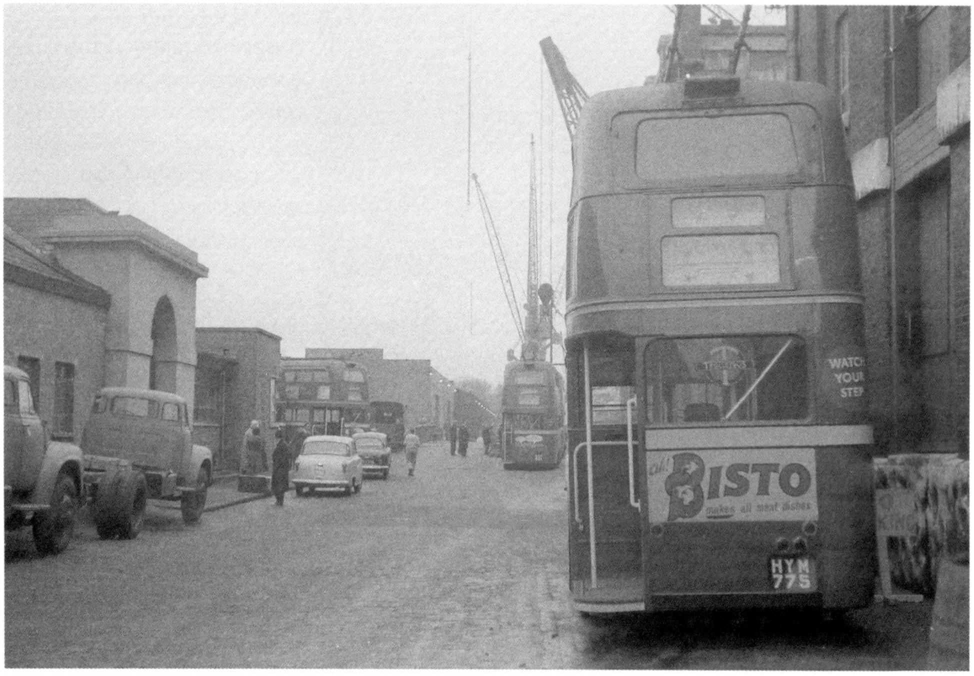

Q1 class 1775 has been towed from west London to the docks and awaits loading at the London Docks (Western Dock) with a number of new Bedford lorries also being exported at this time. This scene was recorded on 24 February 1961.
John Shearman

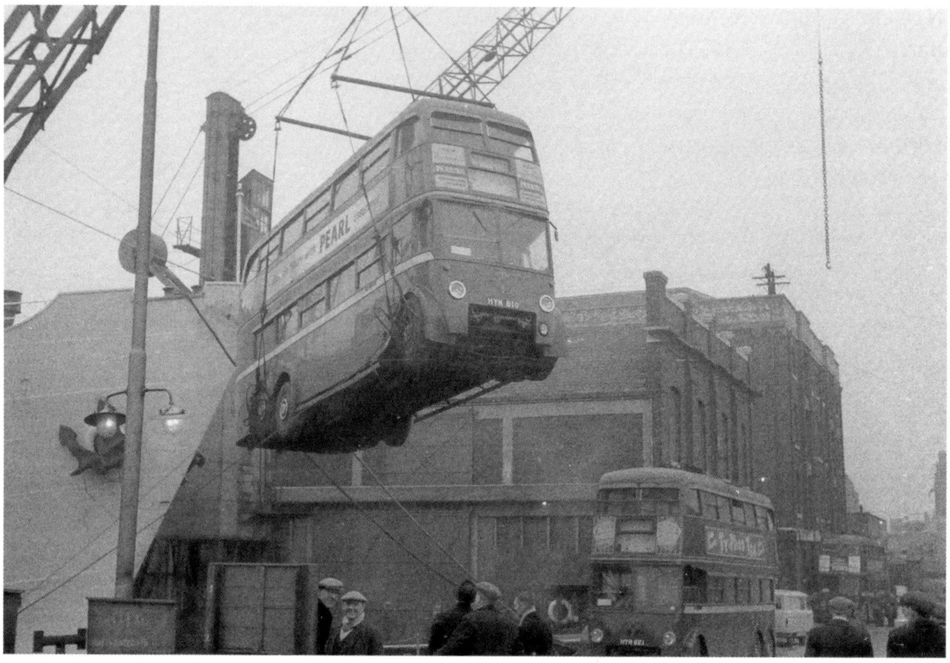

Q1 class 1810 is seen being craned onto MV Pozarica on 24 February 1961 for further service in Spain.
John Shearman

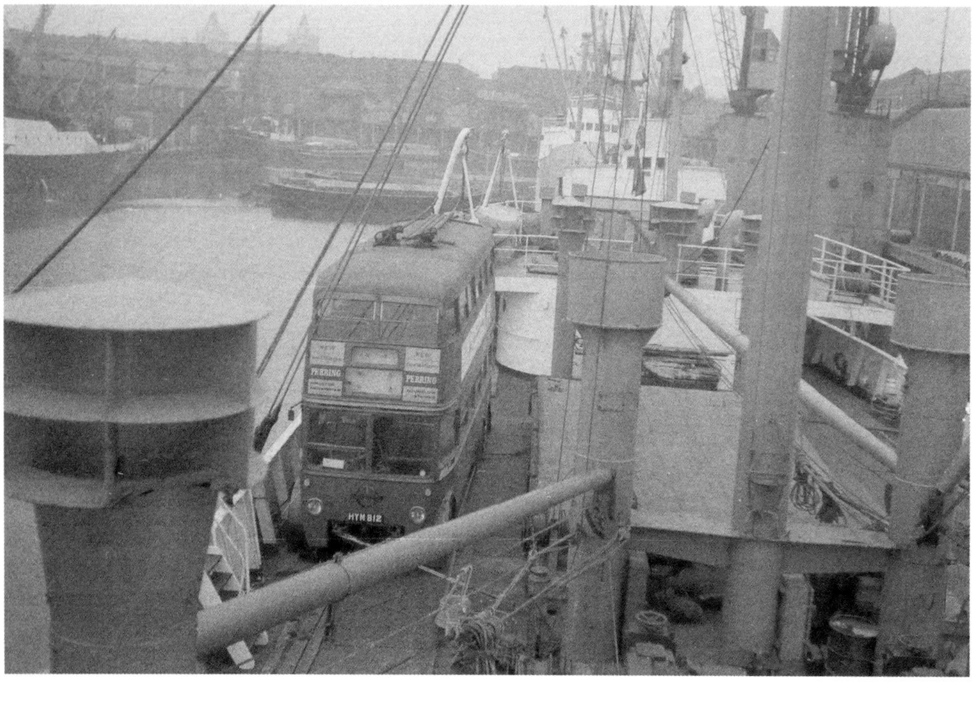

Q1 class 1812 is seen on board ship in London Docks (Western Dock) on 24 February 1961. After service in Spain this trolleybus was repatriated to the United Kingdom for restoration and preservation and is usually to be seen in service at the Sandtoft Trolleybus Museum in Yorkshire.
John Shearman

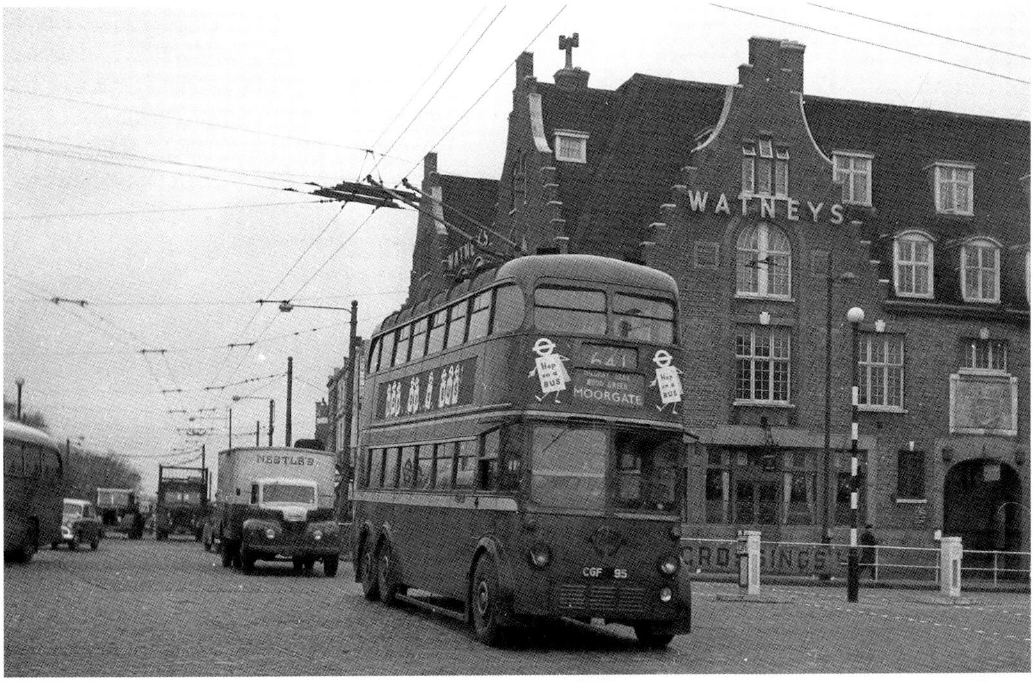

By 1941 a number of trolleybuses had fallen victim to enemy bombing and required rebodying, twelve Leylands and four AECs. These sixteen vehicles received new bodies by Weymann, and to denote such received an 'A' suffix to the fleet number. Included were two which had been short-wheelbase B2 class, but were lengthened to 30 feet and reclassified D2A. 95A threads its way through Manor House junction.
Michael Dryhurst

N1A class 1587A is seen at Barnet on 2 May 1959. This was one of two N1s rebodied by Weymann in 1942 following wartime bomb damage.
John Shearman

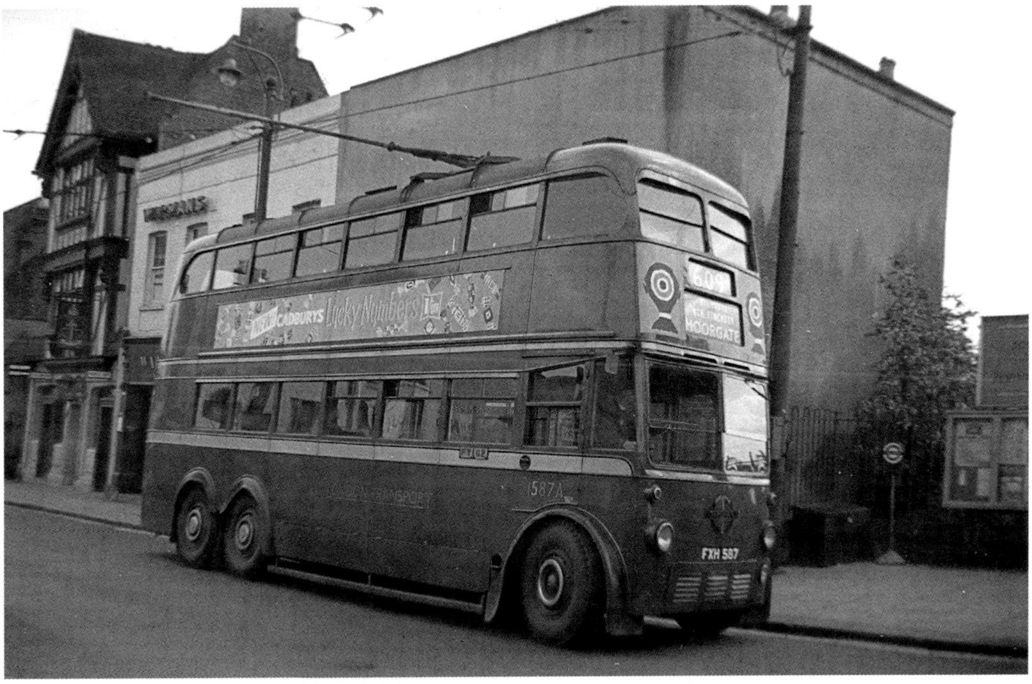

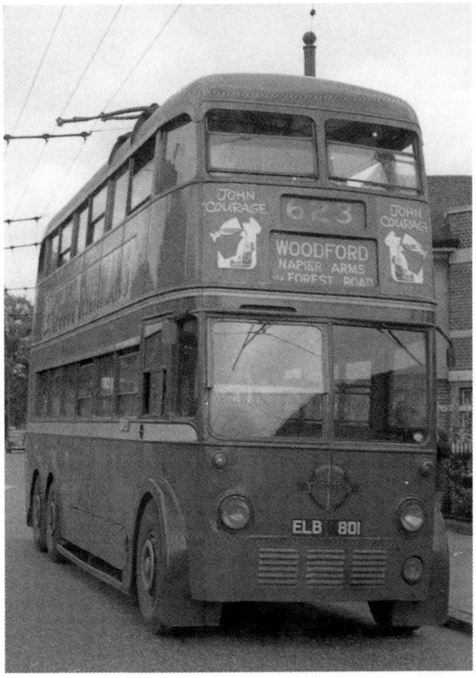

In the rebodying programme of war damaged trolleybuses, East Lancashire Coachbuilders supplied 25 new bodies for nineteen Leylands and for six AECs, and received a 'B' suffix to the fleet number. Class H1B 801B is seen at Manor House.
Michael Dryhurst

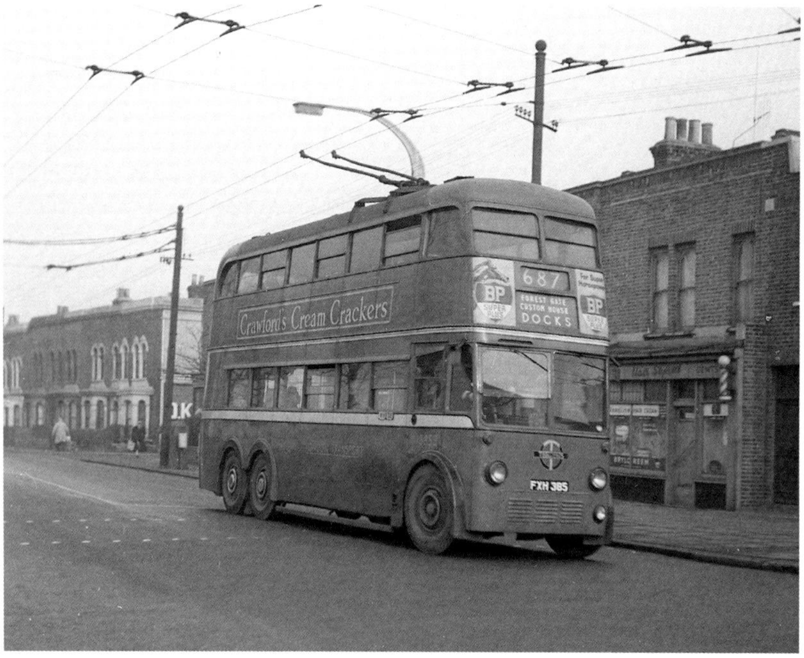

1385B is not all that is suggested by its fleet number. Being an L3, 1385 was a chassisless vehicle, not much of a basis on which to build a new body after its Metro Cammell body was destroyed in the war. Instead, apparently, the chassis frame of 364, the only C class trolleybus which had been written-off by wartime bombing, was salvaged and fitted with electrical and mechanical components which could have been recovered variously from 364 and/or 1385. East Lancashire Coachbuilders then built new bodywork on this refurbished chassis. London Transport chose to give the completed vehicle the identity of the former 1385, not of 364, presumably because for maintenance purposes it more closely accorded with the specifications of the original 1385 than of 364. Further compounding this trolleybus's identity, as it was not chassisless it could not be an L3 so was uniquely classified as N1B.
Michael Dryhurst

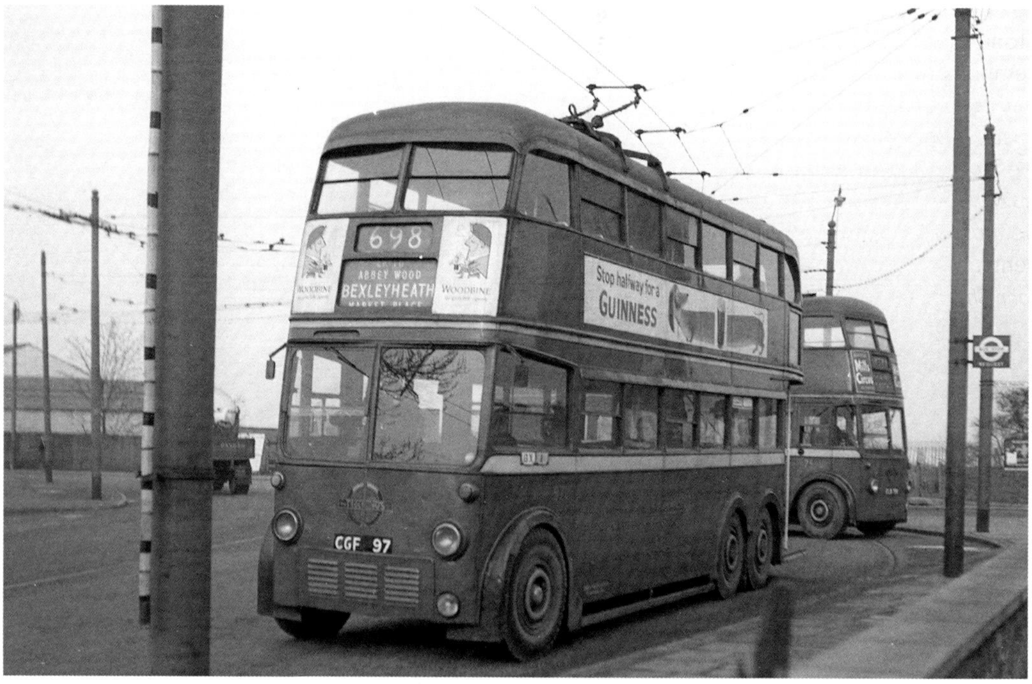

The remaining twenty war damaged trolleybuses which required rebodying were ten Leylands and ten AECs and these received Northern Coachbuilders bodies. They then had a 'C' suffix added to the fleet number. Another short wheelbase B2 class to be reclassified, this as a D2C, is 97C which is seen here on a short-working of route 698 at Erith.
Michael Dryhurst

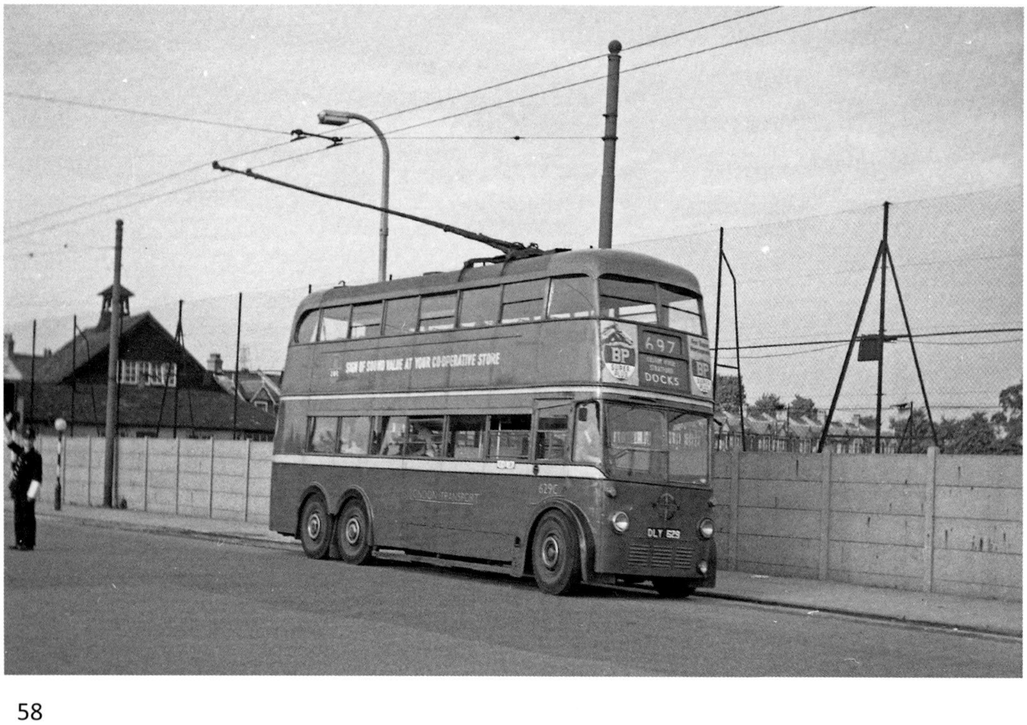

Park Royal bodied the 25 E3 class trolleybuses, but only those rebodied survived later than 1956, such as this Northern Coachbuilders bodied example, E3C class 629C, seen here in Walthamstow.
Michael Dryhurst

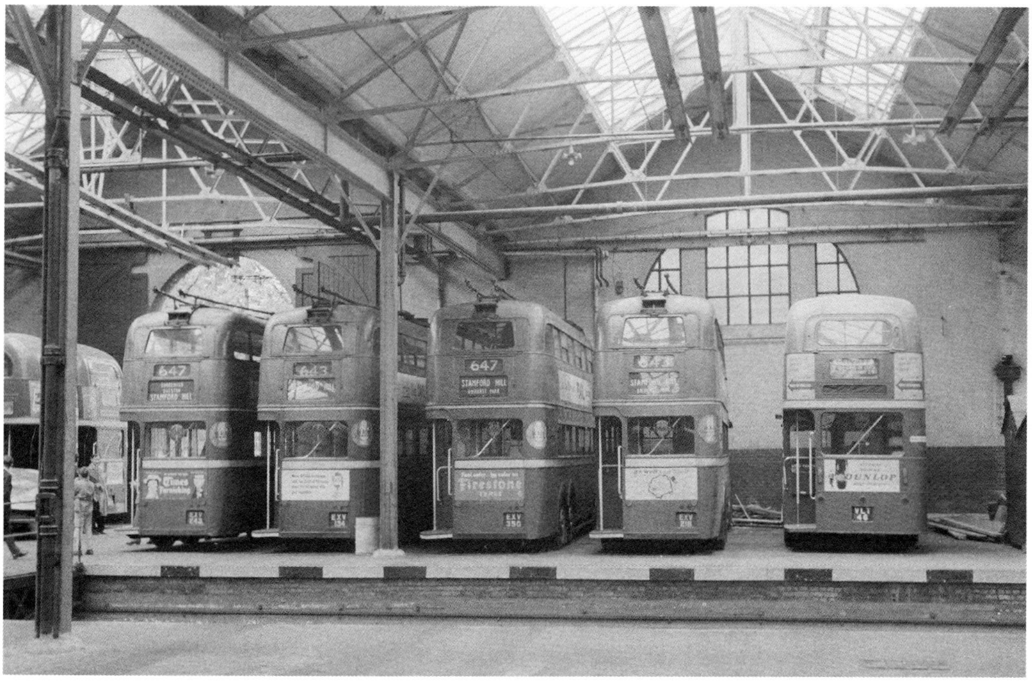

Trolleybuses 1243, 1134, 1350 and 1218 are alongside one of their successors in the form of RM 46 in Stamford Hill Depot on 16 July 1961. This photograph was taken on the occassion of a PSV Circle tour covering routes and depots in North London.
John Shearman

1529 and 1643 are parked at Stonebridge Depot on 30 December 1961. Both vehicles had seen earlier service in east London before transfer west prior to final withdrawal. 1529 was one of five L3s to be fitted with sliding window vents.
John Shearman

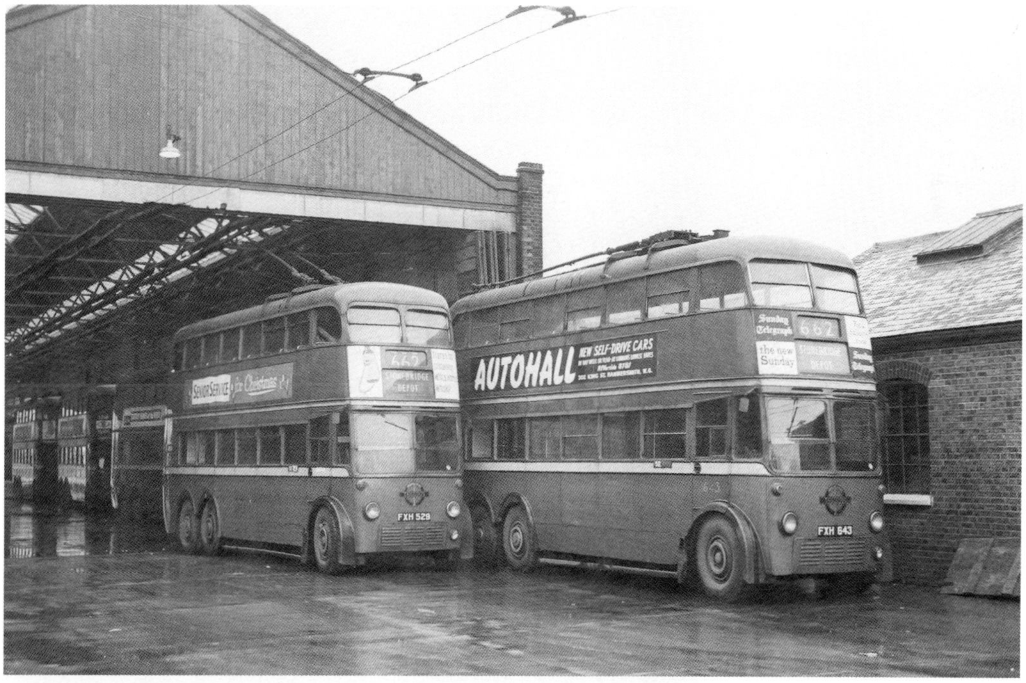

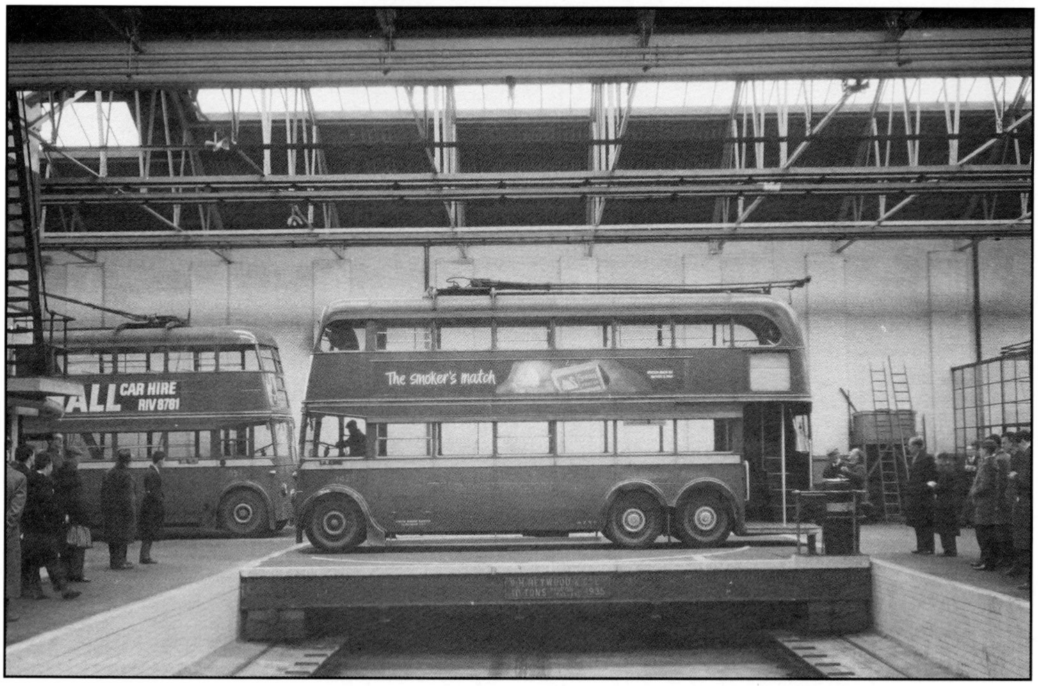

The traverser in Isleworth Depot is carrying 1425 on 15 April 1962. 1425 was one of two trolleybuses hired by the PSV Circle for a tour of the remaining London system on that date.
John Shearman

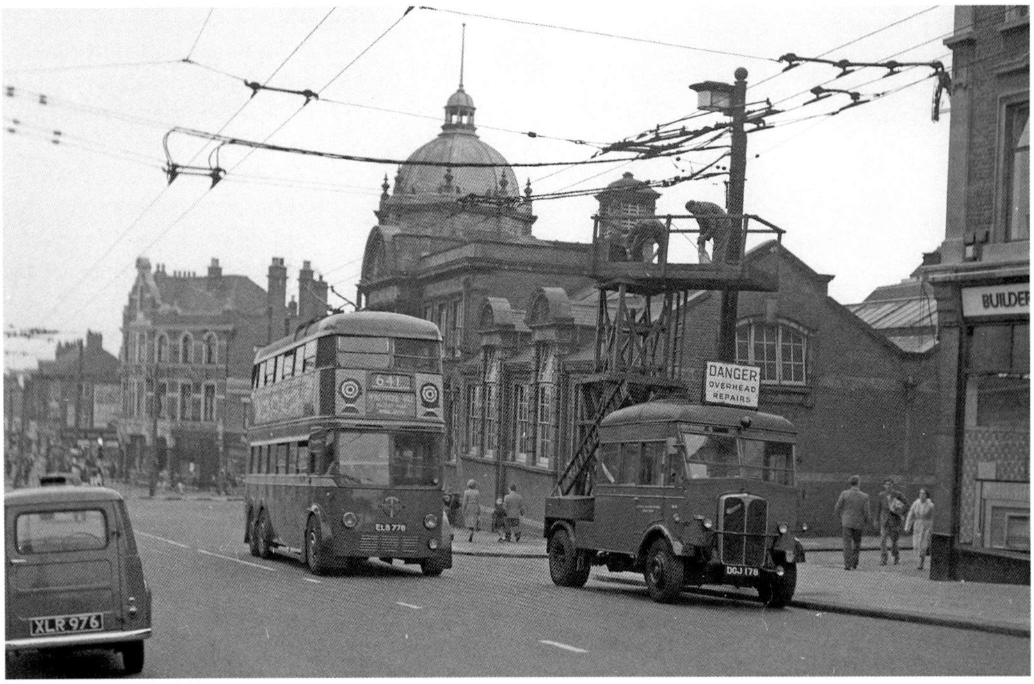

In 1935/6 London Transport purchased 16 new tower-wagons, based on the AEC Mercury lorry chassis. One of these was 86Q, seen here at work on Jolly Butcher's Hill, Wood Green while being passed by H1 class 778.
Michael Dryhurst

76Q (BYL 401) was a 1935 AEC Mercury 4 ton tower wagon for the trolleybus fleet. It is seen in Mitcham Road, Croydon on 24 November 1959.
Brian Speller

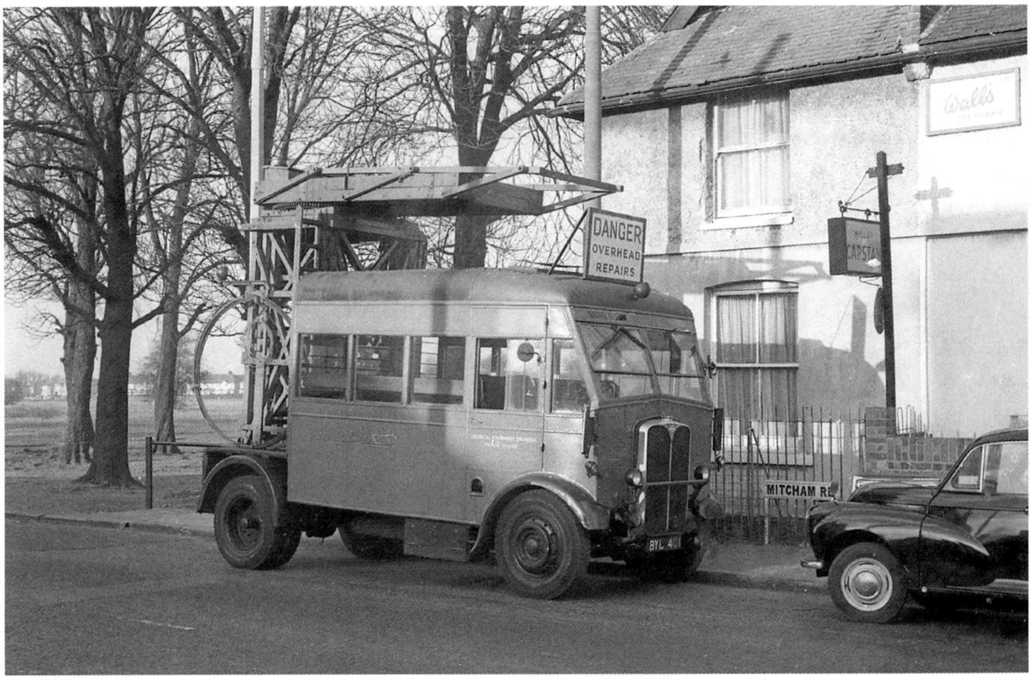

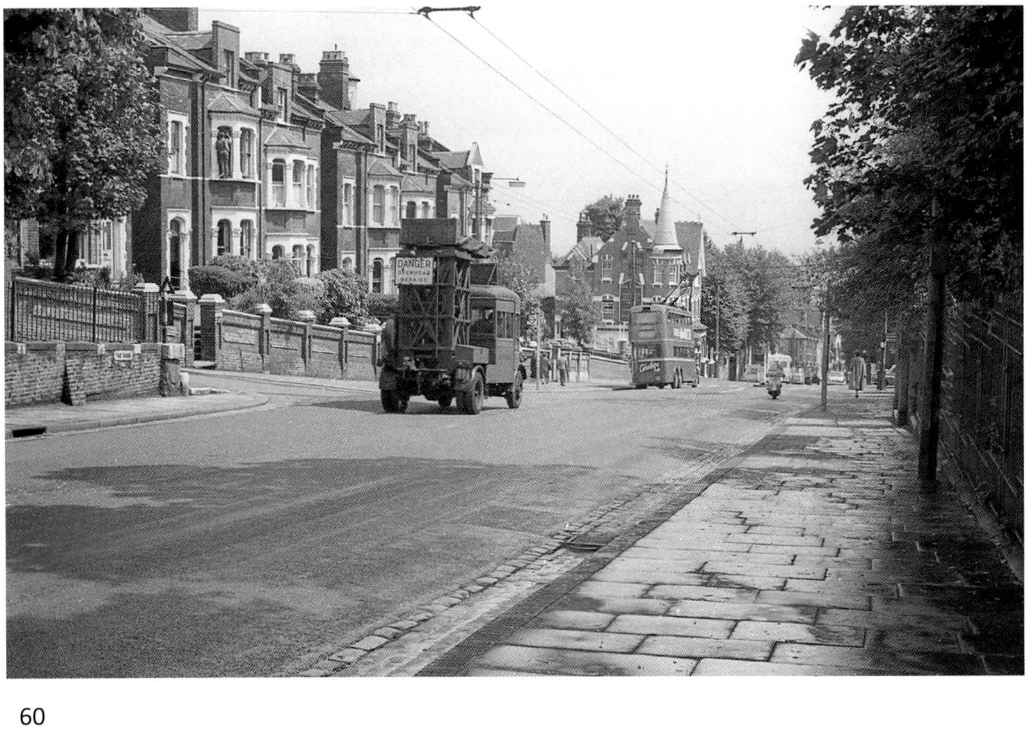

Another view of 86Q (DGJ 178), an AEC Mercury service vehicle this time following L1 class 1363 along Highgate High Street.
Brian Speller

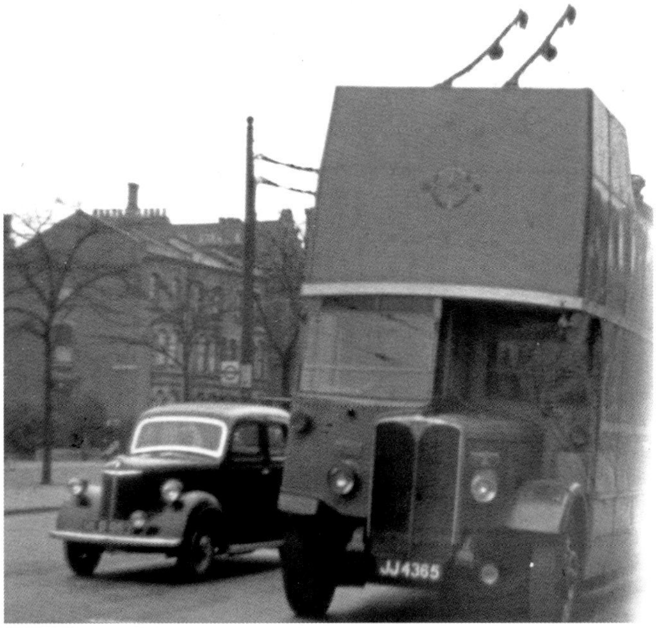

The former STL 12 (JJ 4365) has been converted for use as an overhead wire lubricator. As a service vehicle it carried the fleet number 734J.
SA Newman
Courtesy Julian Bowden

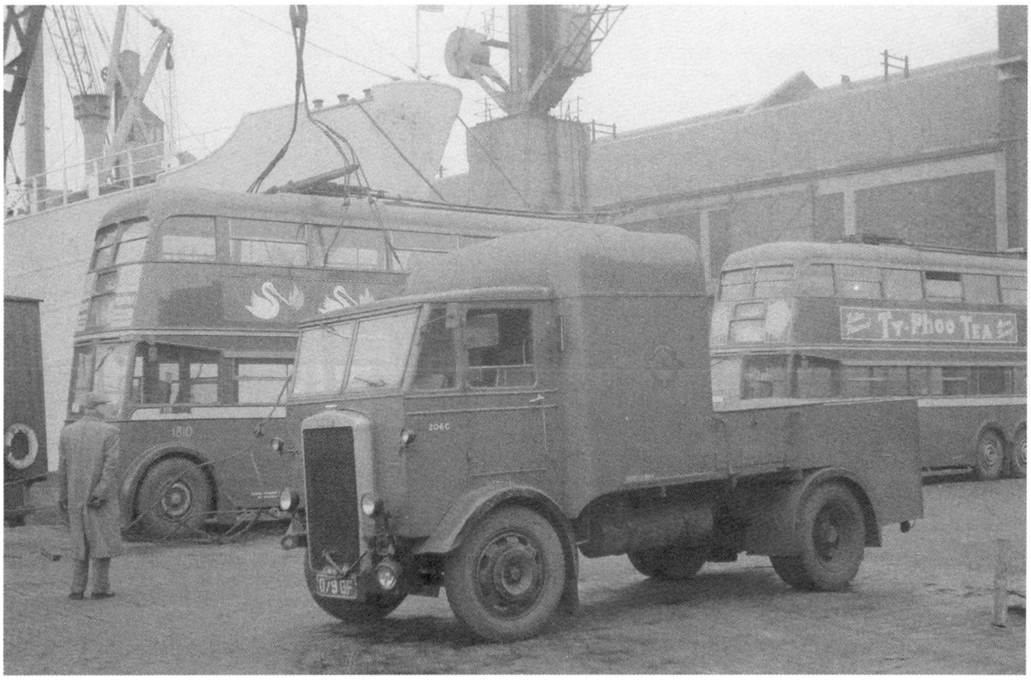

206C, an Albion trolleybus rescue tender, is seen at the London Docks (Western Dock) having brought a withdrawn Q1 trolleybus to the docks ready for loading and export to Spain for further service.
John Shearman

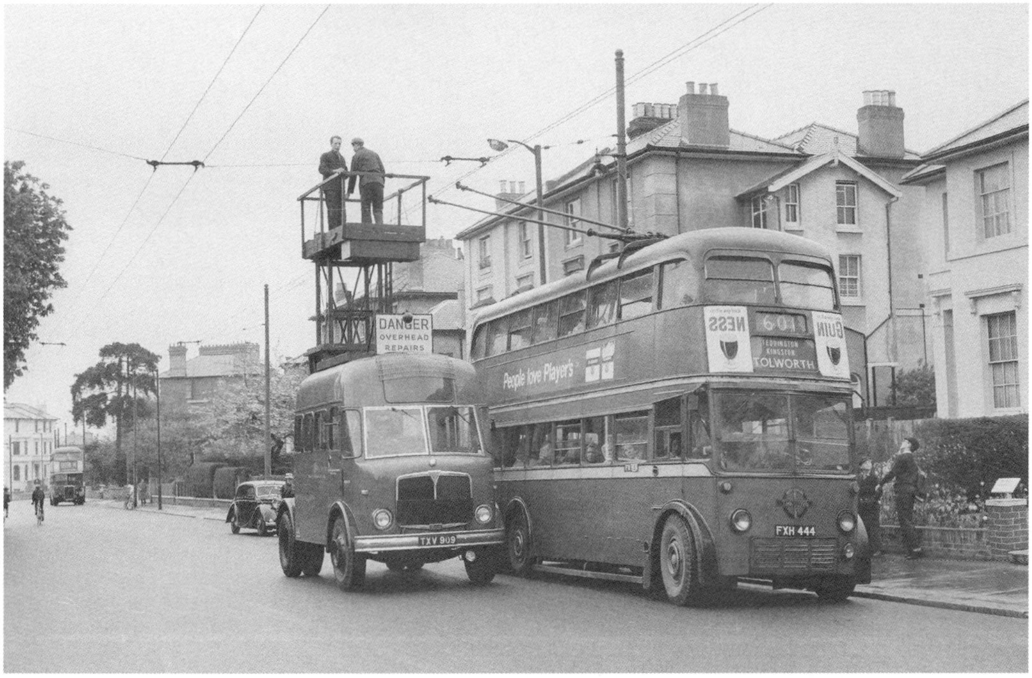

On the last Saturday of London trolleybus service, 5 May 1962, tower wagon 1076Q is seen in Claremont Road, Surbiton preparing to re-attach the overhead running wire back into its hanger while trolleybus 1444 carefully passes by.
John Shearman

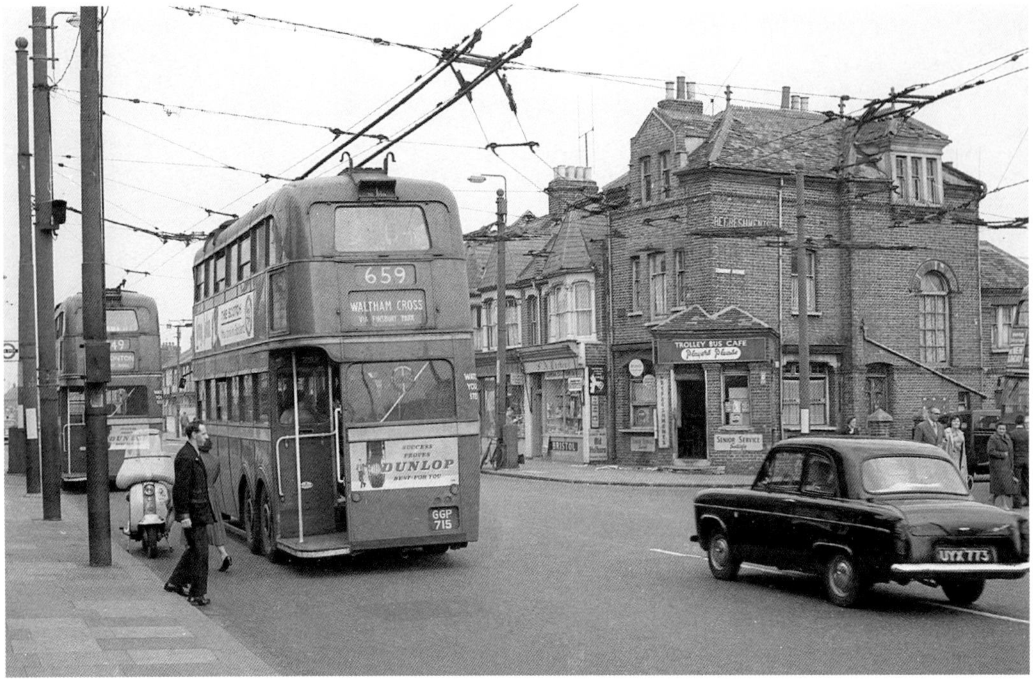

Edmonton Depot was situated at the end of aptly named Tramway Avenue. To complete the transport theme, the cafe on the corner was named Trolleybus Cafe. Three views are shown here, P1 class 1715 (top) and P1 class 1702 (centre) were taken 16 April 1961, and K2 class 1155 (bottom).

Brian Speller (Top & Middle)
Geoff Lumb (Bottom)

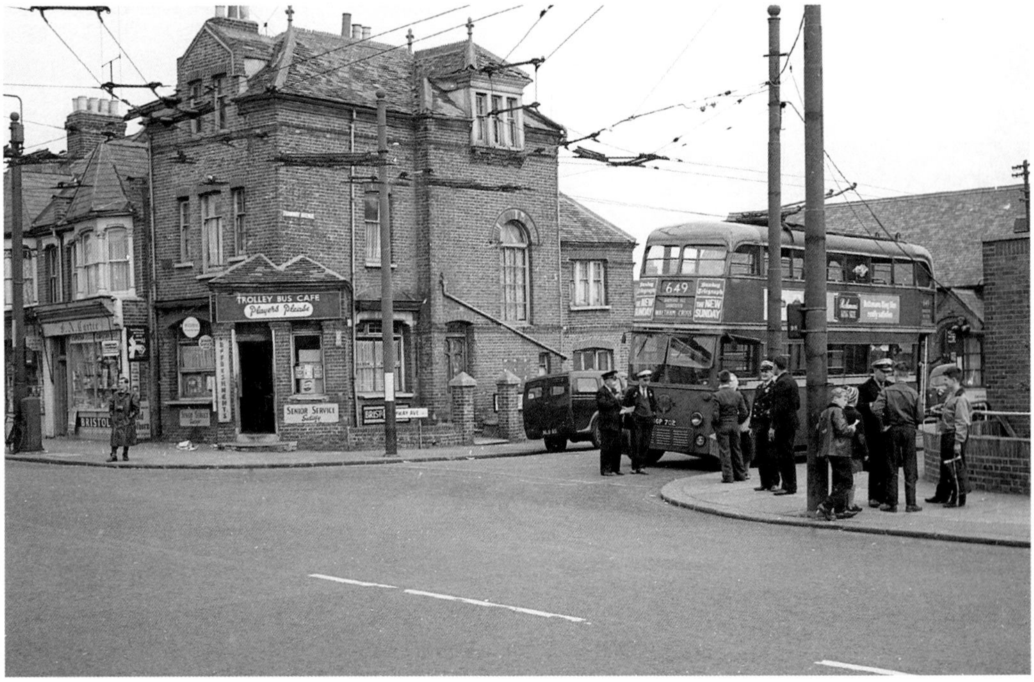

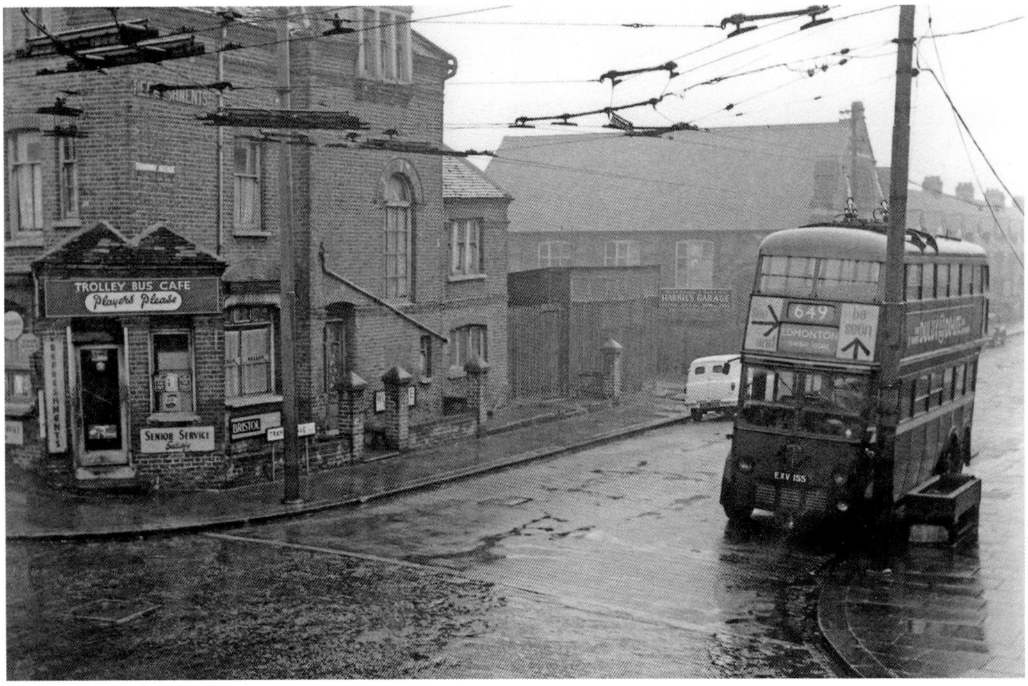

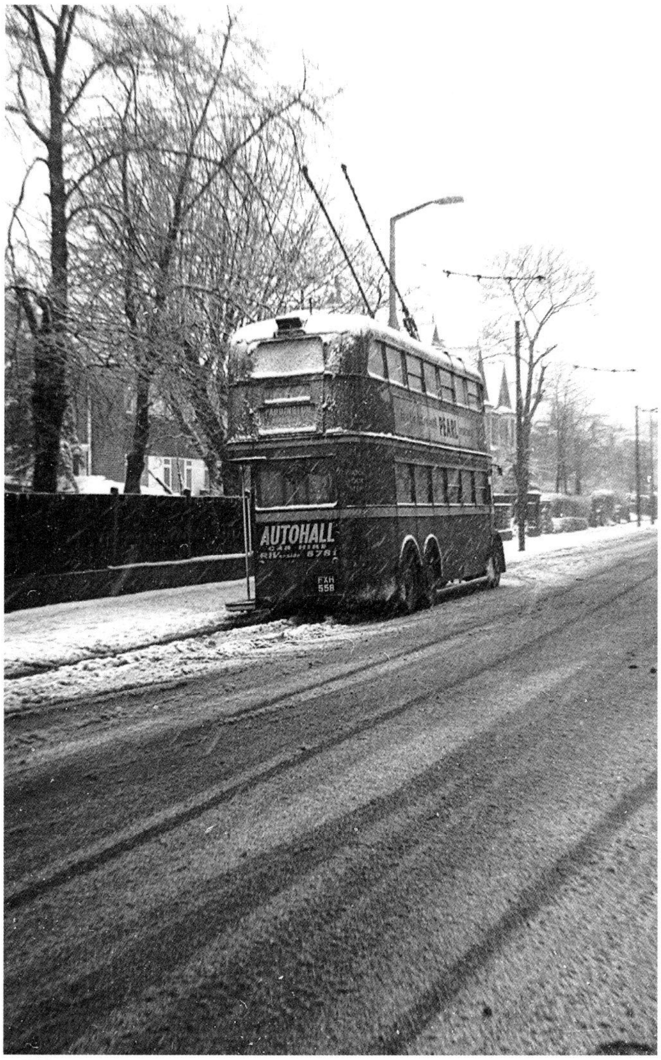

New Years Eve 1961, and Craven Park looks deserted as the snow takes over. N1 class 1558 has turned short on the 662, and the driver will soon attempt to turn and head for Paddington, although one would suspect he would rather go back to the canteen at Stonebridge Depot.
Peter Horner

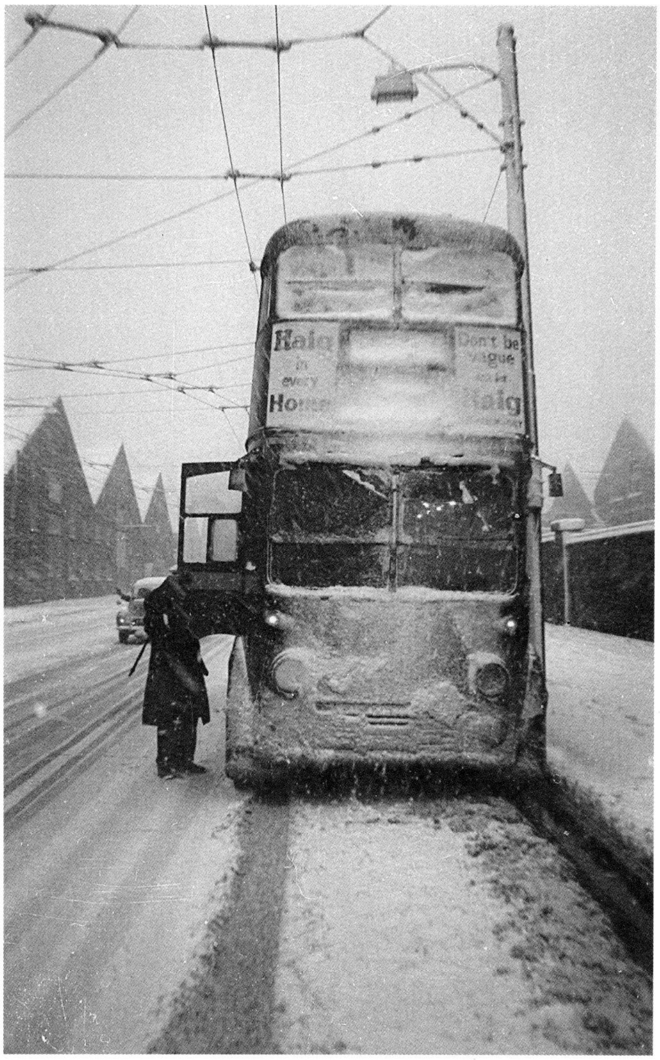

An unidentified N1 awaits a crew change opposite Colindale depot. It is New Years Eve 1961, and London had suffered heavy snow falls which seriously disrupted the bus services. The routes in the area finished on 2nd January 1962.
Peter Horner

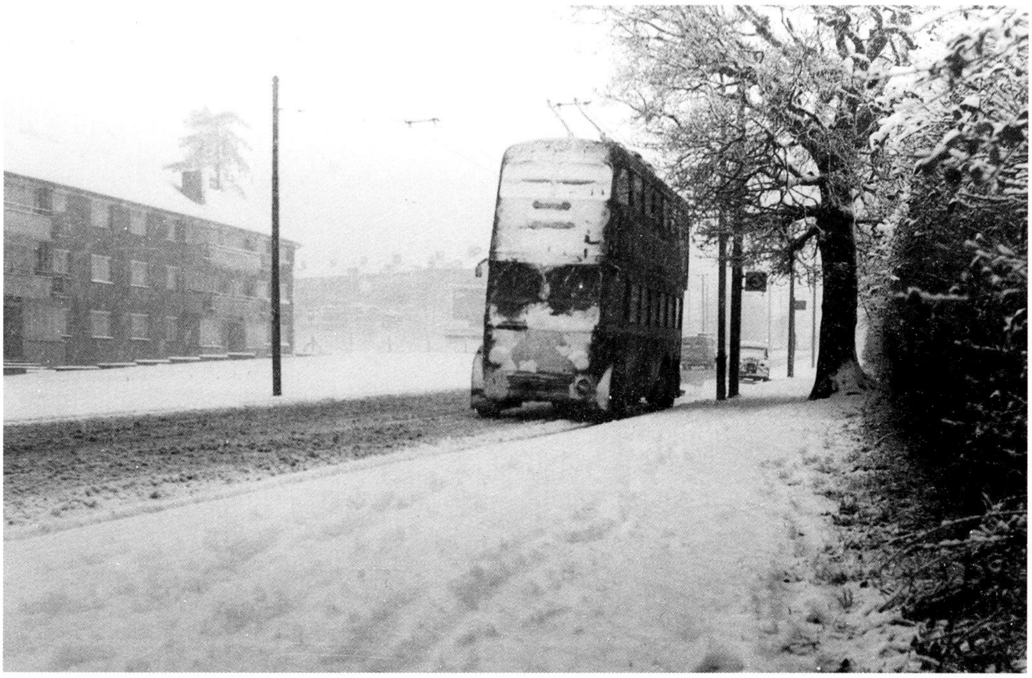

New Years Eve 1961 at Canons Park terminus. L3 class 1469 is covered with snow, as it waits to try the return trip to Barnet. In three days time, it will be in the scrapyard awaiting its fate. Not a happy new year.
Mick Webber Collection

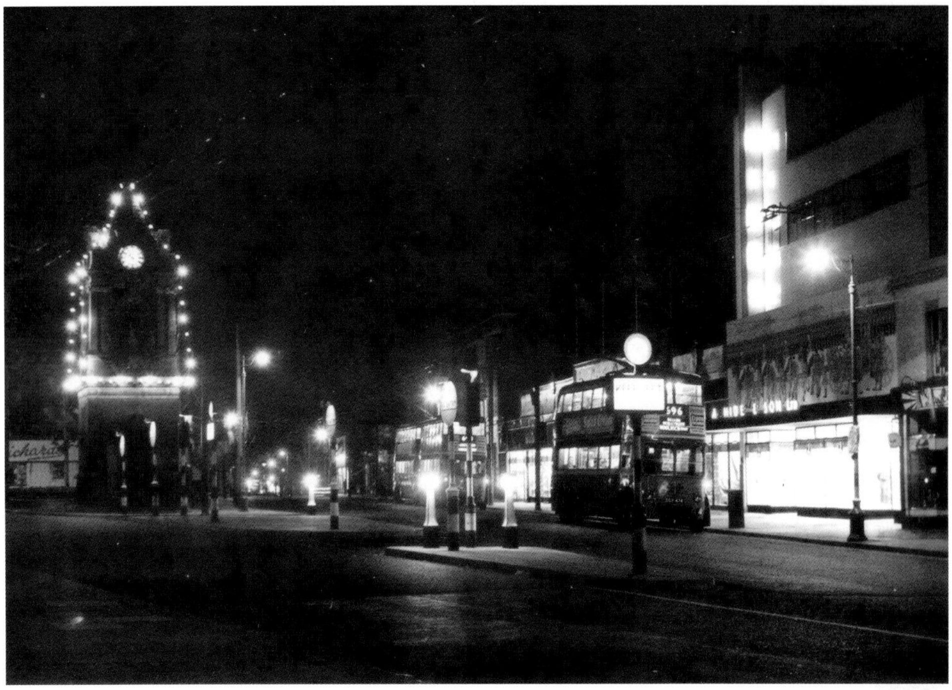

The Coronation in June 1953, was marked by coloured lights on the clock tower in Bexleyheath, and D2 class 474 stands by on the 696 ready to depart for Woolwich. A terminating 698 lurks behind also ready to leave for Woolwich, but by way of Erith and Abbey Wood.
Mick Webber Collection

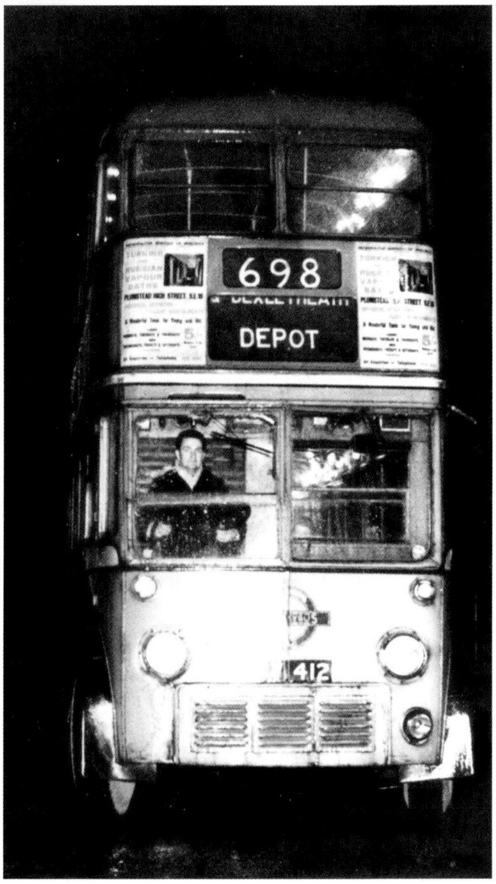

It is the night of 3/4 March 1959, and rebodied 412B makes its way back to Bexleyheath Depot from the extra working to Dartford on the 698. Trolleybus operation will then be at an end in this isolated part of the system, and the Depot, which was the only completely new one to be built for the trolleybus system, will become a bus garage.
Mick Webber Collection

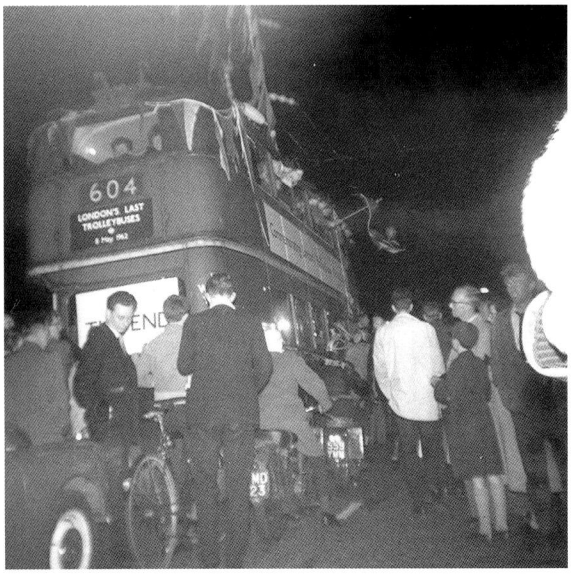

It is the early hours of 9 May 1962, and L3 class 1521 crawls back to Fulwell Depot, to bring the system to a close. Hundreds of people turned out to welcome the trolleybus back, and parts of the vehicle were disappearing fast, to become souvenirs. 1521 now works again at the East Anglia Transport Museum.
Mick Webber

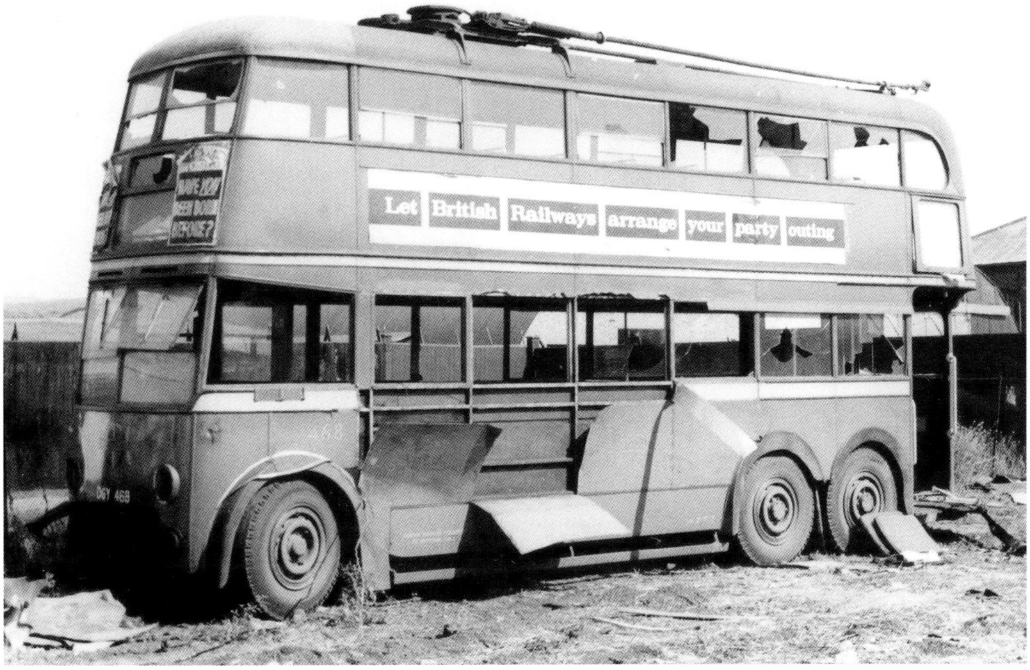

The company most associated with the scrapping of the fleet, was George Cohen & Son. They carried out this task at three locations, their own yard at Canning Town, and London Transport land at Penhall Road, Charlton, and behind Colindale Depot. D2 class 468 was dealt with at Charlton, which was also the site where the same company had scrapped the last London trams in 1952.
Mick Webber Collection

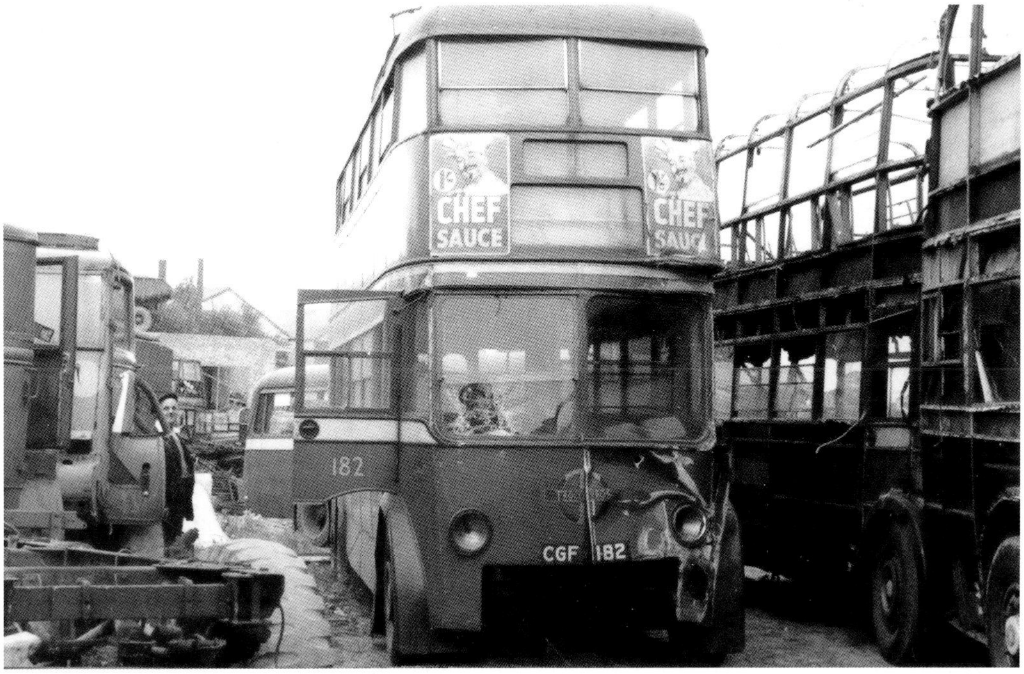

Birds of Stratford upon Avon, scrapped many of the London trolleybus fleet, and C1 class 182 was one of the casualties seen here in May 1956. Towing buses from London must have been a costly business, but they obviously made it pay.
N.Rayfield/LCCTT

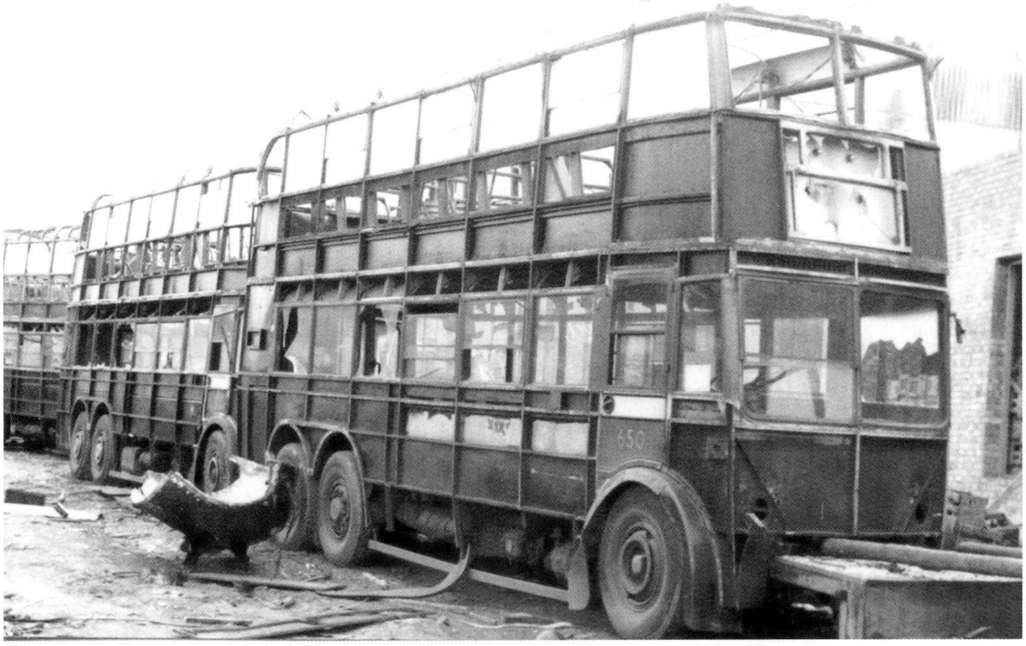

E3 class 650 was another vehicle dismantled by Birds, shown here in May 1956.
Mick Webber Collection

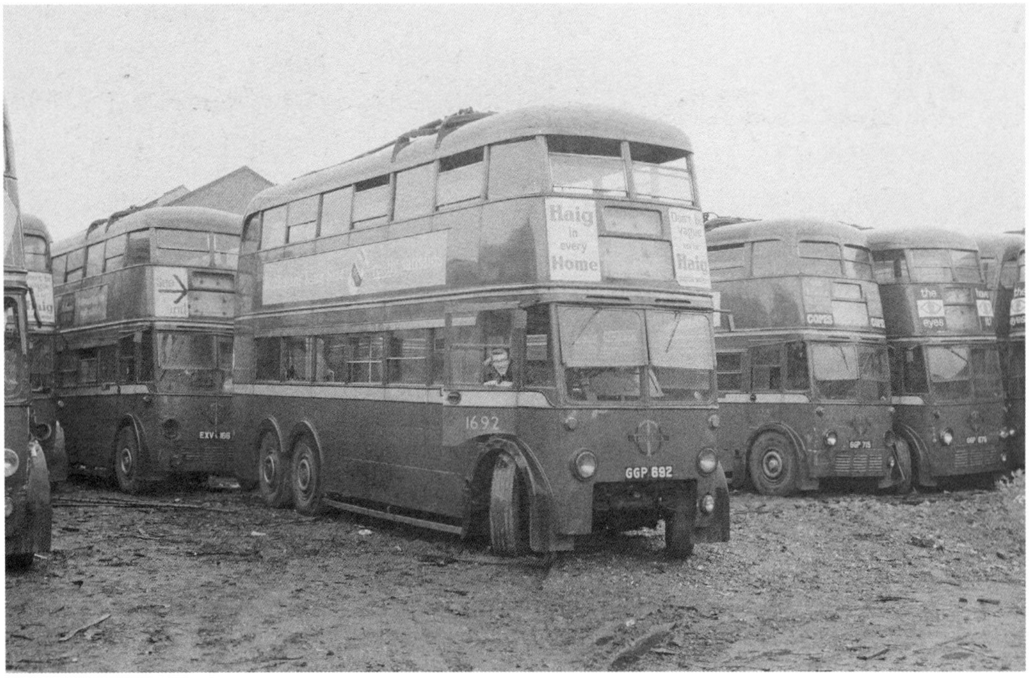

K3 Class 1692 looks to be a recent arrival at the Colindale scrapyard along with 1166, 1715 and 1676 in the background on 16 July 1961.
John Shearman

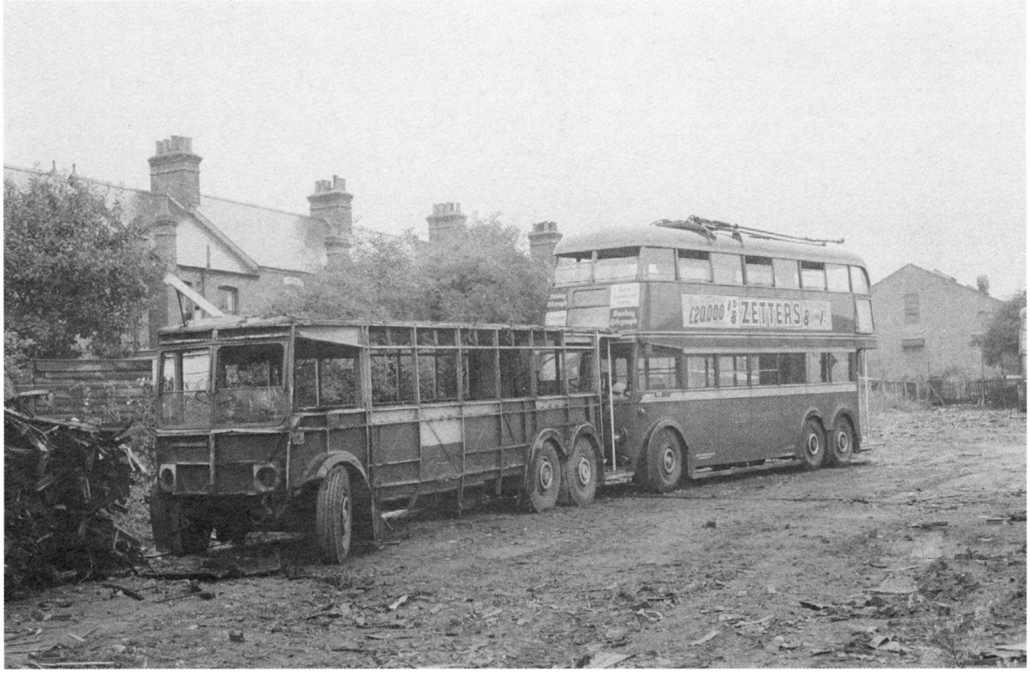

During the PSV Circle tour of north London on 16 July 1961 a stop was made at Colindale Depot and the scrapyard used by Cohens to dispose of a large part of the London fleet. This view of 1362 shows how the Metro Cammell bodywork of these vehicles was constructed in two separate halves. Leyland bodied 1338 stands behind.
John Shearman

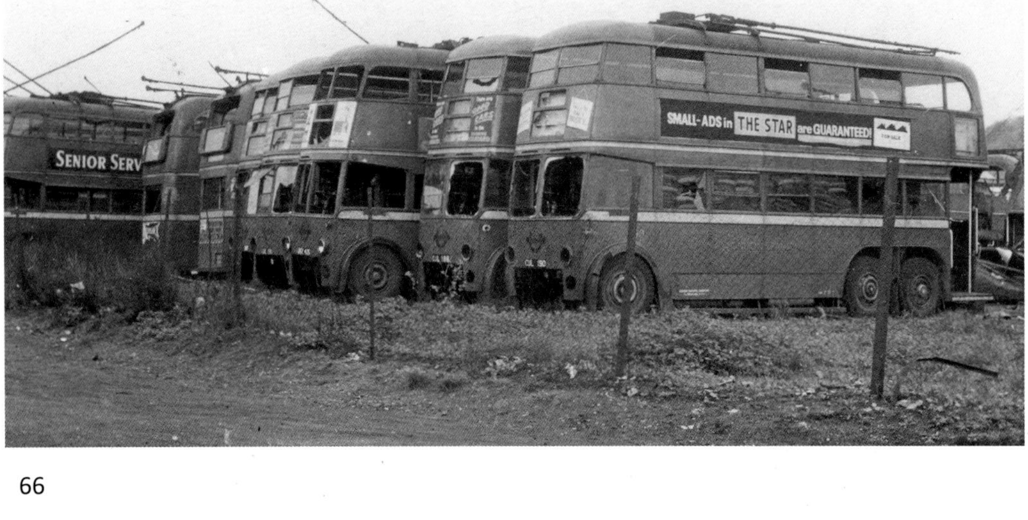

This depressing view of the demise of trolleybuses, taken at the Charlton scrapyard on 29 April 1959, has interest in that not only are there D class trolleybuses very recently withdrawn from the nearby 696 and 698 routes operated by Bexleyheath Depot, but there are also C class vehicles withdrawn from service north of the Thames. For the most part, policy was to withdraw the oldest trolleybuses firstly, regardless of whether or not they were working on routes due for early withdrawal. The trolleybuses in this photograph are (from right to left) 190, 186, 405B and 191.
Fred York